TEENAGERS
When to Worry and What to Do

TEENAGERS
When to Worry and What to Do

Douglas H. Powell

HARVARD UNIVERSITY

DOUBLEDAY & COMPANY, INC., GARDEN CITY, NEW YORK
1986

Library of Congress Cataloging-in-Publication Data
Powell, Douglas H.
    Teenagers, when to worry and what to do.
    Bibliography: p. 277
    Includes index.
    1. Youth—Conduct of life. 2. Parenting. I. Title.
BJ1661.P67 1986   155.5   85-16214
ISBN 0-385-19325-4

TO
Carolyn and Douglas Jr.
Who light up our lives

Contents

Preface

"How worried should I be about my teenager?" and "What can I do to
help?" are the two questions most often asked by parents who consult
me. I'm a clinical psychologist with a long interest in understanding the
differences among normal adolescents, one passing through temporary
difficulties and another in serious trouble. Also my colleagues and I are
regularly asked for advice as to what kind of help is best for a particular
young person.

How worried we should be about a particular teen rests largely on our
understanding of what constitutes normal behavior. For more than a
quarter of a century I've had a growing interest in learning how to tell if
people are normal. This training began when I was part of the team to
select astronauts for the Gemini and Apollo programs. Since then this
interest has continued in clinical work assessing whether students are
sufficiently recovered from emotional difficulties to return to school and
college, in teaching undergraduate and graduate courses on the theory of
normalcy, and in writing about this complex process.

In this book I will share with you my understanding of what characteristics you can look at to provide a general sense of your youngster's
mental state. In the problem-oriented chapters we will look at qualities
separating the green and yellow zones of lesser concern from the orange
and red of more pathological conditions. In each of these chapters ficti-
tious cases—constructed from the lives of youths whose lives I've been
privileged to share—provide examples of the more serious manifestations
of these problems.

Following a consideration of characteristics highlighting the zones of
concern, a follow-up for each case is provided. This often will portray a
teenager who refuses professional help, goes reluctantly, or abandons it
at the first opportunity. These follow-ups also illustrate how useful assis-

tance comes from unexpected sources—getting a job, going to church, discovering a sympathetic cousin, leaving the country. Also shown in these cases are occasions when professional help is necessary and must be obtained. The reader will note that when professional intervention is suggested it reflects the author's bias in favor of bringing to bear multiple therapeutic techniques.

Such a program might include medical input and family counseling, as well as a mix of insight-oriented and cognitive-behavioral treatment. These case follow-ups open the way for suggestions to the parents for helping these young people. The emphasis is on what parents can do to help their children who are in trouble. General guidelines are offered: paying attention to overreactions, ideas for raising low spirits or controlling tempers, and ideas for combating more serious forms of the problem.

References supporting many of the major points in the chapters are found at the back of the book. Superscripts have been eliminated from the text to provide for smoother reading. A serious effort has been mounted to record the primary references whose thinking bears upon the ideas in this book. However, it is also true that ten times as many could have been included among the authors cited. I've attempted to include references that either review a body of data or are original studies that seem relevant to the point under discussion.

ACKNOWLEDGMENTS

First and foremost, thanks to my wife, Virginia Stone Powell, for her large and varied contributions to this book. Over the three decades we have been together—as wife and husband, mother and father, and co-workers—I have absorbed much of her wisdom about normal people, adolescent development, relationships among the generations, and what parents can do on their own to help their young. She also has a superb ear for the voices of parents and their teenagers as well as an unfailing memory for anecdotes. The pages ahead draw deeply from her thoughts.

A number of groups of people and specific individuals have been helpful in listening to and criticizing these ideas. Chief among them are my friends and colleagues at the Harvard University Health Services, at Powell Associates, in the Lowell House Senior Common Room, and the faculty and participants of the Northfield Counseling Institute.

I am grateful to individuals who have read and contributed ideas to portions of this manuscript: Dr. Irving Allen, Jessie Baum, Dr. Susan Blumenthal, Dr. Winthrop Burr, Dr. William Coaldrake, Dr. Dale Corbett, Dr. George Goethals, Donna Hill, Ellen Porter Honnet, Dr. Adrienne Larkin, Dr. Margaret McKenna, Kiyo Morimoto, Dr. George Ross, Dr. Warren Wacker, Dr. Paul Walters, and Virginia Williamson. Special thanks are due to two especially close friends—Drs. Randolph Catlin and Patricia Light—who have read the book in its entirety. Their perspectives have been very useful. The responsibility for the ideas presented in this book, however, is the author's alone.

Thanks, too, to those on the publishing end who have been so much help: Donald Cutler of Sterling Lord, and at Doubleday, Kathy Antrim, Lindy Hess, Katharine Phillips, and Susan Schwartz.

This book has benefited enormously by the opportunity given me to work on portions of this manuscript at the Rockefeller Foundation's Bellagio Study and Conference Center at Villa Serbelloni in October 1984. The exquisite setting, superb care provided by Roberto Celli, Angela Barmettler, and their excellent staff, as well as the leisure to share ideas with scholars and artists in other fields transformed an arduous task into pure pleasure.

This manuscript was prepared by Kathleen Lawton. Without her continuing enthusiasm for the task, attention to detail, adaptability, high energy level, and unfailing good humor, the project might never have been completed.

Concord, Massachusetts
November 1985

TEENAGERS
When to Worry and What to Do

1

Helping Your Youngster Through the Teenage Years

> *My teenager spends most of her time looking at herself in the mirror, says she hates school, has a fit if I ask her to get off the phone after she's been talking for an hour, and provokes me continuously. Our doctor says she is normal. Is this possible?*

> *Our son acts more like a kid than his fourteen-year-old sister when he comes home on vacation from law school. He's lazy, messy, sleeps all day, stays up all night, and totally takes us for granted. Is there something wrong with him we should be worried about?*

> *Everyone agrees our sixteen year old has problems, but he refuses to see a psychiatrist. The therapist says that treatment won't work unless he wants it. What can we do?*

This book is for mothers and fathers of adolescents. Its purpose is to address the questions all of us who are parents have about our children: (1) How do we know whether our youngster is normal, passing through a temporary phase, or is in serious trouble? (2) What can individual parents do to help these boys and girls through this period when they seem so resistant to adult guidance? (3) How best can we manage our own complicated reactions to the dramatic changes in our teens to keep family relationships intact while preserving everyone's sanity?

Much of what makes being the parent of a teenager so interesting is witnessing the rapid physical growth, psychological development, and social changes accompanying this life stage. But it also can be a period of challenge and worry if school difficulties harden into real trouble, if the circle of friends leaves much to be desired, if childlike regressions supplant yesterday's maturity, if moodiness, anxiety, and a hair-trigger temper spring out of nowhere, and if provocation, defiance, and experimentation strain the bonds of affection between the generations.

According to mental health professionals only about one teenager in ten has significant emotional or behavioral problems, a statistic that would be news to most parents. Whereas the difficulties may not seem "significant" by psychiatric standards, mothers and fathers report that their youngsters regularly face them with worrisome fears, depressions, learning problems, misconduct, and crises.

Since only a tiny fraction of troubled youths receive professional help, to whom do they turn for comfort and guidance? The answer is you, their parents. In spite of protests to the contrary, a son knows that his friends probably are not the best people to advise him about a broken heart. A college sophomore can't discuss with roommates why the college experience that seems so exciting to them does nothing for her. Eventually many of these teens want to talk to their parents about their problems. Contrary to generation gap theorists, three out of four adolescents look to their families with the expectation of help in times of question or stress. For them their mothers and fathers are the front line —for many, the only line—of mental health support.

A difficult problem for parents of teenagers is to know how worried to be about them. On one hand, we don't want to overreact, pressing psychotherapy on a daughter with a momentary hitch in her development, thereby undermining her confidence and depriving her of the benefit of learning how to overcome the problems life has in store for her. Yet neither do we want to misread a son's emotional disorder as a passing phase, ignoring it as a condition that worsens into a serious maladjustment.

Though the writings about severe adolescent problems are extensive, much less has been published about normal variants of these severe maladjustments. This book focuses on how we can tell the difference between normal behavior and more serious pathological states. In these pages we will look at characteristics that will help us distinguish reasonable academic performance from underachievement, temporary misconduct from delinquency, an eating "order" from an eating disorder, and responsible drug use from drug abuse.

The emphasis will be on what *you* as parents can do to help young people maintain normal adjustment. Also we will consider things that mothers and fathers can do, short of seeking professional help, to help adolescents who may be exhibiting signs of more serious difficulty. This is not meant in any way to diminish the importance and value of professional assistance from mental health workers with troubled youths. A good deal has already been written about how to find expert help when the need arises. The emphasis here is on what parents themselves can accomplish, on their own, to improve the emotional adjustment of their offspring.

Finally we will look at how parental overreactions may worsen problems young people have and effectively block our being able to help them. These often are set up by our own underlying anxieties, conflicts, and dreams and hopes for our children. Being able to assist our teenagers in moments of need depends on being able to respond objectively and compassionately. To a large extent our objectivity and compassion turn on being aware of the unexpected and powerful emotions young people trigger within us. These feelings can interfere with our ability to understand what a youngster experiences. Instead of reacting sympathetically to a son who brings home a D+ in biology, we may find ourselves overwhelmed by the dread that he will never survive in higher education unless something is done instantly, and we suddenly hear ourselves threatening him rather than listening to how he feels. These excessive emotional reflexes can block us from being able to aid the child and taking corrective action. Instead of trying to help a daughter understand why she shoplifted from a nearby mall, we may find ourselves threatening her with dire punishment if she ever does it again.

Who Is the Teenager?

The word "teenager" describes the group of young men and women who are no longer children but who are still short of adulthood. It is a generic term as are "adolescent," "youth," or "young person." While most of these individuals about whom we are concerned are thirteen to nineteen, the age boundaries are elastic, because "teenage" is a state of mind and activity.

For example, within the same family might be an eleven-year-old girl and her twenty-three-year-old brother. She begins menstruating and soon adopts the dress, interests, and attitudes of older female friends with whom she spends all her time. Her older brother, still living at home since graduation from college and working odd jobs, is still trying to find himself. Both resemble teenagers more than the majority of their age-mates as far as what they feel, think about, and do.

Who is and who is not a teenager is defined by a number of factors. The beginning of this life stage is signaled by physical and psychological changes, by the educational system, and by the peer group. The close of this era is even more flexible.

To a very important extent the physical changes of puberty mark the beginning of the teenage phase of life. Hormones secreted either for the first time or in much higher amounts than previously cause an acceleration in growth rate resulting in increased body size and strength. The onset of menstruation in girls and nocturnal emissions in boys, the development of secondary sexual characteristics—pubic hair and breasts, beards and a deepening voice—signal growing maturity.

While on the average in the United States a girl's first period occurs at about twelve and a half, a glance at the candidates trying out for a seventh grade girls' basketball team will tell us that enormous variability exists as to when puberty begins and how rapidly sexual maturation happens. It is possible to find a twelve year old, apparently fully grown, playing with prepubescent girls a foot shorter and seemingly light-years behind her developmentally. We could see the same considerable diversity in size and maturation in a group of fourteen-year-old boys.

Psychological changes characterize this period of life almost as clearly as does puberty. A youngster moving into the teens exhibits less dependence on parental guidance and greater self-scrutiny than at other stages of life. One of the surest signs that the teenage years have begun is reflexive opposition to what yesterday seemed the unquestioned truths of the older generation. Thirteen year olds quarrel incessantly with mom while older teens can argue any position that is contrary to pop's. Their opposition to parental values and demands is for these young people the first step along a lengthy road to autonomy.

Greater self-absorption is a hallmark of the teenage experience. In young adolescence this appears as increasing preoccupation with appearance. Teenagers inspect their bodies feature by feature, hour after hour in front of mirrors, trying on everything in their closets and repeatedly practicing particular smiles, expressions, postures, or ways of moving so they have a kinesthetic feel when they project the image they desire.

Wondering "what kind of person I am" is a teenage infatuation. Younger boys and girls spend considerable time inventorying their talents and traits: To what extent are they athletic, attractive, smart, sociable, dominant, or amusing? With older teens these questions focus on issues of identity and occupation: Who am I? What am I going to do? Where am I headed?

This constant inward looking results in periods of obsessive dissatisfaction with the self, even among those with the least to complain about. The prettiest girl in school can be convinced she is ugly because her left eye is microscopically larger than the right. Her friend who is rich *and* smart hates living in a neighborhood with no other kids her own age and wishes the teachers wouldn't always expect her to do so well. When their parents don't seem to respond sympathetically to their "misfortune," they react with the universal teenage lament, "My parents don't understand me."

The educational system in the United States opens the way to teenage status in the form of middle or junior high school. Moving into this portion of school presents the youngster with greater freedom and a much wider assortment of choices for attitudes and behavior. Unlike grammar or lower school where the children work under the minute-to-minute surveillance of one teacher, these adolescents now have a different instructor for each subject. No longer are they scrutinized continually by a single faculty member who knows them well and reinforces adult values. Unhampered by close faculty monitoring, teenagers at this age now have far more latitude to follow their own instincts, experimenting, challenging, experiencing as much as they dare.

Much greater freedom occurs when these teens enter high school. Here the atmosphere is even under less direct adult control. Although most secondary institutions fall well short of being a "jungle," new students apprehend on the first day that the environment is different. Larger older students knock aside smaller younger ones with impunity; often-raunchy graffiti decorate the bathrooms where teenagers smoke in contempt of the rules; even in the best schools vandalism, cheating, stealing, and drug use are not uncommon.

Also unlike the earlier grades where little diversity existed, high school abounds with students who seem to young adolescents to model a mind-boggling array of opinions about how important it is to do well academically, to follow rules, or to treat teachers with respect. There is much variety in their classmates—a fervent churchgoer, an Eagle Scout, and a computer buff may all share the same social studies class with a pupil who opposes *everything* an adult in authority says, a girl who has been sexually active for two years, and a boy who heavily uses drugs. Whatever their conviction or conduct, each seems to have credible backers.

Making choices among dissonant beliefs, values, and actions, many of which run counter to those held by one's family, is the business of this stage of living. A powerful force helping to make these choices is the peer group.

The growing importance of being a member of a peer group distinguishes the teenage years from childhood. The process starts in early childhood with the finding of a best friend. The best friend is someone of the same sex who provides a boy or girl with the first experience of being sensitive to and caring deeply about a nonfamily member. This relationship affords opportunities for intimate sharing and collaboration. These best friend duos become the basic unit of early adolescent peer groups, which at first almost always seem to be even numbered.

Cliques reinforce sameness. Their members dress alike (often checking with one another the night before), develop an in-group vocabulary, and share common interests and biases. The groups minimize and discourage differences. They play down dissimilarities in maturation, intelligence, athletic skill, and family income, especially in conversations with parents who can't understand *what* these kids could possibly have in common. Too much success in the classroom or other activities, causing the teenager to stand out significantly above other group members, is frowned upon. Many youngsters, rather than running the risk of forfeiting social acceptance, disparage their high-level achievement. Others lower the level of their performance to conform to the standards of the clique.

Perceived similarities among teenagers in a group give rise to a shared identity. Almost every high school has its elite crowd: wheels, BMOCs, or leading citizens; its athletes, jocks, or animals; and its strong students: brains, grinds, or wonks. The labels "swingers," "greasers," "heads," "nerds," "born agains," or "mathletes" suggest other common qualities a group projects.

Continued clique membership provides young adolescents with leverage to support independent behavior which may run counter to their families' wishes. An adolescent girl may insist that she be permitted to wear grubby-looking jeans and a torn sweatshirt "because all the other kids do." Her younger brother often uses the same argument for permission to attend a punk rock concert in the city.

The end of this life stage comes with entry into young adulthood. Just when this period starts varies enormously because it is strongly influenced by custom, law, and socioeconomic status.

It was not many generations ago that the Protestant confirmation and the Jewish bar and bas mitzvahs, held when children are about thirteen, ushered youngsters into adulthood. They now are more commonly the official entry into teenage status. Until the twentieth century most high school boys and girls had little experience with a carefree adolescence. They were pressed into productive work early. During the Civil War only four states had minimum age work laws. As late as 1900, one child in eight was in the labor force. Gradually a combination of forces, including disgust at industrial exploitation of child labor, a growing desire from older workers to protect themselves from being displaced by the young, and a recognition that greater education led to greater opportunity, came together to regulate the labor of young people under eighteen years of age.

Complicating the question of when we are no longer teenagers is the mixed message society gives us as to when we are considered adults. We can serve our country in combat at age eighteen but may not be served in a bar. Around age seventeen we are adult offenders and no longer juveniles in the criminal courts, though we can neither vote nor marry. At about the same age we can operate a car but will have to reach our twenty-fifth birthday before we can drive without an insurance surcharge.

Entry into young adulthood is a matter of taking on the tasks of this stage. For most this process entails settling down, launching a career, getting married, and having a family. When young adulthood begins is highly correlated with the individual's socioeconomic status, because wealthier families can afford to subsidize the education of their progeny longer, thus prolonging the adolescence of these children.

Staying in school may extend the teenage years well into the twenties. An example is a twenty-three-year-old law student who is still covered by his parent's Blue Cross/Blue Shield health insurance and listed as a dependent on their tax return. When he visits his mother and father he may find himself treated like his sister a decade younger. To his astonishment he may find himself responding with the same behavior. Contrast this experience with the law student's high school classmate who didn't go on to college. Instead he got a job, married his high school sweetheart, and started a family. At twenty-three his adolescence is a distant memory.

Words of Caution

Learning how to tell the difference between a youngster who is normal from one who isn't, understanding the emotional reactions they evoke in us, and learning methods to influence teenage conduct can be helpful to our teenagers. Since we are talking about a complicated and very personal endeavor, a few words of caution are in order.

First, a little knowledge about a subject as complex as human adjustment is like reading about a trail up to the top of a mountain we wish to climb. The printed pages rarely do justice to how complicated and challenging the path really is. The material presented in this book outlines general principles for making broad distinctions between states of emotional adjustment and identifies criteria that distinguish normal from more troubled behavioral patterns. This summary gives us a start in learning both how states of adjustment and particular disorders differ from one another. However, we must remind ourselves that, like the hiker with a trail guide, we will find that any distillation omits a great deal of detail and may not fully tell how arduous the process of understanding teenagers can be.

The second caution is that this book is not a substitute for instinct, common sense, or professional judgment. If you sense something is wrong with your teenager, act on this feeling, even if the adolescent does not exhibit the warning signs of maladjustment given in these pages. Young people rarely suffer lasting psychological harm because their mothers and fathers are overly concerned. It is also true that adolescents can exhibit a number of signs of emotional distress and their parents will know that they are basically all right. This information is not intended to take the place of advice from a family doctor, pediatrician, teacher, priest, minister, or rabbi. They know the child and the family and are in the best position to evaluate a teen's mental stability.

Adolescents have much to gain from our concerns and from our contact with them. In spite of their protests to the contrary, they don't always know what's best for them. A fourteen year old is not the best guide for another fourteen year old. Sometimes youths merely lack information—what's the best way to study for high school final exams or lose ten pounds and keep it off. When things are not going so well they need a mental boost, and we may know some things that help: regular exercise, keeping busy, and focusing on positive rather than negative events all help to raise low spirits. Sometimes our teenage children need us to knock around with, even to knock up against, to help them clarify values and attitudes that will influence lifelong behavior patterns.

And we have much to gain from remaining in contact with our teenagers. Their enthusiasms energize us. Their activity stimulates our interests. Their clear-eyed questioning opens our minds to issues that we have had neither the courage nor wit to probe. And their experiences reawaken long-dormant feelings and thoughts, even conflicts, giving us a second chance to live them. Without them our lives would be infinitely poorer.

2

Is My Teenager Normal?
Telling the Difference

ALEX

Alex never fully worked up to his ability. His teachers always said that his grades would be higher if he tried harder. His current marks were three Cs and a B. Alex was an eighth grader at a parochial school in Albuquerque, New Mexico. When his parents occasionally pestered him to spend more time on his work, Alex smiled, put in a little more effort for a few days, and then tailed off.

Alex had several good friends. They took turns sleeping over at each other's houses. He and his best friend, John, spent hours playing a baseball board game. They compiled extensive statistics on their imaginary players. More than once Alex's mother commented that if they both devoted as much time and effort on their homework they would both be A students.

Alex attended a nearby Catholic church. Though he was lukewarm about CCD classes he was there most weeks. "My parents make me go" is how he explained it to his friends. Alex also was not an exceptional athlete but he played most sports.

In the spring Alex suddenly started paying much more attention to his appearance. Hours were spent in the shower and in front of the mirror. The reason was Rosa, an attractive classmate. Their telephone calls went on for hours and occasionally one of their parents drove them to a movie.

On a warm spring evening, his father drove Alex and Rosa to an eighth grade dance. When he came at 10 P.M. to pick them up, they were nowhere in sight. The father and several of his friends looked for them without success. Frantic, the father drove home. As he arrived, Alex was on the phone talking to his mother. Could his father come and pick them up at school?

His father held his temper in check until they were in the house; "Where have you been and what have you been doing?" he then demanded. "What did you used to do on a beautiful spring evening with a beautiful girl when you were young, Dad?" smiled Alex.

LISA

In November, Lisa's best friend in Portland, Maine, called her mother to say that she was really worried about Lisa. Since entering high school that fall, Lisa had changed a lot. She had gone from being a demure, friendly, and hard-working ninth grader to a faintly outrageous sophomore, contemptuous of old friends, and disinterested in school.

Her mother was glad to hear from Lisa's friend because she'd been worried too. Since September, Lisa's behavior toward her had been increasingly hostile; Lisa made her mother feel she could do nothing right. She made fun of her mother's clothes and slight obesity, interrupted her constantly, and sarcastically challenged her values. Lisa felt that her mother was hopelessly old-fashioned and could never understand the younger generation. These kinds of confrontations often ended with Lisa crying in her room and her mother sobbing in the kitchen.

On the other hand, Lisa still thought her father was terrific and usually behaved herself around him. She also regularly visited her aging grandmother in a nursing home, the only grandchild to do so.

Her mother could see that Lisa was very unhappy. She found her weeping more than once. Lisa started twisting her hair again when she read and began to have stomachaches more often than in the past. Lisa also lost interest in confirmation class and gave up the piano.

Throughout most of the fall, Lisa's behavior was uneven in school. Some days her dress and actions were flamboyant and provocative. Other days her demeanor was much more modest. Lisa's teachers noticed that she seemed poorly prepared for class some of the time and her grades slipped. They also suspected that she composed several of the notes excusing her from school because of illness.

Finally the principal decided to call Lisa and her parents in for a conference. The call relieved her mother, confused her father, and drove Lisa into a frenzy of rage.

FIONA

Fiona hadn't had a meal with her family in a year and a half. Midway through the eighth grade she started eating by herself. It was about then that the antagonism between Fiona and her parents reached the flash point. From her point of view nothing she could do or say pleased her father and mother, so she ate by herself. From their perspective Fiona had a terrible temper, dressed like a freak, hung around with the dregs of society, lied to them constantly about where she was going, was probably using drugs, and seemed destined to fail most of her courses.

A tenth grader in Vancouver, British Columbia, Fiona was aware that something was very wrong with her life. Somewhere along the line she lost interest in school, drifted away from old friends, and began to feel restless and irritable much of the time. Midway through the ninth grade Fiona developed insomnia in addition to headaches. About the same time she began smoking, drinking, and using illicit drugs. These diminished her discomfort for brief periods. Since she couldn't sleep very well anyway, Fiona came home late or told her parents she was staying overnight at a friend's house. She had sex with three different boys. About these experiences she later said to a friend, "No rockets went off."

One Saturday night Fiona and three friends were coming home from a party, all of them drunk. The car skidded into a tree. The front seat passenger died and the driver was paralyzed from the waist down. A third had a head injury. Miraculously, Fiona emerged unscathed physically. Psychologically, she was a wreck. "My god, what's happened to me?" she sobbed to her parents.

PETER

Peter was a capable high school student and had a real talent for computers. As a result of this ability he earned a scholarship to Carnegie-Mellon University in Pittsburgh, only a few miles from his home in subur-

ban Sewickley. Peter was the youngest of three. His older brother and sister were all strong students at other colleges in Pennsylvania. Like them he was premed.

They had been raised by their mother alone since their father's death from a coronary when Peter was eight. Though the father's insurance left them in comfortable circumstances, Peter worked through high school to pay his own expenses. Actually he had three jobs: he taught regular classes for his neighbors to learn to use their personal computers; he set up a computer system for a local theater chain to estimate the requirements for popcorn, candy, and soft drinks; and he was a summer assistant in a medical research laboratory. All who knew Peter were impressed with his energy, capability, and personality.

Shortly after college began, Peter's personality began to change dramatically. He was unhappy living in the dorm and began to be depressed and withdrawn. The lack of privacy bothered him and he felt intimidated by his highly talented roommate. By November everyone who knew Peter was worried about him. He looked disheveled and dirty, stopped eating and sleeping regularly, seemed confused, and had trouble concentrating on his academic work. He began to act strangely. One entire evening he sat rigidly in front of his computer and wouldn't reply to his roommate's questions. The next day Peter began to make undecipherable sounds and strange ritualistic movements with his hands and arms. The roommate called the resident adviser who contacted the health service. When the doctor came into the room Peter began to make weird incoherent statements. When the two-hundred-pound doctor told Peter he wanted him to come to the infirmary, Peter lifted him up, threw him against the wall, and ran out of the room.

It's been said that only a little difference separates one person from another; but these little differences can make a great deal of difference to that individual's mental health and enjoyment of life. Nowhere is the truth of the statement more apparent than during the teenage years. These youngsters can seem very much the same—clothed in the garb of their clique, sharing innermost thoughts with one another, by turns enthusiastic and apathetic, becoming incensed when we are reluctant to swap our values for theirs, exhibiting the same trouble controlling fresh impulses as coordinating new physical powers, and alternating adult behavior with regressive countermarches. Most of these adolescents are normal. A few are not.

Considerable disagreement exists among specialists as to what is "normal" teenage behavior. Some mental health clinicians believe that emotional disruption rebellion toward parental values and identity crisis should be expected. In their minds adolescence is a "developmental disturbance" and maintaining a stable mental equilibrium is itself abnormal. Others who studied normal young people in their natural settings—in high schools and colleges rather than in doctors' offices—reached different conclusions. Instead of finding the majority of these youths in turmoil, and at odds with themselves and others, they discovered that the vast majority pass through this phase of life without turmoil. These teens maintain good relationships with their parents and friends, function effectively in school and at work, adapt without unusual distress to physical changes, and grow into maturity through quiet evolution rather than dramatic revolution.

A closer look at the evidence suggests some truth on both sides of the argument. For instance, about one in five normal high school seniors studied in a Chicago suburb were characterized as having "tumultuous" growth patterns and another third had notable periods of unhappiness and difficulty with adults. Whereas most college youth were normal at the moments in the life cycle when they were studied, a significant minority experienced what was called a "crisis" or "delayed maturation." More than 15 percent had emotional difficulties severe enough to seek psychotherapy. Moreover, a number looked back on their early teenage years with displeasure, saying that this was the worst time of their life they could imagine prior to old age.

For most, these unstable episodes pass quickly and they return to normalcy within a few days or weeks. For some, the turmoil lasts for several months before they are themselves again. For a small fraction, these unstable periods harden into emotional disorders. Distinguishing those boys and girls for whom this unrest and confusion is part of the usual two-way traffic of adolescence—a momentary backward step before continuing the forward progress of maturation—from those for whom this disequilibrium signals the onset of real trouble is one of the most challenging tasks in the mental health field.

TABLE 2.1
Zones of Teenage Adjustment

GREEN ZONE—Normal Adaptation

Balance of satisfaction
- Usual balance
- All spheres reasonably satisfying or not unpleasant

Quality of responses to stress
- For the most part high-level reactions
- Awareness of stress and effects
- Ability to appraise qualities of response
- No impedance of direct action

Stability
- Generally stable
- Attempts at new behavior, attitudes
- Characteristic mood
- Sense of humor
- Feeling of relative well-being

Mental organization
- Variation with personality style
- Independent choices
- Rapid learning from experience

Resources
- Intact
- Accessible

YELLOW ZONE—Temporary Adjustment Reactions

Balance of satisfaction
- At least one troubling area
- Family relations strained
- Inability to accept criticism
- New, unfamiliar, questionable companions

Quality of responses to stress
- Extended periods of lower-level reactions
- Reduced awareness
- Adverse influence on other areas

Stability
- Childlike, challenging, negative traits
- Emotional overreactions
- Heightened physical sensitivity
- Symptom present

Mental organization
- Variable
- Dependent on whim and external stimulation
- Slow profiting from experience

Resources
- Shrinking range of enjoyable leisure activities

ORANGE ZONE—Neurotic Symptoms

Balance of satisfaction
- Acknowledgment of alien distressing symptoms
- Persistent, predictable, and portable
- Marked decrease in pleasure from all areas

Quality of responses to stress
- Excessive, low-level reactions continue
- Stress obscured
- Self-protective reactions cause other problems

Stability
- Crippling symptoms
- Overdriven traits
- Low energy
- Increased physical complaints
- New symptom

Mental organization
- Chronic inefficiency
- Requirement for others' accommodation

Resources
- Few
- Huge effort required
- Little afterglow

RED ZONE—Severe Maladjustments

Balance of satisfaction
• Nothing going well
• Parents giving up
• Isolation
• Passing acquaintances with criminals, addicts,
    down and out

Quality of responses to stress
• Stress relief mechanisms nonfunctional
• Responses major problem themselves
• Drug dependence

Stability
• Out of character
• Disabling depression, anxiety, rage
• Poor self-care, health
• Exhaustion

Mental organization
• Great impairment
• Near impossibility of doing required tasks

Resources
• Depleted

Table 2.1 provides three kinds of information. First, it identifies primary features of adolescents' behavior most likely to reflect the quality of their adaptation to life. These are: the extent to which the young person realizes pleasure from family and friends, school/work, and play; the maturity of ways of reacting to stress; the degree of stability of personality, moods and physical health; mental organization; and, access to resources. Second, the table separates adolescent behavior into four zones of adjustment. Third, it shows that as the psychological well-being of a youngster deteriorates, the primary features generally reveal this.

Let's look at the characteristics of these four states of adjustment.

The Green Zone: Normal Adaptation

Normal teenagers enjoy pleasant relationships with family and friends. Most of the time they feel close to their mothers and fathers, believe their parents are happy with them, and expect these positive emotions to persist into the future. They have a say in family decisions and can disagree comfortably with the older generation.

As Alex's example suggests, being with friends is important to them. Most have no trouble becoming friendly with others. Like Alex, they have had a best friend in early adolescence and experienced the first deep caring for someone outside the family. They may incorporate particular phrases or gestures into their conversation with one another which evoke shared feelings of intimacy and exclude more casual friends as well as parents. Four out of five older teens belong to a group and would rather be with others their own age than alone. They give and receive support from these contemporaries. When an intimate is hurting they are there to help. When they confide troubles to a chum they can anticipate a supportive response. The majority believe the opposite sex finds them attractive and want a romantic attachment.

The primary occupation of boys and girls through their teens, and for many well beyond, is school. Normal youngsters find going to classes reasonably satisfying or at least not regularly disagreeable. Some find school interesting, challenging, and a place to exhibit their competence. Others travel with Alex in the lower half of their class without chronic displeasure, though they don't particularly care for school. About half of these adolescents also work part-time. Employed young people often enjoy working far more than they enjoy school.

Young people in the green zone can play. Activities that are playful as opposed to working or loving are nonobligatory, don't require high achievement, and can be abandoned for something else as interests change. Alex has fun playing board games, but he can skip a day here and there without withdrawal symptoms. He enjoys sports even though he is not particularly gifted athletically. If the whim strikes, he can give up board games in favor of computer hacking, baseball for tennis.

Psychiatrists have long observed that the life experiences, thoughts, and feelings of mental patients are no different from those of us who somehow resist mental breakdown. It might be imagined that teenagers remain normal because fortune has been good to them: they love their parents and vice versa; their friends are numerous and expressive; they enjoy being a straight-A student while starring on the basketball team; and they have no melancholy or bizarre fantasies. In fact, normal adolescents—like the rest of us—rarely go for long without being frustrated by loved ones, blocked from obtaining a desired goal, or upset by a run of bad luck. Being normal does not exempt them from frightening thoughts, unacceptable desires crying for release, flurries of temper, or common misery. The difference between these youngsters who remain mentally stable and those who develop emotional disorders is how they handle these stresses.

Normal teenagers manage emotions triggered by external frustrations or inner conflicts effectively. That is, they know they feel tense or angry or helpless, and they know why. Rosa, Alex's girlfriend, cares very much about her grades. She's upset because she has five final exams in two weeks. Green-zone teens can examine how they are reacting to the stress, appraise whether their responses make sense, and can change as needed: though it is painful, the girl knows her high degree of nervousness about exams prods her to study harder, so it's worth putting up with. Finally, ways of controlling stress don't seriously compromise other areas of satisfaction: Rosa knows that to study for her finals will mean she'll be unable to see Alex as much as she would like and she is likely to be irritable at home, so before exams she'll warn them all and afterward she'll do something nice for her parents and spend more time with her boyfriend.

If we watch these youngsters combat the stress in their lives, we will notice them using some of the higher-level self-protective responses summarized in Table 4.2 on pages 59 and 60: Rosa employs anticipation and a sense of humor to help her with exam tension, and she may drift off into brief fantasy excursions to relieve the grind of studying. Adolescents in this zone also will use various forms of direct control and direct action: the young woman increases her carbohydrate intake because it makes her feel better even though she knows the result will be some weight gain she'll have to take off.

Youths in the green zone exhibit stability of personality, mood, and physical health. They will experiment with new attitudes, values, and behavior, trying them out to see how they work—much the same way as with a stylish new piece of clothing. A sweet, compliant boy may affect a provocative, challenging style for a while, whereas his sister may try her hand at dressing the role of the temptress. Shortly these adolescents discard these roles to play another part: the girl might imagine herself as a missionary and practices asceticism and her brother with a minor talent in basketball may begin to rehearse walking like a jock. These new behaviors change rapidly, with only a few aspects remaining as part of the youngster's growing identity.*

The overall mood of youth tends to be relatively consistent. The amount of depression, guilt, shame, and aggression is no greater than at other stages of life. As Alex's final comment illustrates, teenagers can also show a good sense of humor. Indeed, of all the signs of mental health, a sense of humor is the most reliable. It permits us to acknowledge the origin of feelings of distress and dissipate it through laughter. Clinicians treating disturbed youths look for the return of humor as a sign of mental stability in the same way Northerners see the first robin as a harbinger of spring.

Normal young people feel pretty well physically. In the words of the immortal American songwriters Lester Santley and Thomas "Fats" Waller, "looking good but feeling bad is hard to do." A correlation exists between poor physical health and less well-adjusted mental states. The more emotionally disturbed, the thicker the medical record. When normal youngsters don't feel well, it is for a reason—for example, the flu, menstrual cramps, an allergic reaction to ragweed, or chicken pox. Other reasons may be: this boy has trouble sleeping in the fall; that girl gains weight in the winter; someone else's skin problems kick up in the spring.

To express their growing independence from adult direction, teenagers exert more control over what happens to their bodies. In an effort to set themselves apart, they wear unusual hairstyles, clothes, or jewelry. Control of their bodies expresses itself in ignoring parental admonitions for health care—gorging themselves on junk food, playing their stereos at 100 decibels, trying licit or illicit drugs. These experimentations are usually relatively brief.

The mental organization of normal teens allows them to do what they want to do. High school students may force themselves to complete hard courses—which they loathe—and hold down miserable jobs, for example, as dishwashers, after school because they want to go to college. They learn quickly from experience. They may experiment with a range of potentially harmful behaviors, situations, or people on the way to becoming individuals separate from their mothers and fathers. But it doesn't continue. A poor math grade may cause a boy to do his homework when he is fresh and the TV is off. After getting drunk with a middle-aged alcoholic dishwasher two nights in a row after work, he declines an offer the next week to go drinking.

Until recently an evaluation of someone's mental state consisted largely of finding out what was wrong with that person. Early trauma, frustrations, conflicts, and failure to resolve developmental tasks were surveyed while noting the presence of nervousness, depression, or irritability. Clinicians devoted nowhere the same effort to the *plus* side— discovering what was going right in a person's life. On the plus side are pleasures from working, loving, and playing. Also on the plus side are resources. Resources encompass anything we can call upon to cushion the impact of failure, bad news, or loss. They provide compensating experiences when we feel temporarily overwhelmed by life's stresses.

In the green zone, teenagers have access to resources. The most potent resources are friends, a belief in something greater than themselves, or a dream that gives the adolescent a sense of self and a continuity of purpose. Other resources that provide compensating positive experiences to counterbalance unpleasant stress include a strong constitution, physical attractiveness, intelligence, hobbies or skills.

There are far more ways of being normal than abnormal. Teenagers exhibit their normalcy through a unique balance of working, loving, and playing, in with a wide range of personality traits; they cope with stress in a dozen different ways and respond distinctively to the tasks of living. By contrast, mental disorders limit the possible range of behaviors. As the adjustment level of young people deteriorates to the yellow, orange, and red zones, adolescents begin to resemble one another more and more.

The Yellow Zone: Temporary Adjustment Reactions

As the name suggests, temporary adjustment reactions are transient periods of conflict and turmoil. They occur in about one adolescent in two.

During these periods passions surge to the brink of control while episodes of anxiety, depression, and the fearful recognition of being alone in the world fracture mental tranquility. The body is subjected to relentless scrutiny and is found wanting. Primitive ways of coping with stress appear, including outright denial that a problem exists. Goals that yesterday seemed worthwhile now seem murky, and in their place come fantasies of being a rock star. The urge to try sex and drugs is equally terrifying and irresistible. As Lisa's case illustrates, positive feelings toward one or both parents are suddenly reversed—love becomes hate, dependence turns into revolt, admiration converts to contempt, and defiance replaces obedience. In unguarded moments an inner conviction grows in these teenagers that something desperate and horrible is wrong with them. They wonder if they are going mad—an aching apprehension shared by their parents.

This instability can develop in response to easily identified external events—changing schools or communities, death, separation, or divorce in the older generation, maturational lag or precocity, academic or social difficulties in school, or peer influence. Just as often, however, these periods of turmoil seem to jump out of nowhere. Little relationship exists between the severity of the stress and the onset of temporary adjustment reactions.

This yellow zone is marked by impaired satisfaction in at least one major sphere. Moodiness, irritability, and withdrawal behind closed doors sever contact with family. Interest in school abruptly disappears. Enthusiasm for having fun wanes and is replaced by whining complaints of having nothing to do.

Teenagers in the yellow zone may be bitingly sarcastic toward their mothers, or convey the conviction that they believe their fathers to be totally inadequate. These comments, however, are not intended to cause their parents grief—though the senior set may suffer in earnest. In fact, when Lisa's mother breaks down weeping, Lisa is shaken. She didn't know she had this much power to upset the older generation.

Though it comes easily for them to be confrontational, sarcastic, and critical, these boys and girls don't take counterpunching very well. Any suggestion that their expectations may be unrealistic—for example, "How do you expect to become a doctor, Lisa, with grades that make high school graduation questionable?"—they belligerently shout down, as though saying something loudly enough makes it more likely to be true.

Lower-level self-protective responses appear for extended periods. As is shown in Table 4.2 on pages 59 and 60, we are likely to see rationalization—"My grades really don't indicate how much I've learned, Mom," says Lisa with three Ds and a C. Appearing for the first time will be projection—"You are always yelling at me," might scream a boy to his father who asked him gently to cut the lawn.

A distinctive self-protective response of the yellow zone is acting out. This is the use of action as a means of warding off anxiety and uncertainty. The fifteen-year-old boy who insists that he must free himself of his "smothering" mother by hitchhiking to Chicago with an older friend to find work for the summer, who rejects offers of money as a grubstake because he's sure he can support himself, who spurns the phone number of an old family friend in the Windy City in case he needs a warm meal, is exhibiting a teenager's trust in the special magic of action to overcome doubt and fear. This means of coping with the usual stresses of adolescence is ubiquitous and usually transient. At eighteen the same boy, setting out to hitchhike to Denver, doesn't mind having his mom pack him a lunch and gladly accepts cash, a credit card, and the phone number of a distant relative along the way because he's more certain of his own competencies.

The prefix "hyper-" best describes other responses to stress: hypervigilance (exaggerated awareness), hyperkinesis (restlessness and an impulse to stay on the move), hyperintellection (obsessive worrying without a solution), and hyperperfectionism. In addition, yellow-zone adolescents use fantasy to excess—for example, dreaming of being a country and western star while avoiding problems at school or at home.

Denial occurs as an alternative to logic. Lisa assures her mother that she and her boyfriend can sleep together without using birth control because she "knows" she won't get pregnant. Denial sets the stage for counterphobic behaviors—plunging into acts that a youngster most fears. These may appear as brief flurries of deviant behavior with friends. Together Lisa and her friends skip school, try drugs, and shoplift. Should they be confronted by adults while acting up, remorse and a commitment to self-correction follow.

Lower-level responses to stress reduce awareness that a problem exists. A shy fifteen-year-old boy can cope with anxiety triggered by entering the ninth grade in a new town his family moved to over the summer by computer-assisted avoidance. Instead of trying to make new friends or involving himself in school or community activities, he might withdraw to learn new languages to program his computer with. As a result the problem remains, though it is felt less painfully. Moreover, low-level self-protective responses adversely affect other areas. Because this boy uses the computer as a refuge, his social maturity begins to lag behind that of his contemporaries.

Instability runs through personality, mood, and physical health. Mature behavior suddenly peels away, revealing childlike traits—a 15 year old regresses to sucking her thumb while Lisa reverts to twisting her hair while studying. Defiance erupts in a formerly placid teen who now challenges every parental request. The ability to laugh at oneself vanishes though a sense of humor about others remains. Physical health might decline slightly. Familiar stress symptoms appear—headaches, stomach problems, insomnia.

In this zone mental organization deteriorates. It's harder and harder for adolescents to make themselves do what they wish to do. A tendency grows to make school performance contingent upon external factors. Lisa says she has no trouble doing her homework in history because the teacher is "stimulating," but she can't drive herself to study other subjects because the teachers of those are not. Another example is a boy who says he can obtain decent grades only when a class turns him on because he can't motivate himself.

Youngsters in this category profit somewhat more slowly from experience than do normal teenagers. It takes her being called into school with her parents because Lisa's teachers are tired of her coming late to classes, not showing up at all, sliding grades and nastiness, before she understands that she needs to "clean up her act."

In the yellow zone the absolute number of resources shrinks, thinning out the cushion of positive experiences to buffer stress. Because of the turmoil in her life, Lisa gives up confirmation class and the piano; a classmate of hers forsakes the 4-H Club and his stamp collection. Their lives are poorer for it. Later, when they recover, they will be sorry they didn't pursue these interests.

It should be said here that taken as a whole the behaviors and attitudes of youngsters in the yellow zone are just as often mature and positive as regressive and oppositional. Lisa's good relationship with her father and dutiful attachment to her grandmother are examples. Also, although the regressive patterns of the yellow zone would be ominous in an adult, the remarkable resiliency of the youthful psyche enables teens to recover their emotional balance relatively quickly and return to normalcy.

Questions that puzzled parents ask about transient adjustment reactions are "How long does this go on?" or "When should we start to be worried?" While this obviously depends a great deal on the individual adolescent, a reasonable outside limit is three to six months. If the troubling behavior continues beyond that length, the youngster may be frozen in neurotic symptoms typical of the orange zone of adjustment.

The Orange Zone: Neurotic Symptoms

Parents and mental health workers have far less trouble identifying youngsters in the orange zone of neurotic symptoms than normal teenagers or those in the yellow zone. As with Fiona, the distress is obvious, recognized by the teenagers and adults alike. The psychological impairment is persistent, predictable, and portable. Instead of a spontaneous return to normalcy after three to six months, problems solidify or grow worse than ever. We can predict with depressing accuracy that Fiona will not be able to eat with her family without blowing up. Others unfailingly drink to excess at parties, or suffer panic attacks which cause them to fail exams. Changing schools doesn't help; neither does sending the adolescent to live with an aunt and uncle in Oregon. Before long the same maladaptive patterns begin again.

The orange zone is marked by decreased pleasure in all areas—antagonistic relations with family, loneliness, poor grades in school, and the inability to find or keep a job. For these youngsters the pleasures that come so easily to normal adolescents seem as unreachable as flying to the moon. Some recall better days, and the contrast is painfully and sharply apparent: things were great for Fiona until the eighth grade when the bottom fell out. For others decreased satisfaction grows gradually: over the years hostility replaces affectionate family relationships between the generations.

Occasionally things look fine on the outside but the inner experience is quite different. Highly talented teenagers with neurotic symptoms have emotional reactions to their accomplishments that are dramatically at odds with what might be anticipated. The girl at the top of her class can react to an A with only the relief of disaster averted, of having fooled her teachers once again. She knows that one day they will find her out and give her the C she is convinced she deserves. The state debating champion might be positive that his father respects him for his achievements but doesn't really like him. A fourteen-year-old backstroker may deeply resent that her ability converted the swimming she once did for pleasure into an inescapable drudgery which isolates her from normal teenage life. But she doesn't see how she can escape because she feels it's a sin to waste her talent.

Sometimes orange-zone youths have a guilty secret that strips away any pleasure from their achievements. The most attractive girl in the junior class will maintain her figure by binge eating and throwing up.

Without four joints of marijuana every day the best-liked kid in high school would be unable to be friendly to anyone. Other examples include those apparently well-functioning young people who can't resist chronic, alien, irresistible impulses to gamble, steal, or make obscene phone calls. It doesn't always have to be an action no one else knows about which causes distress. Unrelenting, frightening thoughts serve the same purpose. Some teens can't shake the thought of taking a chain saw to their younger siblings, obsess about their parents being killed in a freeway crack-up, or feel that no matter how good things look disaster is just around the corner.

Excessive, immature ways of coping with stress—especially denial, displacement of aggression, and projection—become fixed self-protective responses. Avoidance increasingly typifies how these youngsters respond to problems. Fiona handles her worries about school by "forgetting" to bring her book home, spending her free time talking on the phone to her friends, and then cutting those classes in which she has the most difficulty.

Compulsive disobedience makes an appearance in the orange zone. All adolescents defy their parents once in awhile. But these teens regularly disregard authority. Frequently their disobedience seriously compromises pleasure from living: ignoring her mother's insistence that she do her homework each night and get a job after school, Fiona fails most of her courses and becomes increasingly depressed with nothing to do. Defiance often takes the form of teens' hurling themselves into those very dangerous activities parents warn most vociferously about: diving off a 30 foot cliff into an abandoned quarry, snorting cocaine, having casual sex without using birth control, or driving recklessly without seat belts, especially after downing a pint of vodka at a party.

Though these lower-level self-protective responses provide the adolescent with momentary psychic relief, these ways of reacting to stress obscure the very thing that promotes the need for these psychological defenses. They restore inner peace at the price of diminishing upsetting feelings that something is wrong and needs to be examined and corrected. Thus Fiona's seduction of several boys as a way of shutting out her own anxiety about sexual feelings and her mother's stern prohibitions never honestly deals with the problem. She also causes difficulties in other areas—parental distress, bad reputation, estrangement from her female friends, the possibility of venereal disease and pregnancy as well as unfulfilling sexual experiences.

Lower-level self-protective responses are supplemented by external means of feeling better. Abuse of food, tobacco, caffeine, alcohol, stimulants and sedatives, or illicit drugs become necessary in order to function.

Crippling symptoms—anxiety, helplessness, or explosive anger—infiltrate the personality. They emerge without reason. Fiona has a temper tantrum when asked to come to dinner with the grandparents and stomps off to her room. If we were to ask her later what set her off she would be hard put to tell us. Phobias, panic attacks, tics, stuttering, or compulsive rituals emerge. Because they so limit the range of the individual's freedom they become an additional burden.

A recognizable feature of the orange zone is the intensification of particular aspects of the personality. Often this overdriven behavior is a reaction to a subconscious conflict. For example, a normally aggressive, dominant fourteen-year-old boy turns into a bully, terrorizing other youngsters because he feels socially inadequate and doesn't know how to make friends. For him being feared is being somebody even if it isn't what he wants. Overdriven behaviors are indiscriminate—the boy has an insatiable need to bully everyone—he needs to have people fear him over and over again, and blocking this need causes great frustration.

Fiona likened her psychological problems to walking around continuously wearing a forty-pound pack. Getting through each day burdened by this heavy load is tiring—one reason that teenagers in the orange zone have notably less energy than do their contemporaries. They also will exhibit a number of physical complaints—some of them new. In addition to her headaches Fiona develops insomnia. Trips to the doctor increase and medicine intake grows without long-term relief.

The mental functioning of these teens resembles that of those who have recently experienced frontline combat or another form of severe stress. They have trouble processing information—concentrating, shutting out unwanted thoughts, remembering—are impaired in their capacity to make and stick with decisions, and exhibit limited confidence in their capacity to take action. Procrastination dogs the beginning of any work. When they start, they proceed slowly, easily losing momentum, and falling victim to obsessive worrying or compulsive pointless checking and rechecking. New tasks are viewed as potential catastrophes rather than as challenging opportunities to exhibit competence.

Adolescents in the orange zone require that others accommodate their neurotic behavior; for example, for a principal to permit a sixteen-year-old boy with school phobia to miss Mondays and the first day after holidays because of phantom stomachaches for she feels he is not able to conform to the same rules as are other students. Fiona's parents give up trying to encourage her to eat with them and resign themselves to the fact that they no longer have a say in what she does out of the house.

Young people with neurotic symptoms can't find much to do that brings them pleasure. The effort required to get to church makes it more trouble than it's worth. The dream of being a lawyer fades somewhere along the way. If a father insists that his son play golf with him, the boy will find that he still enjoys it. But the afterglow—those good feelings which used to last several hours afterward—quickly wanes. Old friends tire of their excesses, quirks, moodiness, limitations, and self-centeredness, and they pull away.

The Red Zone: Severe Maladjustments

Very few teenagers develop the severe maladjustments characteristic of the red zone—fewer than one in a hundred. At this level of serious trouble are well-known mental disorders—schizophrenia, depression, and mania. In addition are numerous adolescent behavior patterns carried to the extreme: paralyzing fears, self-starvation, drug dependence, delinquency, or personality fragmentation. We'll look at these specific severe maladjustments that make their presence felt in the teenage years in later chapters. For now we'll examine several general features demarcating the red zone.

Young people at this level cannot wring sustained satisfaction from any sphere of life. They wear their parents out with their pain, neediness, self-destructive behavior, volatile emotions, and inability to think about anyone but themselves. It's not unusual to find mothers and fathers making a decision to preserve what's left of their own sanity and save the rest of the family. They place a seriously troubled son in the hands of a professional or allow their daughter to go her own way. The household is so peaceful and enjoyable when these teens are not around.

Good friends are long gone. Passing acquaintances come from the underbelly of society, and they frequently victimize these teenagers. Unstable heterosexual and homosexual alliances of convenience form but are devoid of romance. Youths in the red zone forget what it's like to play.

Because they are so much at the mercy of their emotions and are mentally confused much of the time, most cannot function successfully in class or hold a job. If they go to school they frequently sit dispiritedly in special classes for the handicapped, learning disabled, and psychologically crippled. If they have jobs they are dead-end drudgery with high turnover.

Self-protective responses to stress function poorly, offering little relief. Cascades of depression, destructive rage, and anxiety periodically deluge these adolescents but these emotions appear to have no cause and no way of being stopped. Like Peter, they can become violent when pressed. Often the ways these youngsters use to relieve their distress become part of the problem. A fifteen year old may create an elaborate fantasy that a certain professional basketball star will fall in love with her and make her life all right, and so she gives up trying to straighten herself out. Another may project his own sense of worthlessness on the world around him, seeing everyone and everything as without value, alienating his remaining friends.

Drug abuse riddles this group. Many teenagers have been prescribed compounds to calm them down, pep them up, or provide surcease from disquieting thoughts. Most have access to illicit substances. Not a few organize each day around the task of finding chemical peace of mind.

The personalities of people in the red zone may bear little resemblance to their former selves. This occurrence is most apparent when well-functioning young people suddenly become mentally disturbed. As Peter's case suggests, these unexpected disorders—called reactive psychoses—often happen at a point of transition in their lives: The first year of college, military basic training, during a semester abroad. These psychotic states are called reactive because the individual was functioning well enough before the onset of the disorder, the disturbance came in response to a clear-cut environmental stress and worsened rapidly. Recovery from these states comes to pass almost as rapidly as it developed.

For other young people the severe maladjustment seems to result from slow deterioration. Adaptive qualities wear away and underlying pathological features gradually assert themselves. These are called "process" psychoses—as opposed to reactive ones—because of the insidious onset. Among these individuals the dominant personality traits may bear a closer resemblance to the personality when normal: the girl who becomes seriously depressed may have always had a pessimistic style; or the boy who develops schizophrenia may have had a tendency to overthink problems for years.

Depression, helplessness, and anxiety disable. While an adolescent in the yellow or orange zones can be upset and continue to attend school or relate to parents, red-zone teenagers are incapacitated by these same emotions. Their moods, however, may swing wildly from a depressive abyss one moment to an excited high the next. The mood doesn't quite fit the circumstance. A girl may maintain resolute good humor in the face of serious losses and then break down weeping over an episode of an afternoon TV soap. Some might find their emotions flat and blunted. They speak in listless monotones which display the emptiness inside. A boy will bang his head against the wall or burn his arm with a cigarette saying, "I can't *feel* anything."

Youths in the red zone frequently are in poorer health than are their age-mates at higher levels of adjustment. To some degree this is because their personal preoccupations leave little time for them to care for their physical condition, so they have a higher incidence of cavities, skin conditions, GI problems, and the like. We see the effect of substance abuse in the smoker's hack, caffeine nerves, alcoholic's liver, as well as the bruises, breaks, and sprains resulting from the higher incidence of accidents which befalls this group. Weighed down by the problems of coping somehow with an unsatisfying external world and an unpredictable inner life, these young people are constantly exhausted.

The mental functioning of teenagers with severe maladjustments is greatly impaired. Some like Peter who are in the grip of a psychotic disturbance will become disoriented: they lose track of time, place, person, or situation. This disorientation may be rather dramatic as in the case of a schizophrenic who believes that he is the new Christ and it is his job to convert everyone to Christianity. It may be a more subtle process as when a runaway teenage girl is unsure of whether it's May or June, to or from where she is hitchhiking, and who she is since she's left home and given up on becoming a lawyer.

In this state of mind it's very difficult to get very much done at all. When one is distracted by internal preoccupations and real difficulties in day-to-day living, it's nearly impossible to process information, to make plans, and to act. The simplest task—cooking breakfast, taking a shower, retrieving the mail—seems insurmountable.

One of the most striking qualities of the red zone is the absence of resources. Being too preoccupied with inner feelings and thoughts, or too

disorganized to maintain an interest in leisure pleasure, results in their
having very little to cushion or comfort them against daily stresses.

Desperate and debilitating as these conditions can be, we need to be
aware that these individuals do not exhibit signs of their maladjustments
all the time. They may have weeks, even months, of behaving at a level
approximately normal. Even adolescents hospitalized with serious mental
disorders can appear far better adjusted than we might imagine. A Harvard professor knowing he had to teach a course on abnormal psychology
decided to spend several days with inpatients in a mental hospital to try
to understand firsthand how they differed from the students he taught.
He was astonished to discover how at first the youthful patients resem-
bled their contemporaries in his classroom. They talked pleasantly,
played cards, watched TV, and even conducted a form of patient government. On closer scrutiny, however, he began to recognize delusional
thinking and impaired-reality testing in specific areas among these young
people, but these symptoms were not as obvious as he thought initially
they would be.

No matter how troubled their teenage years, most adolescents become
effective, reasonably well-adjusted thirty-five year olds. As parents, we
can foster this normal growth process by helping our youngsters identify
and avoid major problems that have a high potential for closing down
future options. A messy room is not a red flag, nor are a skimpy bathing
suit, an F in geometry, coming in two hours after curfew, or being
caught smoking marijuana. Only a few behavior patterns have the potential for lasting harm—endangering oneself, isolation from friends and
loved ones, falling well behind academically, trouble with the law. Even
among youngsters in real jeopardy, most recover their mental equilibrium because the teenage years are a time of maximal support from
others and many second chances.

Far richer, more varied qualities and behavior patterns distinguish
green-zone adaptation from stages of declining adjustment. There are
many ways of being normal. Each normal teenager finds his or her
unique pattern which is as unique as his or her fingerprints. By contrast,
when adaptation deteriorates these youngsters look more and more the
same.

The portrayal of normalcy is descriptive, not prescriptive. These
sketches of the characteristics of normal adaptation, temporary adjustment reactions, neurotic symptoms, and severe maladjustments are in-

tended to convey an overall feeling for the differences among these mental states. We should remind ourselves, however, that any teenager will exhibit characteristics that are not encompassed by this or other descriptions.

These pictures of differing states of adjustment provide a context in which to appreciate the variations among specific teenage problems described in the next chapters. We may not be quite as alarmed at an otherwise normal fourteen-year-old boy who experiments with marijuana as we are likely to be with a teenage girl with orange-zone characteristics who is also starving herself.

These zones of adjustment resemble four snapshots laid side by side. It is not assumed when a teenager's mental health declines that the deterioration will follow an orderly sequence—from green to yellow, then to orange, and finally to red. There may be a transition from normalcy to a temporary adjustment reaction which sets the stage for a neurotic disorder. Just as often, however, an adolescent is functioning in the green zone one moment and suddenly exhibits the signs of a serious maladjustment the next. Recovery from emotional difficulties can follow the same abrupt, unpredictable pathway.

Chapters 5 to 13 focus on specific issues common to teenagers—for example, transitional anxiety, sexual precocity, learning problems, and dealing with loss. Each chapter will discriminate normal manifestations of this behavior from more serious versions in the yellow, orange, and red zones of severity.

3

The Effect of Teenagers on Adult Mental Health

> *Our youth now seem to love luxury. They have bad manners and contempt for authority. They show disrespect for elders, and they love to chatter instead of exercise. Children are now tyrants, not the servants, of their households. They no longer rise when elders enter the room. They contradict their parents, chatter before company, gobble up their food, and tyrannize their teachers.*

This quotation is from the ancient Athenian philosopher Socrates. Though voiced close to twenty-five hundred years ago, these words catch the sentiments of many modern parents about the younger generation: aggravation, resentment, and fear. Now as then, something about having a teenager can badly affect the emotional stability of previously well-adjusted adults.

Much has been said about the effects of mothers and fathers on adolescent mental health. Rarely do we pick up a newspaper or magazine without an article tracing a youngster's breakdown to parental mishandling. Library shelves bulge with well-thumbed books about how to avoid having disturbed children. Even if we follow these directions we are told that adolescent emotional upheaval is a normal event.

Little has been said about the other side of the coin—the impact of youths on the mental health of their parents. Only recently has the ancient Persian legend of Rustam and Sohrab received attention. This is the tale of Rustam, the famous warrior, who unwittingly kills his son, Sohrab, in a battle. As Sohrab lies dying, a charm bracelet on his wrist which his mother gave him as a child reveals his true identity to the now grief-filled Rustam. This story of parental antagonism toward their offspring is called the Rustam Complex. It is a spectrum of negative parental sentiments about their children: from indifference and rejection, through resentment, envy, and bitterness, to overwhelming fury and destructive rage.

The last two decades provide ample evidence of adult hostility toward their young. We have, for instance, the startlingly harsh response of some in the older generation who believed the protesting students shot down at Kent State got what they deserved. Then there is the growing recognition that battered children are a problem of considerable magnitude. Hot lines and support groups regularly advertise themselves as a resource for mothers and fathers who have had all they can take from their kids.

A growing body of research supports the notion that parents and children each influence the emotions and actions of the other. On this two-way street youngsters alter the older generation as they are in turn changed by them. As the title of the book, *Child Effects on Adults,* suggests, developmental psychologists find ample evidence that children determine the behavior of their caretakers. As an example, temperamentally active and aggressive youngsters can drive otherwise placid mothers and fathers to apply high-scale physical punishment to try to control them, the mirror image of the popular thesis that punishing parents cause aggression in their progeny.

Intergenerational conflict increases in early adolescence. The emotional tenor of relationships between young males especially and their parents changes significantly at puberty. The majority of boys are less respectful of their mothers, interrupt them more often, and explain their reasons for wanting to do something with decreasing frequency. In apparent reaction to this behavior the mothers become more assertive toward these teenagers, interrupt them more often, and more frequently demand compliance to rules without explaining why. Fathers tend to behave much like the mothers toward their sons—in spite of the fact that these early adolescent boys are *not* more assertive toward them.

Sources of Instability in Parents of Teenagers

What is it that causes otherwise sane adults to destabilize around teen-agers, giving way to wildly swinging moods, emotional outbursts, and erratic behavior? What causes a mother and adolescent daughter to be unable to share a meal together for years, a father's despair at his son who cheerfully underachieves in school, or parents who need tranquiliz-ers, alcohol, or psychotherapy to diminish the pain the youngsters gener-ate in them? Let's look at four sources of this distress in the parents of teenagers.

CLASHING TEMPERAMENTS

In a number of families the temperament of a particular youngster is incompatible with the personality styles of the older generation. Clash-ing temperaments is a problem from birth onward, typically intensifying at puberty. By then parents of offspring with dispositions at odds with their own have experienced considerable emotional wear and tear. The accumulated frustrations of raising a child with a differing or difficult personality can result in excessive parental anger or withdrawal from the teenager over relatively minor incidents.

Our own temperament includes consistent ways of emoting, thinking, and acting. If we know our daughter's basic personality, we can predict with considerable accuracy how she will react to meeting new people, being told "no," seeing a sad movie, being asked by her brother to borrow her bike, or having nothing to do. In contrast to other character-istics that change over the life cycle, temperament remains stable.

That the basic disposition of human beings differs in important ways was recognized by the ancient Greeks. Pediatricians have long noted that infants typically exhibit one of three types of temperament—easy, slow to warm up, and difficult. The easy babies quickly develop regular eating and sleeping patterns, accept frustration with little fuss, are outgoing and energetic, and adapt quickly to new situations. By contrast those in the second group are often placid, milder-mannered, shy, slower to engage in unfamiliar experiences, and adapt cautiously. As the term implies, diffi-cult infants exhibit irregular eating and sleeping patterns, are given to tantrums when frustrated, and react badly to new experiences.

More recently, evidence gathered by child psychologist Jerome Kagan and his Harvard colleagues indicates that differences among children with specific traits such as aggression, dominance, dependence, or socia-bility remains consistent through adolescence. Efforts to change young-sters' behavior have met with mixed results and do not appear to alter the underlying temperament.

A major source of potential intergenerational conflict develops when a youngster's temperament is very different from everyone else's in the household. For example, placid, cautious parents, who have produced two equally placid, cautious offspring, have born to them an active, extro-verted girl. As an infant she's energetic, outgoing, and restless. By her second birthday she refuses to take naps anymore and is into everything. At three she breaks her collarbone playing on a jungle gym with the older kids—the first of four fractures prior to adolescence. In school she makes friends quickly and is a leader, though she can be nasty when she doesn't get her own way. Her grades are fairly good considering how little she studies. Lots of interests absorb her energies, but she doesn't stay with anything very long—except playing ice hockey with the boys.

Imagine how her parents must feel trying to raise her. Her activity level wears them out. Her resistance when they try to contain her drive them into an upsetting and uncharacteristic rage. After four trips to the emergency ward they live in constant fear that her life will be ruined because of her failure to anticipate the consequences of her adventure-some spirit.

Powerful as the influence of parents is, and as much as a child may want to please them, the girl has within her personality a core that resists alteration. Moreover, the temperaments of her father and mother aren't going to change much either. Even if they wish they could, they are unlikely to feel comfortable with her carefree rather than cautious atti-tude, her tendency to be superficial rather than thorough, her catholic rather than selective taste in friends, and her desire to follow her own instincts rather than be guided by knowledgeable adults.

By adolescence the nerves of both the youngster and her parents have been frayed by the inability of one generation to accommodate the other. The normal acceleration in the teenager's efforts to seize greater control of her life by opposing parental values, choosing her own friends, and making unilateral decisions about what she puts on, and in, her body can cause her parents' anxiety level to go through the ceiling. The more they try to regulate her the more antagonistic and defiant she becomes.

The problem with difficult children is not that their temperaments clash with parental personalities, it is that they are *very* hard to raise.

Their unpredictable eating and sleeping patterns are exhausting. They want, want, want, but nothing pleases them. Hour after hour they shriek. Even when they are happy, their loud and explosive laughter grates. The most predictable characteristic of these youngsters is they have difficulty adjusting to any new situation. Whether it is different food, toilet training, unfamiliar playmates, beginning school, a trip, or summer camp, their initial response will be the same—fear, crying, withdrawal, and regression.

Since adolescence requires a great many new adaptations, we can predict this will be a tough period for both generations. Teenagers have to cope with a constantly changing school environment—new teachers, buildings, subjects, increased competitiveness among classmates, a reshuffling of the peer group, and relationships with the opposite sex. Teenagers with difficult temperaments will have more severe adjustment problems than will others. To the extent that these transitions are well spaced a youngster may have sufficient time to manage them with parental support.

Should these difficult adolescents be forced to adjust to many new experiences simultaneously—for example, the family moves when the student is in the tenth grade—all of the negative behavior that typified their childhood will reemerge. If they are to make the adjustment to the new situations, the parents—then in their second decade of struggling to raise these frustrating boys and girls—will be required to once again help them out. It is not so surprising that a mother might think to herself when she's had all she can take, "A judge allows me to divorce my husband on the grounds of incompatibility. It's too bad a court won't let me separate from my fifteen year old for the same reason!"

CONTRAST IN LIFE CYCLE TASKS

It's said that the two worst times of a woman's life are when she turns thirteen, and when her daughter turns thirteen. The truth of this statement lies in the recognition that a large part of what makes dealing with a teenager so upsetting are the issues parents must cope with in their own stage of the life cycle. These stand in sharp contrast to the developmental tasks confronting the adolescent.

From Chapter 2 we recall that a component of normal adjustment is being able to find satisfaction from a balance of work, love, and play.

What causes middle-aged parents to be happy with these spheres of their lives is usually vastly different from what makes their teenage children happy. The struggles of each generation to resolve its own life stage challenges can so change the atmosphere at home that it takes very little to ignite an emotional conflagration.

Visualize this scene. The middle-aged father is focused narrowly on being as successful in his work as he can be. Like most of his contemporaries his energies are absorbed by thoughts of being promoted, making partner, filling a practice, and accumulating money. Under stress, worried about workaholism and burnout, wondering if he isn't a candidate for the same coronary that struck down a neighbor, the man staggers home after another twelve-hour day. And what does he see his fifteen-year-old son doing? Watching a rerun of M*A*S*H, of course, having done nothing else but sit in front of the TV since 2:20 P.M. when he arrived home from school. He hasn't emptied the kitty litter, mowed the lawn, or set the table which he is supposed to do. After supper the boy has to be forced into his room (which is a mess) to study. He says he doesn't like school. The only thing keeping him there is that he has no idea of what he would do if he dropped out.

We can imagine the emotions this creates in the father. It's nearly impossible for him, who has grooved his habit patterns and yoked them to an occupation in the two decades following his own youth, to remember what it was like to be unable to sit still, to have his mind resist concentrating on a book, to become preoccupied with his own thoughts and "forget" to carry out his chores, and to live in cheerful chaos.

Moreover, it's the rare forty-five-year-old man who is not wondering whether the occupation in which he has invested himself is worth it. Consider the man who enters the family business for security instead of becoming the journalist he dreamed about in his adolescence. Now he's wrestling with the question of whether he's done the right thing: What's he missed by taking this route? Does he want to do this the rest of his life? This distressing reappraisal may occur just at the moment his son has his own identity crisis: What on earth is he going to do when he grows up? Because the teenager's problems resonate with his own unresolved career issues—past and present—the man may become overly anxious about his son's unfocused career plans. In an effort to help, to ensure the boy doesn't make the same mistakes he did as a youth, he will have a hard time resisting becoming overly intrusive. When his son resists his efforts to help, the father is extremely upset—in large part because his son's pain mirrors his own.

Middle-aged adults need to feel generative too. Generativity has been defined as a blend of creativity and productivity. It also includes passing the torch to the next generation. What does it do to mothers and fathers when their teenagers reject adult values as a first step at discovering their own? In the normal course of their own maturation adolescents will disparage the suburban life style that their parents worked so hard to build, say they have no interest in material things, and plan to move to Vermont with friends to start a natural food farm. This attitude can be infuriating to the older generation because of their heavy commitment to the belief that their children should avail themselves of the advantages they have provided to build successful lives of their own.

In the loving area, a predictable source of parental antagonism occurs when overburdened parents become provoked by youngsters who seem to contribute nothing to the household, spend all their time with friends, and don't appreciate what's done for them. Imagine the week of a single-parent mother who works. Sunday morning her mother stops by to discuss her anxiety about having a hip operation next week. That afternoon, while she's weeding the garden, her high school son brings a lawn chair out into the backyard to sunbathe. In the evening her twenty-three-year-old daughter in North Carolina calls: things haven't worked out there and she wants to come home to get her head together. Wednesday, as she's leaving to visit her mother in the hospital, her son says he's decided to pass up college to form a rock group. What does she think of that idea? After she's finished shopping and cleaning the house on Saturday and is about to take a leisurely bath prior to going out for dinner with a new man in her life, the phone rings. It's her father, complaining he has nothing to eat because his wife is in the hospital. As she begins talking to him she sees her daughter from North Carolina pull into the driveway.

It isn't hard for a grownup in this predicament of being caught "mid between the ages" to resent adolescents who can't put dishes in the dishwasher, weed the garden, or walk the dog without being nagged, who are too busy to get the groceries, and whose sensitive caring about their friends stands in such contrast to the indifference with which they accept all their mother does for them. Feeling unappreciated, that it is all give and no get, and that she has no life of her own, this mother is primed to fly into a blind rage when the gas tank of the car reads Empty on Monday morning because her kids forgot to fill it after driving it all weekend.

The final arena in which developmental issues of the generations conflict is play. A large part of the problem is envy. Mid-life adults would like to have more time to play but with working long hours each week on the job and at home they barely have enough time to squeeze in a movie or weekly tennis match. We should not be surprised to find them jealous of their teenagers who seem to have unlimited free time. Moreover, we would not be amazed if they are a little hard on the adolescent who believes he or she has nothing to do while surrounded by several thousand dollar's worth of playthings. The parents *know* what they would enjoy doing if they had the leisure time; they fantasize about it continuously.

And part of the problem between the generations arises from a parental misunderstanding of what play is. Two characteristics of play are the freedom from obligation and freedom from the necessity of high achievement. Most youngsters understand this instinctly. But a father seeing a daughter with a natural facility in ice skating may believe it is the girl's "moral obligation" to develop her aptitude to the fullest. "Anything worth doing is worth doing well," he will say. After all, that's what he'd do if he had it to do over again, he thinks. He will encourage her to practice regularly, accept private coaching, and skate in competition. If her interests begin to flag, he will be horrified: "You have a God-given talent and ought to use it." Coaches are all too familiar with the teenager who gives up a sport because of excessive parental zeal. As one veteran coach put it, "Whenever some parents see a spark of ability they drench it with their own enthusiasm."

FRUSTRATED PARENTAL NEEDS

Raising small children is enormously gratifying. Part of the reason is that it provides an opportunity to fulfill so many of our own needs. Many of us have strong desires to be in control, to be right, to rescue others from distress, to have a special friend, and provide opportunities denied to us. In the child-rearing process we control much of the experience that shapes their lives, know the answers to most of their questions, rescue them from unhappiness, are special beneficiaries of their trust and love, and are able to give the younger generation benefits their parents never had. In few other areas of life do we satisfy these needs so fully.

There are mothers who take as their vocation the total shaping of their children's destiny. In so doing they enjoy the sense of being able to program what their youngsters feel, think, and do. A mother directs her son toward those experiences she believes are best for him: she selects playmates, schools, and activities with care; she involves herself with everything he does—volunteering as an aid in his classroom, being a den mother, teaching in Sunday school, taking him to violin practice and Little League games—so she can understand what he experiences. Of course he never is sent to overnight camp. Instead, he attends a local day program which encourages parent participation. When he comes home from school, his mother has a glass of milk and a plate of cookies ready. As they talk she seeks to correct any attitudes that run counter to her beliefs.

For a father a large part of what makes having a family enjoyable can be the opportunity for him to exhibit his superior knowledge. He has an opinion about everything—politics, sports, religion, education, you name it. Over the years his friends have learned to avoid getting into discussions with him because they always turn into heated arguments when others disagree with him. Nothing pleases him more than to come home and engage his kids in discussions on any subject and to show he is right. He knows the answers to questions about drugs, abortion, gay rights, the national debt.

Other parents exercise their rescue fantasies through their children. They are constantly on the lookout for signs of distress so they can make it well. These mothers and fathers cheer up their children when they are unhappy, entertain them when they have nothing to do, find friends for them when they are lonely, and tutor them if they are having trouble in school. Not necessarily overprotective, parents like these enjoy the feeling that comes from intervening and relieving a child's unhappiness by the force of their actions.

And we see parents for whom their child is a special friend. A bond of trust and love exists between them like no other in the adults' experience. An example is a father whose affection for his daughter grows year after year, a warm feeling increasingly reciprocated by her. In his spare time they do everything together and share their deepest thoughts.

Finally many parents are heavily invested in providing their offspring with those benefits they wanted as children but never had. There are two varieties of this desire. The first is the "make-up" need: a father insists on the kids having the playthings, clothes, and travel he so much coveted as a youngster. A second expression of this need is to guide their progeny around problems they experienced as adolescents. If indifference to school and bad friends caused a mother grief in her own teens she insists her daughter avoid these pitfalls. In return, parents anticipate their children will be grateful and accept their warnings.

Children's normal development brings a halt to these pleasures. Usually it is a gradual erosion: bit by bit parental control over their children's experiences diminishes as peers exert increasing influence. Youngsters see that teachers and other adults have other ideas about what is right that differ from their parent's and that are adept at rescuing them from unhappiness. Energy invested in forming and maintaining solid relationships with friends is subtracted from the attachment to parents. And children may take for granted material things given them while resisting parental admonitions about the long-term negative consequences of poor grades and bad friends.

For the most part the older generation accepts the growing autonomy of their offspring in the natural order of things. For those parents, however, whose subconscious needs have been gratified through their children, this growing independence can leave an agonizing void in their lives. Some are able to postpone this inevitable loss to the child's college years and even beyond. But a sharp, painful break usually results: adolescents wrench control of their own lives out of their mother's reluctant hands by behaving exactly the opposite of her wishes. They violently disagree with their father on every matter when two opinions are possible. They resolutely cling to unhappiness while refusing all offers of aid from grown-ups; they break their father's heart by shutting him out of their lives. Their quest for autonomy propels them toward the same wrong choices that brought so much unhappiness to their mother as a teenager.

ILLUSIONS ABOUT TEENAGERS

The excessive responses of adults to teenagers are frequently conditioned by their preexisting illusions as to what adolescents are "really" like. When a thirteen-year-old son—dressed for school in a leather jacket, combat boots, and cartridge belt—refuses to change clothes, his mother screams, "I won't have you looking like that! Take those clothes off this instant!" The source of her overreaction partially has to do with her belief that her son looks like a fool in that garb, but it more strongly emanates from a number of subconscious fantasies she has about adolescence.

For example, the illusion that adolescents are out of control, and are therefore dangerous and to be feared, grows in some parents as their youngsters enter the second decade of life. As puberty transforms weak and helpless children into strong and independent youths who increasingly wish to control portions of their own lives these parents misread this pursuit of autonomy as a threat. The perceived threat can be to a parent's position—the mother becomes angry because her son's outfit seems to defy her authority. Or the subconscious fear may be that the young will seize the power of the older generation—the boy after all seems dressed for combat.

Another illusion about teenagers that causes grown-ups to act irrationally is rooted in envy. Merchandisers in modern society emphasize youthfulness; ads for men's jeans copy adolescent fashions while women's dresses are modeled by sophisticated fifteen year olds. Rarely do we find people over forty—and acting their age—on TV commercials unless they're selling floor wax or denture cleaner.

It is the unusual mother who has not felt more than a twinge of jealousy of her sleek teenage daughter who eats everything in sight while the mother can't lose a pound on eight hundred calories a day. The girl's enthusiasm contrasts with her boredom, her freedom of action mocks her mother's growing conviction of being trapped, and her daughter's plans for the future focus her attention on the unpleasant reality of her diminishing days.

A third source of erratic and excessive reactions is the illusion that the teenagers will act out the subconscious fantasies of the parents—about which they experience considerable inner conflict. Typically these mothers and fathers have unfinished business with a particular psychological issue—for example, sex or aggression. They project onto their young their own ambivalent desires, imagining their adolescents to be just as obsessed with sexual matters or roughing up people who cross them.

As a result of their own preoccupations, these parents give their youngsters mixed messages in the extreme. For example, a mother with conflicts about her own sexual feelings may rage at her fourteen-year-old daughter going out in a skintight outfit to a party with a boy, calling her a "little whore" for dressing like that. She may yell that her daughter should stop being so "promiscuous" and if she's sleeping with him "she had better not end up being pregnant." (The girl is barely at the holding-hands stage with the boy and the only reason she is going to the party is to be with her friends who are girls.) Not a few girls have responded to this double message by launching themselves into premature sexual activity, "because if that's what Mom expects, then I might as well do it."

Then we have the father with his own problems with frustrated aggression who encourages his son not to let anyone push him around, but who then overreacts when his son follows these directions. One week the boy breaks the nose of a classmate who makes a joke at his expense and curses a teacher who criticizes his weak classroom performance. The father's response conveys his own unresolved subconscious attitudes: in the same breath he chews out the young man for his uncontrolled hostility, grounds him for a month, and then says with a smile, "But then you can't let the bastards castrate you."

Managing Our Emotions During Their Teens

Continuous hand-to-hand combat is rare in the great majority of households. The generations get along reasonably well, and bonds of affection and respect are maintained through the adolescent years and beyond.

Still, young people do evoke in us stormy moods and excessive irrational behavior. Since we are their primary caretakers, our distress can cause them considerable grief. What guidelines might we follow to manage our own emotions and actions so that we can be more effective parents?

First, recognize the potential problem. Be aware of the continuing possibility that reactions to the younger generation are influenced not only by the objective merits of their behavior but also by clashing temperaments, contrasting life cycle tasks, frustrated needs, or illusions about teenagers. It is valuable to realize that obsessive worry because a shy sixteen-year-old son has only one friend, that constantly nagging him to "do something with other people" may be rooted in our assumptions about sociability coming from our own active, extraverted personality style. This recognition helps us keep our own feelings in check so we don't alienate our child from us and they allow us to evaluate more objectively whether or not he or she has a problem.

As we recognize the potential for distorted responses to our young-sters, we are better positioned to react to our teenagers as good or "good enough" parents. We may be better able to see a daughter as an individ-ual for whom school isn't that interesting instead of someone who is "weak-willed" because she doesn't work fourteen hours a day the way we, her parents do. We may give her better guidance about birth control if it comes from the here and now of her experience rather than being prompted by the "there and then" of our own adolescent conflicts. And we may be a lot more helpful to our daughter when she elects to drop out of college to try to make it as an actress in New York City if we can react to her plan on the basis of the realistic issues rather than our needs to rescue her from the certain unhappiness we see ahead.

Second, find something youngsters can do to please us. Even when we do our best to recognize the reasons that teenagers have destabilized our psychological adjustment, there are moments that the attitudes and ac-tions of our progeny propel us into rage, tears, or a migraine. For in-stance, imagine being the parents of a sixteen-year-old girl with problems everywhere: her report card is a mass of Cs and Ds with low effort grades; she has no interest save gothic novels which she reads while munching junk food; she's forty pounds overweight; and she whines continually that she's bored. In this situation it's very hard to be a "good enough" parent.

Suppose that in an effort to help her do something that would enable us to feel positively about her we encourage this young woman to volun-teer to read to a blind middle-aged single neighbor one afternoon a week. The girl may be willing to give it a try because she enjoys reading and the chance of failure at this activity is minimal. Also she may figure this will get her parents off her back for a while and it might look good on her college application.

After a month or two she may discover to her surprise that the activity gives her some pleasure. The woman is always glad to see her and values what she does, providing the girl with an uncritical adult to talk with. A bond of affection may grow between the two. Before long the girl has reason to think more positively about herself.

This tiny amount of success can cause the parents to feel better about themselves, because they encouraged something that helps a troubled child. Because they see themselves in a better light, the parents may begin to view the teenager less negatively and become more loving toward her, creating an upward, positive spiral in which success is reinforced rather than negative behavior always being punished.

The third guideline is to try to think positively about teenagers. Differentiate between your dislike of a youngster's behavior and dislike of the youngster. We may strongly disapprove of a son's self-centeredness, but that's not the same as seeing him as an inherently narcissistic personality. This perceived difference allows us to help him reshape his behavior in the direction of being more considerate of others rather than to see him just as unchangeable.

Sometimes relabeling an adolescent's especially frustrating actions helps us to think more positively about him or her. For example, a daughter's constant disagreeing with whatever her mother had to say caused the woman to conclude the girl was a little "bitch." When an aunt who had not seen the daughter in several years came to visit, she praised the girl's "assertiveness" and "independent spirit." Jokingly she asked whether she was planning to go to law school. This positive relabeling startled the mother into recognizing how much of the antagonism she felt toward her daughter was based on the one-word summary "bitch." As she began to see the girl as strong-willed rather than willful and nasty, the momentum of their relationship swung in a more positive direction.

Fourth, keep in mind that most of the time teenagers think pretty well of us. Our sons and daughters don't set out to cause us to suffer as they move from childhood through adolescence to their adult years. Their disagreements "with authority" more often are intended to provoke an acknowledgment of their growing powers rather than to harm. Typically a girl's choices which seem so wrong to her mother are mostly a quest of her autonomy, not a plot to frustrate her mother's dreams. The nineteen year old home from college who challenges his father to a racquetball match and thoroughly trounces him for the first time is happy at his winning, not at his father's frustration in losing. What they "win" we don't necessarily lose.

Finally, consider the possibility that conflict with teenagers may provide an opportunity for our own renewed growth as adults. For instance, a mother recognized that she and her daughter always wound up screaming at each other about the girl's choice of friends. The pain from these arguments caused her to begin the process of exploring the origins of her need to control her daughter's peer experiences. She was able to piece some parts of the picture together—though she had complied with her own mother's having the say over who her friends would be, she had always resented it. Eventually the mother sought professional counseling which enabled her to understand more about her own maternal relationship and put to rest some old grudges.

Finally our goal as parents is to enable our children to become autonomous adults. We try to accomplish this task of helping them to become independent, yet still be lovingly connected through mutual affection and respect. Clinicians have long noted that continuing hostility between the generations glues them together. The animosity of mothers and fathers toward their grown-up youngsters causes the "children" to be unable to let go. And no matter how far away they move, no matter how old they are, the adult children never become self-directing because their actions continue to be motivated by conflicting emotions left over from adolescence or before. In order to unglue themselves from each other, so both generations can proceed with the business of their present phases of the life cycle, the warmth of love is needed.

To the extent that we can recognize the potential for our youngsters to be the architects of, as well as dwellers in, the family climate that so much influences their growth, and to the extent that we can understand the forces in ourselves that hinder the expression of love toward our youngsters, the continuing growth of both generations is enhanced.

4

Creating Your Own Helping Environment

All I do is fight with Cathy. Whenever I ask her to clean up her room, get off the phone, or put the dishes in the dishwasher, she has a tantrum. Last night when I told her to stop watching TV and start her homework, she called me a "witch," and I slapped her. Sometimes I just hate her. I feel terrible about that, but I've had all I can take.

I don't know what to do about Brenda. The phone never rings, no one ever comes over to see her, and she's never invited anywhere. All she does is mope around the house and complain that she doesn't have any friends. I don't know what to do. I can't make friends for her.

Since Nick's girlfriend broke up with him, the bottom's fallen out of his life. He's so miserable. He drives around in his car aimlessly. When he's at home all he does is lie in his bed listening to music. Sometimes we hear him weeping. We've told him that he'll get over this pretty soon and he'll find someone else. Now his grades are going down and Nick says he doesn't care about school anymore. I feel so helpless.

Alice has been in four different schools in three cities in the past five years. And now we have to move again. We feel terrible about having to uproot her once more. Is there anything that can help her cope with all this disruption?

My son, Willy, is a thief. For the last three years I know he's been taking money out of my purse but he always denies it. Lately I've noticed other things missing—a nice pen and some jewelry. Yesterday I found my gold lighter in his room. When I asked him about it, he yelled, "Why are you looking in my room?" He's bigger than I am and I don't have a husband.

Norman's schoolwork is just terrible. His teachers say that unless he pulls his grades up he'll have to repeat the year. And he's already done this once. We've tried everything we can think of —and I mean everything—but nothing works. He's been in the resource room, he's had tutoring, and he's gone to summer school—all with no success. We want to take him to a psychiatrist but he refuses. We are worried sick.

All of us who are parents know the awful sensation of feeling powerless to help our troubled teenagers. These youngsters are obviously upset, problems are mounting, and their ways of coping leave much to be desired. We've tried everything we can think of but nothing works. They refuse professional help, and our own mental health is declining.

While we all have experienced these emotions when our adolescents pass through difficult periods, the truth is that we are *not* powerless. We have a great many ways of helping our troubled teens. Here is a list summarizing six general principles that have a positive influence on the development of young people.

Principles for Influencing Positive Normal Development

Maintain (Loving) Contact
Foster the Ability to Enjoy Working, Loving, and Playing
Promote High-Level Adaptation to Stress
Encourage the Development of Resources
Secure Sources of Support
Keep Trying New Approaches

Maintain (Loving) Contact

Years ago a group of social scientists set out to discover how different patterns of child rearing influenced the later development of boys and girls. To their surprise they discovered that it mattered little whether a baby was breast- or bottle-fed, whether toilet training was permissive or strict, whether the parents spared the rod or used it, or whether the emotional climate of the parent-child relationship was warm or cool. What did matter—what was associated with healthy maturation—was the mother's loving contact with these youngsters.

More recent studies of healthy families reveal the same truth, namely, that caring and affection between the generations are crucial components. In other ways normal families are dissimilar. As with normally functioning youngsters, healthy families come in far more varieties than troubled ones.

Others studying why some adolescents are highly resistant to stress discovered that good relationships with parents are associated with higher levels of emotional adjustment. Looking at the value of loving contact from another perspective, psychiatrists working with mental patients note that reestablishing loving relationships with family and others is one of the strongest forces nourishing recovery.

These observations confirm what we all know intuitively—namely, the warm loving contact with parents is a critical influence on the positive development of young people. Unfortunately, even though we understand its value, it is hard to be affectionate with a teenager like Cathy whose nasty behavior and surly attitude antagonize us. Under these conditions how can we express the fondness we know she needs when our instinct may be to slap not hug, withdraw rather than try to talk?

In these moments we need to recognize the importance of maintaining a relationship no matter how much these youngsters might upset us. The contact need not always be positive. The opposite of love, after all, is not hate, but indifference. A relationship—even an adversarial one—is better than no relationship at all. Remaining in communication rather than brooding silently, staying engaged with these youths rather than pulling away, and being committed to enhancing their welfare—in spite of their recalcitrance and recidivism—rather than becoming bitter and giving up makes an enormous difference in the lives of these young people.

Foster the Ability to Enjoy Working, Loving, and Playing

Affectionate contacts with family create an emotional foundation in
which children can learn to gain satisfaction from central sources of
pleasure, namely, working, loving, and playing. Fostering the ability to
work and to love and to play is a central task of parenting.

In the words of Mark Twain's character Tom Sawyer, "Work is whatever a body is *obliged* to do." For most teenagers what they are obliged
to do is carry out household chores and perform satisfactorily in school.
Many educational institutions also require students to participate in ex-
tracurricular activities, clubs, and sports. A growing number of adolescents hold down part-time jobs. These forms of working benefit young
people in both the long and short run.

All of these reinforce habits. Habits are automatic, repetitive behavior
patterns. Because they require no new learning or acts of will to carry
out, they are energy efficient. If youngsters are in the habit of getting up
in the morning, planning ahead, doing things they don't feel like doing,
and finishing what they start, their lives are infinitely easier than if they
wrestle themselves out of bed each day, wonder about the whereabouts
of a book they need, bind themselves to a chair in order to begin their
homework, and fight to maintain enough enthusiasm to complete anything.

Do all you can to reinforce good habits. A surprising number of young
people never learn habits at home because no one invests the time and
energy to teach them. As early as possible show them the merit of hanging clothes up, putting dirty laundry where it belongs, and keeping their
rooms reasonably tidy. Insist on self-care—keeping clean, combing hair,
brushing teeth. Teach your children systems for organizing drawers and
closets. Give them jobs to do—cleaning portions of the house, caring for
animals, washing and waxing cars, and preparing or cleaning up after
meals. Encourage them to carry out chores in a logical sequence within a
specific time period. Help them set aside a time for studying and point
to the value of doing the hardest task when they are freshest.

Not a few parents have visited a daughter working as a counselor in a
summer camp and discovered her to be the epitome of neatness in
organization—quite unlike the chaotic nature of her existence at home.
Or they visit their college freshman son and they find his room orderly
and clean—in contrast to the pigpen he existed in at home—and hear
him badgering a roommate to pick up his dirty underwear. When they

ask their children why there has been such a dramatic change, the answer is nearly always the same: "I have to do it now." Teaching our youngsters is hard work but the payoff is high and lasts a lifetime.

Teens need little encouragement to go to school. Strong students enjoy it because of the opportunity to demonstrate their skills. The vast majority of adolescents in the lower half of the class don't mind school either. That's where their friends are, as well as opportunities to participate in organizations, sports, and other activities. A few loathe going to school. They are overmatched developmentally, read poorly, have a math block, or find French incomprehensible. Report cards detail their inadequacies. For them every day threatens more humiliation. Few adults would remain long working under these conditions. But, unlike their parents, they can't quit.

Monitor the quality of your child's academic experience. Though generally students with better grades enjoy school far more than those at the bottom, the correlation is not perfect. Just as a caring person might inquire as to the emotional and physical cost associated with a hardworking executive's success, we do well to ask the same questions of our offspring with honors grades.

If a youngster has a learning problem, nine times out of ten this will be obvious in the elementary grades. If you suspect trouble, request a conference with the teacher and determine whether the school has sufficient understanding of the problem to serve as a basis for helping the child. If not, consider having a thorough evaluation carried out. Prompt diagnosis of the difficulty in intervention can result in school's becoming a tolerable exercise rather than daily misery.

Encourage part-time employment. About one fifteen year old in five works part-time. By age seventeen the percentage doubles. In addition to providing spending money, employment benefits adolescents in other ways. Working teens exhibit greater self-reliance and social understanding and have fewer physical and psychological problems than unemployed youths.

Working as a teenager has long-term benefits. Boys and girls forced to work because their families were wrecked financially by the Great Depression achieved greater educational and vocational success than children of families who kept their money. Also they had better relationships with their spouses and progeny, and they exhibited fewer psychiatric symptoms. A group of boys from blue-collar families who in adolescence routinely carried out household chores, performed at an adequate level in school, participated in sports or other activities, *and* held down part-time jobs were in better physical and mental health at mid-life as well as achieved greater success in their careers and family.

Whereas the ability to enjoy working is for many adolescents an acquired taste, most teenagers instinctively move into loving relationships. You may need to do little else than monitor your youngster's progress. Pay attention to the many channels in which he or she demonstrates love.

The term "loving" embraces all forms of tender caring. For the teenager loving encompasses expressions of affection in the family, in friendships, and in romance as well as altruistic love. Loving is an active process—the ability and willingness to give to others—not merely being its recipient.

The family into which we are born remains the center of our caring and affection through our teens and beyond. It has been wrongly assumed that a gap opens between the generations in adolescence that makes reciprocal loving impossible. The evidence is otherwise. One teen in two classifies a parent among his or her confidants. Eighty percent of all the adolescents say they get along well with their parents and value the approval of their mothers and fathers more than that of their friends.

Involvement with a chum and then with a group of friends is a hallmark of adolescence. At some point during this period the first big romance occurs. For some, altruistic love appears first in the teens. These youngsters exhibit their selfless passion in fervent churchgoing, in a commitment to being a missionary, in volunteer work with the down-and-out, or in a crusade to save baby seals from the pelt hunters. Young people who become involved in these altruistic expressions will tell us they adore God, service to others, or to all living things. The intensity of their emotions and the gleam in their eyes tell us they mean it.

If a teen, like Brenda, is isolated from normal friendships and feels that no one likes her, encourage the youngster to think about developing the ability to care about others. In order to have friends, we need to be able to be friendly. Friendliness can be learned by observation and practice.

Brenda's parents might help her by telling her to observe the different ways well-liked girls behave around classmates, how they respond to the needs of others, and how they deal with frustration and snubs. Before long Brenda may start to recognize what it takes to be friendly and also become aware that this is hard work.

Brenda's parents can also assist her in improving her social skills by practice. A systematic approach for making friends is shown in Table 4.1.

TABLE 4.1
Making Friends: A Systematic Approach

WEEK 1: ☐ Practice in the mirror talking to others with a tape recorder.
         ☐ Play back and improve skills.

WEEK 2: ☐ Join a folk dancing group at school.
         ☐ Attend a house of worship and stay afterward for coffee.
         ☐ Make a phone call to two people for information.

WEEK 3: ☐ Continue with folk dancing.
         ☐ Join another activity—a religious youth group.
         ☐ Engage in casual conversation with at least three people, expressing what you think and feel.

WEEK 4: ☐ Make an effort to be pleasant, useful, or interested in three people's welfare.
         ☐ Call four people for casual conversation.
         ☐ Invite one person every other day to do something on the spur of the moment—have coffee, go to a movie, attend a game, go for a ride.

WEEK 5: ☐ Invite several members of the folk dance youth group to your place for a snack after the meetings.
         ☐ Plan a party.

Basically these are a sequence of things Brenda can do to improve the probability of making friends. Essentially this approach begins with low-risk actions and gradually prompts the youngster into greater social contact.

It's not difficult to know when teenagers are working or loving. More complicated is the problem of identifying play. Is the girl canoeing through the Allagash wilderness in Maine with other summer campers playing or working? How about the college student whose basketball scholarship pays for his education? Do daily practice and the games provide the same enjoyment as the summer informal games in the park with friends?

Three characteristics that distinguish play are lack of obligation, freedom from the necessity of high achievement, and malleability. For an adolescent's activity to qualify as playing, it should be voluntary, motivated more by an inner desire than economic necessity or responsibility to others. For the girl, canoeing is recreation because she chose to do it. For the counselor heading the trip, it is work.

Winning, doing well, finishing in the ninety-ninth percentile is not essential to having fun. By these criteria basketball may not be any longer play for the college student. But shooting pool and singing with a group—neither of which he does especially well—are. This doesn't mean that skillfully performing a leisure-time activity isn't important. Many like to do everything as well as they can whether it's making the highest score in darts, lowest in a round of golf, or sewing a perfect piece of bargello.

The third feature of play is that it is malleable. That is, young people can do with their leisure time just about whatever they wish, being constrained only by law, opportunity, and talent. Teenagers can fit their play to changing whims. One fourteen-year-old girl's major form of recreation moved from the cello to ice skating to photography in a twelve-month period.

Watch to be sure that the playful activities your youngsters engage in are volitional: Can your daughter take a day off from jogging or shopping at the mall without feeling guilty or having withdrawal symptoms? Can she enjoy the jogging even though she doesn't do it especially competently? And can she replace it with some other recreation when the whim strikes?

Promote High-Level Adaptation to Stress

The ability to find pleasure in working, loving, and playing is half of the definition of normalcy. The other half is how people adapt to stress. Like their parents, few teenagers go for long without being frustrated in school, upset by a friend, or conflicted by competing emotions. It is how they handle these outer and inner stresses—not the events or feelings themselves—that determines whether a young person will continue to function normally or begin to show evidence of maladjustment.

Mental health workers have been fascinated by the amazing capacity of some youngsters to maintain their emotional balance while living with enormous deprivation, brutality, and hardship. While their brothers and sisters may succumb to these stresses one after another, somehow these boys and girls continue to function normally. By contrast, a girl from an affluent, loving family starts to have panic attacks because she has trouble learning French. Nick, with everything else going for him, feels his life collapsing around him when his girlfriend drops him. What makes some young people highly resistant to enormous stresses while relatively trivial difficulties cause others to break down?

The answer is adaptation. High-level adaptation to stress is a fluid process of quieting inner discomfort without creating greater difficulties in ways that permit learning from experience. By a fluid process we mean that adaptation is a day-to-day, sometimes hour-to-hour, practice of dealing with smaller tensions as they arise rather than waiting for them to build up so that heroic measures are required. An example is the student in the French class who doesn't comprehend the subject from the first day. She will be better off reacting to her anxieties right away—asking questions, talking to the teacher after class, getting outside tutoring—rather than putting her worries out of her mind until a rush of anxiety before a midterm drives her to try to master the material. At that point her tensions are more likely to paralyze or disrupt the learning process than stimulate it.

Just as any medication has its side effects, each adaptation to stress has its cost. One cost is the extent to which pleasure from areas unrelated to the stress is compromised by how a teenager copes with it. Another cost is how the youngster's future is negatively affected by ways of adjusting to today's problems. The girl who finds French very tough going might react to her mounting frustrations by devoting more and more time trying to learn it. If she does this something will have to give somewhere else: there will be less effort in other courses; she may see her friends less often; she won't be able to try out for a play; and her parents will find her more difficult to live with.

If the stress leads to a desirable goal—three years of a language is required by the colleges the girl wishes to attend—she may tolerate the other problems because of long-term benefits. On the other hand, she may conclude that feeling pressured in other courses, being separated from friends, not being able to do other things in high school, and taking out her frustrations on her parents is not how she wants to live. Instead, she may drop the idea of learning a language altogether and set her sights on a college program that doesn't have this requirement.

A high-level process of adaptation to stress involves learning from experience. Initially adaptation involves becoming aware of discomfort and the events causing it. Nick, whose girlfriend has broken up with him, knows he's unhappy and knows why. Because of this awareness Nick is in a better position to take corrective action than is an equally distressed youngster who forces his depression out of his mind, blithely saying he's fine and that there are other fish in the sea.

Learning from experience also means being conscious of immediate reactions to stress and modifying them as is appropriate. Imagine Nick after his girlfriend leaves him for someone else. He feels desolate, that he can't live without her. Then Nick begins to gather himself, looking at how he is reacting. Is his depression justified? He reevaluates the stress and his response to it. Sure, this has been a terrible blow. But from talking to his friends, Nick knows that others have experienced similar losses. Somehow they have coped. He's managed to survive other difficulties in the past, such as moving into a new house away from his old friends when he was eleven. His parents still love him and he has friends with whom he's close. Gradually Nick starts to think of the loss in less catastrophic terms to imagine that he might survive after all.

How might we help this boy or girl and other teenagers recognize self-defeating patterns and teach them more effective strategies for reacting to stress? This process is more difficult than we imagine because many psychological self-protective mechanisms snap into place automatically, without our knowing it, masking an unpleasant reality or soothing inner tensions. They resemble the mental equivalent of a knee-jerk reflex. The student with trouble in French "forgets" her homework assignment and becomes certain her teacher hates her. The girl has *not* made a conscious decision to feel relief by putting French out of her mind or projecting her anger onto the teacher, thus seeing the benign French instructor as a tyrant. These self-protective responses have functioned without her conscious intent.

The first step in promoting higher-level adaptation to stress among our teenagers is to understand how self-protective responses to stress differ. We can identify three levels of self-protective reactions. From lowest to highest on a scale of adaptability they are ego defenses, coping devices, and adjustment mechanisms. Table 4.2 shows examples of each.

TABLE 4.2
Three Levels of Self-Protective Responses

Ego Defenses

STRESSFUL EVENT: A girl has trouble in French class.

REPRESSION: Forcing an anxiety-arousing perception out of awareness
Example: Student "forgets" to do her French homework.

DENIAL: Rejecting the existence of an unmistakable reality
Example: Though she's failed every exam and has stopped studying, the student insists that she'll pass the course.

PROJECTION: Assigning an unacceptable impulse to others, converting inner urge to an outer threat
Example: Angry at herself because she can't learn French, the girl sees the benign teacher as hating her.

DISPLACEMENT: Redirection of an impulse toward a safer object
Example: Frustrated at school, the girl torments her little brother.

Coping Devices

STRESSFUL EVENT: A boy's girlfriend breaks up with him.

SUBLIMATION: Transforming an alien impulse into an acceptable expression
Example: Boy converts his anger toward her to a strong desire to excel in soccer.

SUPPRESSION: Consciously pushing an unsettling reality or thought out of direct awareness
Example: Student chooses not to think about how much he misses his girlfriend while he does his homework.

MOTILITY: Evading stress by remaining physically in motion
Example: Driving around aimlessly with friends at night causes him to think about her a little less.

RATIONALIZATION: Acknowledging a portion of a distressing reality but omitting a larger unpleasant truth
Example: Boy tells himself and others that breaking

up is for the best because he shouldn't be
tied down at his age.

Adjustment Mechanisms

STRESSFUL EVENT: A student moves to a new town and high school.

FANTASY: Voluntary, pleasurable, or gratifying daydreams

Example: Student tolerates being with new people now by
drifting in and out of pleasant thoughts about past
experiences.

HUMOR: Relieving stress by being aware of its amusing aspects and expressing it

Example: Student with an overprotective mother tells humorous stories about struggles for independence.

ANTICIPATION: Imagining the effect of current choices upon future satisfactions

Example: Student manages a heavy academic course
load by thinking how enjoyable college will be.

SUBSTITUTION: Putting one goal in place of another

Example: Failing to make the debate team, the student
tries out for the school newspaper.

The ego defenses—repression, denial, projection, and displacement—
relieve discomfort momentarily. However, the price that ego defenses
exact for restoring mental tranquility is considerable. The girl with problems in French may feel better momentarily if she "forgets" to do her
French homework or insists the teacher has it in for her. But the problems created elsewhere will be monumental. Moreover, ego defenses
limit learning from experience: she is unlikely to recognize on her own
that her repression or projection is excessive. And, not being aware of
how maladaptively she is handling stress, she will have trouble spontaneously improving the quality of her self-protective responses.

Coping devices fall in the middle range of self-protective responses.
They allow us to recognize unpleasant events and our reactions to them
as well as how we try to comfort ourselves. Nick, who transforms his
anger at the girlfriend who left him into a competitive desire in soccer,
or forces himself to put her out of his mind so he can study, knows he's
upset and knows why. A negative feature of coping devices, however, is
that they may cause problems in other spheres: driving around aimlessly
results in his doing less homework, getting lower grades, and causing his

parents to become upset with him. Another negative feature of coping devices is they limit learning from experience. By rationalizing to himself that the girlfriend breaking up with him was "all for the best," Nick doesn't look at why this happened and how he might prevent a romance from fracturing in the same way next time.

The highest level of self-protective responses are adjustment mechanisms. Though they are at first automatic, they permit a relatively continuing awareness of the stress itself and the emotional response to it. The student sitting with other unfamiliar classmates in a new school can float in and out of pleasant daydreams about past experiences and friends, paying attention when necessary. The deployment of adjustment mechanisms doesn't create problems in other areas: the teenager with the mother nervous about her child's starting a new school can diminish building tension by joking about her overprotectiveness. Finally, these high-level devices permit a relatively smooth process of learning from experience. The adolescent using anticipation to moderate anxiety about a difficult course load has insight into inner discomfort and the origin of it. Adjustment mechanisms allow for a more accurate appraisal of how effectively stress-reduction techniques are working and making a change if necessary. The student who goes out for the school newspaper after failing to make the debate team may find this works pretty well to salve inner disappointment. If not, he tries something else.

Should you observe that a teen is reacting to stress badly, wait for a short period to see if the youngster realizes that a change is necessary. The girl with problems in French takes steps to avoid forgetting to do her homework and recognizes that thinking it's the teacher's fault has painful consequences. This is a reasonable course of action because studies of youths grown into adulthood show that young people improve their ability to handle stress as they get older.

What happens if nature doesn't seem to be taking its course and an adolescent doesn't make spontaneous self-corrections? A second step is to present a personal perception—supported by more than one example —of self-protective responses operating in an ineffective, costly manner. Nick's parents might confront him with several illustrations of staying on the move. This discussion could lead to insight into what he is doing— along with its negative consequences—and ultimately help him come to terms with the loss, lessening the need for the coping device of staying on the move. Parents can also make suggestions to Nick for ways to speed the healing of a broken heart—talking to friends who have had similar experiences, or channeling energies into substitute activities.

In addition to what you tell teenagers about how to manage stress, pay attention to what kinds of anxiety-reduction techniques you model. Strong evidence indicates that children follow the lead of their parents in reacting to difficulties. If they see their parents controlling the urge to scream at a waiter who overcharges and quietly asking him to recalculate the total, or responding to being laid off by systematically organizing a job search rather than doing nothing and hoping something will turn up, they are more likely to use these same ways of managing their own problems. High-level ways of coping with stress beget higher-level adaptation to stress in children.

The correlation between the self-protective responses of parents and their progeny is far from perfect. Other powers influence how young people adjust to distress. The strongest nonfamily force is friends. The peer group whose solution to their unhappiness about being mediocre students is to deny that grades in school matter, and find ways to avoid thinking about it, is a powerful role model for a teenager. But so too are the contemporaries with equally modest academic achievement who enliven what would otherwise be a humdrum, unproductive existence by involving themselves in community activities, service organizations, sports, and paid work.

You also can promote high-level reactions to stress by encouraging proactive behavior. "Proactive" means acting upon an unpleasant situation by relieving its negative emotional impact and trying to modify it, rather than being acted upon and responding passively to whatever problems the environment presents. An example is the fourteen-year-old boy from a Chicago suburb whose father's company moves to the research triangle in North Carolina. He copes proactively with his unhappiness by going to the library, checking out an atlas, and learning as much as he can about that state. As he learns that this is one of the fastest growing areas of the country, that the schools are first-rate, that it is less expensive to live there and warmer in the winter, the lad begins to feel less discouraged and develops a more positive attitude about the move. Contrast this response with his brother who feels overwhelmed at the thought of leaving friends and familiar surroundings, withdraws to his room in despair, resisting all efforts to discuss what it might be like to live in North Carolina, and assumes he will be miserable there.

Parents have a crucial role in providing a climate in which proactive

behavior can develop. The elements of this atmosphere include supporting efforts of the youngsters to relieve their own frustrations, to develop
feelings of competence, and to respond flexibly to difficulties they confront.

Babies whose parents supported their reasonable efforts to overcome
distress—being allowed to struggle to reach a toy, turn over, crawl, sit
up, or walk on their own—coped with stress better than the infants of
parents who "helped" them at the first whimper of frustration. As tod-
dlers these higher-level copers were allowed a safe freedom to explore
their world—to find out what tasted good or bad, what was hot or cold,
or felt hard or soft. These same children were taught how to take care of
themselves within their capability and encouraged in self-management
skills. The mothers and fathers of these good copers respected their
efforts to master problems, applauded their success, and comforted them
in times of failure and frustration.

These young people also were being taught competence. Competence
is an inner feeling of joy at being a cause of, of being effective in dealing
with the environment. The girl struggling to make a dress or comprehend the mysteries of the square root, the boy laboring to fix the gear
mechanism of his ten-speed bike or to learn to type, will feel considerable pleasure when they succeed. Neither requires the praise of adults, or
anyone else, to feel gratified.

And being proactive means having a flexible set of responses to problems. On the Hawaiian island of Kauai a group of eighteen year olds
were studied who were raised in family situations judged likely to cause
emotional problems. Not surprisingly the majority of these young people
did develop serious behavioral, social, or learning problems in their teens.
But a smaller fraction did not. The researchers then compared the two
groups on a number of dimensions. Having a large repertoire of coping
strategies characterized these more resilient Hawaiian youths. Sometimes they were assertive, attacking the source of a problem directly.
Other times they lived with it, using lower-level self-protective responses
to insulate themselves from distress. One moment they were stoic, bearing painful emotions and, in the next instance, they expressed all they
felt.

Encourage the Development of Resources

Until recently the assessment of a teenager's mental health focused largely on finding out what was wrong with that youngster. Problems with toilet training, traumatic nursery school experiences, failure of proper parenting were noted along with the presence of tensions, melancholy, or tantrums. Nowhere close to the same effort was devoted to discovering what was going "right" in the young person's life. This omission is a significant omission because research shows that having a few things go right in our lives has a more beneficial impact on our mental stability than having nothing go wrong.

Each of us is greater than the sum of our minuses. The "pluses" in our lives contribute substantially to overall adjustment. In the plus column are satisfactions derived from working, loving, and playing. In the plus column also are resources. Resources are anything we can call upon to cushion the effects of failure, loss, bad news, or frustration, and they provide compensating experiences.

Among the resources you can encourage young people to develop are the ability to make friends, a belief in something greater than themselves, and skills or hobbies. The resource most clearly associated with normal adjustment is the capacity to maintain friendly relationships with family and others. For example, students at a California college living in socially supportive housing had many fewer visits to the health service than those living in residence units that were both academically and socially competitive.

A belief in something greater than the self both can enrich the day-to-day quality of a teen's life and sustain that youngster in tough periods. For example, a boy in a Jewish family finds strength in living in a kosher home while his born-again Christian classmate feels a powerful joy in living resulting from her recovered faith. Much of the appeal of traditional and nontraditional religions is that they provide solace when little around them brings comfort. A fourteen year old with an alcoholic father and a mother with cancer felt profound relief at hearing those words from the gospel of Matthew, "Come unto me all ye who labor and are heavy laden."

Not all belief in something greater than the self entails religious faith. Other young people are sustained by a conviction of the supremacy of science, of universal ethical principles, of the essential value of life itself, or of the good fortune in being born a Capricorn.

Resources can be skills and hobbies. A teenager who can draw upon an activity, talent, or hobby to provide solace or sanctuary in difficult times has a greater probability of maintaining normal adjustment than those who do not. These resources can include active pursuits: playing music, shooting baskets, going for long walks, or growing something. They can be passive ones, such as in lying in the sun, listening to the stereo, watching a favorite TV rerun, or taking a hot bath. They might be solitary activities: collecting coins or stamps, doing crossword puzzles, working the home computer, or learning the intricacies of applying eye shadow. Or they can include others, such as playing cards or shopping.

Alice's skills and hobbies, as well as her cat, kept her going during all of the moves in her teenage years. She had an excellent alto voice which allowed her to fit in immediately with a high school singing group. If the chorus didn't need any more altos, she also enjoyed sewing and playing the guitar.

For some teenagers pets are a valuable resource. A joyful bark, a thumping tail, and licks of affection can do a lot for the spirits of a boy who's been cut by the soccer coach and his girlfriend on the same day. His dog is a reliable playmate when the boy is lonely, ready to roll around in the family room or chase an old tennis ball. Animals can provide something warm, soft, and responsive to cuddle when young people can't get it anywhere else.

Pets can offer an opportunity for catharsis, as is the case with Alice who enjoys talking about her troubles to her purring cat in her lap. Pets provide diversion: few more natural interesting indoor spectacles exist than multicolored fish swimming around in an aquarium. Pets offer youngsters opportunities to develop competence—teaching a canary to sing or a gerbil to use an exercise wheel. They are a vehicle for meeting other people: walking a dog, breeding rabbits, attending pet shows, or buying equipment. They permit a statement of uniqueness, as in the case of a sixteen year old who raises boa constrictors.

Pets enhance the normal growth of adolescents by reinforcing habits through caring for them. They promote the expression of affection by providing something to love. At times of transition they buffer stress: Alice's shock of moving to yet another town was relieved somewhat by knowing she could bring her beloved cat with her.

Some resources are built-in. Intelligence is an example. Superior perception and memory, verbal and mathematical skills, analysis and reasoning have a moderate connection with successful management of unpleasant events. Another innate resource is a better than average physical constitution. Studies of men and women from their teenage years to adulthood consistently find mental soundness is highly associated with physical vitality. We know that people who work at staying in shape through regular, moderate exercise exhibit improved mood, lower physical tension, better self-concept, and increased intellectual efficiency. The exercise need not involve a competitive sport; it can be weight lifting, aerobic dancing, climbing, jogging, or walking briskly.

Secure Sources of Support

It would be nice if we could tell a troubled adolescent that we are worried and think it would be a good idea for the youngster to see a psychiatrist and have the teenager reply, "Gee, Mom, that's a terrific idea! Can I see someone this afternoon?" Adolescents are far less willing than other age groups to accept the suggestion that they might benefit from consultation with a mental health specialist. Even when the evidence of their problems and unhappiness is undeniable, a large proportion will resist seeing a therapist. If coerced into a doctor's office, many refuse to talk or fail to return for appointments. Parents are then told, "If your youngster doesn't want therapy, there's nothing I can do to help."

Complicating these situations further is that carrying out therapy itself with troubled adolescents is extraordinarily difficult. Partly this is because of their instinctive antagonism to whatever changes parents want them to make as a result of treatment. In some measure the hard going is due to their convictions—based on denial and avoidance—that nothing is wrong with them. It's their mothers and fathers who actually need help.

If a dialogue is started with these teenagers, it is frequently short-circuited by extreme emotional variability, regression, and fluctuating interest in the treatment process. In the therapist's office they may be alternately challenging or compliant, hostile or seductive, open or closed. Their moods swing widely from enthusiasm to apathy, optimism to despair, confidence to doubt. In the grips of an adolescent turmoil a boy may exhibit a frightening array of psychopathology one afternoon and seem perfectly normal after supper. A girl might call her therapist at midnight in a crisis, be given an appointment at 7:30 A.M. the next day, and not appear. Called at home by a worried doctor, she responds that she "forgot" and is fine now. Following their oscillating thoughts and feelings is much like trying to stay with a stunt pilot's aerobatics. Anna Freud, a psychoanalyst whose clinical work with young people spanned a half century, put it accurately when she said, "Treatment of adolescents is a hazardous venture from beginning to end."

These problems don't mean that psychotherapy should be avoided, or once attempted that it is doomed. It is just that the process is far trickier than it is with adults.

You may be unable to locate a suitable mental health specialist or find it impossible to force an adolescent to stay with treatment. If you should find yourself on your own with a troubled teenager, this is the time to secure outside sources of support. Almost everyone everywhere can draw upon at least two types of external assistance: extended family, friends, and neighbors, and problem-focused community support groups.

The point has already been made that other people represent a primary resource enabling each of us to manage stress. These same individuals can lend a necessary hand to parents with teenagers who won't acknowledge their difficulties or whose behavior is out of control. Imagine the divorced working mother of Willy who is a thief. When she discovered Willy with her lighter in his room and confronted him, he yelled, "I can't live on the allowance you give me, so I took your things and sold them. What are you going to do about it?"

In this case his mother called on a brother and sister-in-law as well as two older cousins, all of whom had good relationships with Willy. Imagine his surprise when he came home from school one afternoon and waiting for him were his mother and four relatives. Together with his mother they told him how worried they were about him, and how much distress he was causing them, and how badly they wanted him to change.

Faced with this large group of concerned adults, Willy realized he had a serious problem that they would not tolerate. He broke down sobbing. Eventually Willy was able to say why he stole the money—to buy gifts for classmates in a vain attempt to make friends. Later he found he could talk to an uncle who had had the same social insecurity as a teenager and was helped to find other ways to relieve it.

A second source of external support is community groups. Largely self-help undertakings, they provide an opportunity to discuss a youngster's misbehavior with other adults who share similar worries, comparing experiences as to what works and what doesn't, obtaining feedback from them as to what might be contributing to the continuation of the difficulty, evolving ideas for new approaches and then critiquing the outcome are at the heart of these self-help meetings. These groups come together regularly and advertise in community newspapers. Suburban weeklies regularly announce meetings of Parents of Adolescents Support Groups, Toughlove, Parents Without Partners, Parents Anonymous, Bereaved Parents, Mothers with Custody, Overeaters Anonymous, and Children of Single Parents.

Keep Trying New Approaches

Each time you make an attempt to help a teenager there is a good chance the effort will stimulate a natural self-correcting process. "Baloney," you may say. "I've done everything there is to straighten out my teenager and nothing has worked." Rarely do we go wrong respecting how hard it is to find the right combination of forces that will stimulate a young person to function more effectively. Still, positive changes do occur in adolescents. And nearly all grow out of their youthful difficulties before they reach adulthood.

How does this happen? Environmental changes are an important factor. These can be gradual, sharply defined, or traumatic. The gradual development of Norman's physical competence makes him a strong candidate for the freshman basketball team and gives him a reason to care about staying in school. His bar mitzvah and entry into high school— sharply defined changes—allow him to look once again at his poor academic performance, wipe the slate clean, and try out new ways of forcing himself to study.

Even traumatic events can result in positive transformations. In the same week Norman flunked a course and was caught by the police smoking dope with friends. This forcefully, and finally, convinced Norman that he was not going to make it to college unless he started taking school more seriously. Norman traded in some of his friends for those less likely to lead him into trouble and gave up marijuana.

If beneficial environmental changes don't seem to be happening to a troubled teenager in the normal course of development, you can help the process along by modifying the rhythm, atmosphere, or geography of their lives. Norman may improve his grades when he has to get a job to provide spending money—and so has to use the fewer hours available to study more efficiently, when he is encouraged to study ten hours a week with the telephone turned off, or when he is sent to a boarding school in Colorado.

When talking to teenagers about a needed area of improvement, try to avoid using sentences beginning with verbs and ending with question marks: "Have you started your homework yet?" "Don't you think you should try to get all Bs?" "Aren't you worried about how you are doing in school?" These are indirect commands for compliance, and they are so understood by our children. Almost every time they aggravate rather than motivate, and they frequently provoke resistance on a spectrum from dawdling to tantrums. On the whole we improve communication with the younger generation and create a setting more conducive to shared problem solving when we say candidly, though gently, exactly what we mean. "I think it's time you started your homework." "What's holding you up?" "It would please me if you brought home Bs on your report card." "What do you think of that idea?" "I would spend less time worrying about your school record if you seemed to be more concerned about it. How *do* you feel?"

When trying a new approach to help a youngster break out of a frozen, self-defeating pattern, you raise the odds by sounding the alarm. When both parents, or more than one adult, sit down with Norman and express their worries directly, this has the effect of throwing a pan of cold water in his face: you focus his attention on his poor grades. Norman may see that things are getting worse not better in high school and may begin to think about what life might be like if his grades make him an unlikely candidate for entry into, or survival in, college.

Mental health workers and educational specialists are often struck by the number of teenagers referred to them who improve *after* an appointment is made but *before* the first interview. Many times the reason is that a parental confrontation resulting in the decision to seek professional help is what is needed to arouse the recognition in a young person that a problem exists and something needs to be done about it now.

You don't need a teenager's overt consent as to what should be done to help. Norman, flunking out of the tenth grade, is not likely to be the best judge of what has the best possibility of helping him. But when you try a new approach, it's worthwhile to involve the teenagers in planning what changes are to be made. This permits them to say what they think and contribute ideas that can be woven into the overall plan. Also be open to feedback as to how the new plan is working and make changes as needed. Youngsters' involvement also reduces the feeling of being "done to."

When a new tack is planned small changes should be made as needed. For example, it's agreed that Norman will study two hours a night Sunday through Thursday, sitting upright at a desk in his room, doing his hardest homework first, and with the electronics turned off. But he may find it impossible to sit still in his room for two hours. Norman may have to limit the time period for studying into twenty-minute units with a break between. He also may discover it's easier to concentrate in the kitchen.

Devise ways for teens to obtain rapid feedback as to how they are doing. A problem with most schools is that a huge gap exists between the youngsters' efforts and the response of the faculty. A test taken this week may not be returned for a month. A paper handed in today may not be returned for weeks. Grades and teacher comments come four to eight times a year. Girls and boys trying to improve their schoolwork will have stronger motivation to continue their effort when they receive frequent input that tells them the effect of their efforts.

Parents working in concert with their teenagers and school personnel can devise two kinds of more rapid feedback. The first is associated with recording the effort itself. Behaviorally oriented psychologists tell us that if we simply keep track of how often we do something we will change its frequency. For example, if Norman writes down in a small notebook at the end of each day the number of hours he has studied, he may find that this log of effort spurs him to spend a longer time with his homework. Sometimes merely looking at this record provides enough satisfaction to maintain his enthusiasm. A modest incentive system—added hours of TV viewing or a new video for successfully meeting the agreed quota of study time—may also keep him moving.

A second type of rapid feedback concerns results. Having to wait for weeks and months to find out whether the additional effort is paying off is too long a time span for unmotivated students. They need to see a connection sooner than that. Most school systems can arrange through the guidance counselor or adviser for the teen's teachers to write a short report at the end of every week that evaluates his or her performance. This gives a realistic perspective on the relationship between effort and performance.

Impatience hampers efforts to activate fresh, positive growth. Many of the parents who say they have tried everything have stayed with a new approach for only a few weeks, sometimes merely days, at a time. Seeing no progress they try something else before the first approach has had a chance to work. The problems did not materialize overnight and will not vanish before only a month's end, no matter how powerful and effective is the environmental change.

How long is it reasonable to wait before concluding an approach that is not working? The length of time depends on the temperament of the child, how tenaciously the difficulties are embedded, and the vigor with which you execute the plan. With most adolescents it takes six to twelve months before we can see positive results from any environmental change. In the case of a poor student, the first thing that usually happens when an approach is successful is that the grade decline stops and bottoms out. Then academic performance may begin to improve gradually.

When you believe you've given an approach a fair trial and it isn't working, don't be reluctant to try something different. This activity forces the teenager to recognize once more that a problem exists and it may stimulate the hope that this time perhaps the efforts will begin a self-correcting process. Also young people may be closed to outside intervention at one age and open at another. The boy with poor grades may resist help at fourteen but at sixteen may be responsive when he is less antagonistic to his parents and a little worried about what he is going to do after he graduates from high school.

When you finally find an approach that works, try to avoid spending hours with the teenager analyzing how and why. The boy who used to do poorly but isn't anymore really doesn't want to dwell on the differences until he's had enough success to feel secure thinking out loud about it. Also talking to an adolescent about the progress that came as a result of your ideas may detract from the confidence that the child has developed in his own capabilities. Better for the youngster to be pleased with the progress and unsure of why than for you to risk undermining the growth by excessive speculation.

Maintaining (loving) contact, fostering the ability to enjoy working, loving, and playing, promoting high-level adaptation to stress, encouraging the development of resources, securing sources of support, and maintaining a willingness to keep trying new approaches are components of an environment you can create to help your teenager. Everyone has the potential to affect a youngster at least a little. Often just a tiny amount of change is enough to overcome adolescent inertia and restore the process of normal growth.

5

"I Don't Want to Go!"
Transitional Anxiety

It is the rare teenager who at some point has not been reluctant to go to school, attend summer camp, begin college, or leave home for a job, a year abroad, or boot camp. With most the apprehension is manageable and passes within a short time. For a few adolescents the distress of the thought of facing an unfamiliar experience does not dissipate and causes continuing unhappiness. A smaller fraction become school phobic: they just plain refuse to go to school. Some of these develop separation anxiety and have an overpowering dread of being apart from family and home for any reason.

Formerly, transitional anxiety was considered largely a disorder of children. More and more, however, this problem is being diagnosed in young adolescents and among youths in their late teens and early twenties. It occurs equally in males and females. In one form or another, at one point or another, this difficulty affects 2 to 4 percent of the teenage population.

GLORIA

When her parents split up, they thought it would be best to send fourteen-year-old Gloria to boarding school in the fall. For eight years they had lived in Cupertino in California's Silicon Valley. Once they decided on a divorce, Gloria's father, a microcomputer executive, planned to move into a condominium in San Francisco. Her mother would pursue a graduate degree in landscape architecture. Both assured Gloria they still loved her and would see her regularly.

When they explained to Gloria and her eleven-year-old brother that they were going to separate in the spring of that year, the children were not surprised. There had been a lot of fighting in the last two years. Gloria and her brother agreed that everyone would be better off with less conflict in the house. At the time, Gloria was in the ninth grade in the local high school. She was a B student and thought by her teachers to be well adjusted.

That summer Gloria and her brother attended a six-week camp in Colorado. They had enjoyed the camp for several years and this summer was no different for Gloria. When it came time to leave for the boarding school, about two hundred miles to the south, Gloria seemed a little nervous but gamely said she thought it would be a "good experience." Her father and mother also were apprehensive. On the drive down they encouraged her to call them as much as she wanted and said they would try to see her as often as possible.

The first month and a half was fine. Gloria made friends in the sophomore class. The midfall term grades were Bs with a C+ in science and a D in geometry. The teachers weren't worried, however, feeling that she would improve as she became better adjusted to the new school environment.

By the third week in October phone calls to her mother from Gloria were a daily event. Gloria said she was miserable because the girls she thought were her friends "talk about me behind my back," the courses were "too hard," and teachers, especially the male math teacher, "hate me." Usually her mother was able to cheer her up but then the next day Gloria would call again and sound just as forlorn. By contrast, when her father visited Gloria and took her out for dinner each month, she talked positively about school and didn't appear unhappy.

After Thanksgiving vacation Gloria didn't want to return to school, but she agreed reluctantly when both parents insisted. In her nightly phone calls she seemed increasingly dejected. Gloria said she didn't know how she would pass her fall term finals. Her worse fears were justified when grades for the first term arrived—an F in math and a D in science to go with the Cs in the rest. Along with these marks came a stern letter from the headmaster saying that Gloria was frequently unprepared, never participated in classroom discussion, and generally seemed to have a sour attitude about the school. If she were to continue there Gloria would have to make considerable improvement in the winter.

The headmaster's letter settled the matter in Gloria's mind. She told *her mother that under no circumstances would she return to the boarding school.*

ROGER

It was February of Roger's senior year and he had done nothing about applying to college yet. His parents were becoming increasingly anxious. Finally his mother obtained several college applications but Roger didn't fill them out. The more they thought about this the more the parents were aware that Roger had been reluctant to involve himself in the whole college application process: he "forgot" to take his SATs and achievement tests in the spring of his junior year; he never got around to seeing his college adviser; and he was "too busy" to talk to college reps who visited his school.

Roger was a capable student at the high school in Bloomfield Hills, Michigan. He was especially strong in math and science. He loved electronics. He worked as a volunteer in the audiovisual department and for two years had been the leading "techie" for all of the high school events that required light and sound.

The youngest of three—two older sisters had been graduated from the University of Michigan—Roger had always been especially close to his mother. His father, an ophthamologist, was busy and distant and left the child rearing to his wife. From early on, Roger and his mother spent lots of time together. They shared similar interests in classical music, reading, and board games. At eighteen Roger considered his mother the best friend he had and she felt likewise.

Roger always was "slow to warm up" in new situations. When he went to nursery school at four, Roger was shy and sat by himself instead of playing with the other youngsters. Finally the teacher asked his mother to stay for a few hours until Roger relaxed and became more involved in the activities. Throughout elementary school Roger had adjustment problems at the beginning of each new year, but these gradually abated—usually helped along by his mother's working as a volunteer in the school.

In middle school Roger had the expectable hard time adapting to a different teacher for every subject. Also contributing to his difficulties in adapting was the fact that his mother decided she was being "hovering" and did not seek a volunteer position. During the seventh and eighth grades Roger started a pattern of missing classes on Monday and the first *day after holidays. Usually this was because he had pains in his stomach for which no organic cause was ever discovered.*

It also was during his early teens that Roger's worries about his parents' welfare started. He became obsessed with the fear that something terrible would happen when they went to the movies or out to dinner. Pacing the floor while they were out, Roger was positive they would be killed in a bloody car crash. Roger developed difficulty going to sleep at night even if his parents were at home. He couldn't say why; he just felt "nervous."

In high school Roger's pattern of missing classes continued. He was, however, exceedingly reliable in his audiovisual and technical work. Moreover, Roger made several friends among classmates with similar interests. His parents were delighted to see him invited to parties on weekends.

Eventually in the spring of his senior year, Roger's parents prevailed upon him to apply to Wayne State's electronic engineering program. Because of his record he was quickly accepted. Roger elected to commute from home. Though he said he liked it initially, he began to miss classes with increasing frequency. He told his mother he would get the lecture notes from his classmates and do his reading at home.

Roger passed two of his courses and had two incompletes the first term. He decided to take next term off and think things over at home. A year later he was still thinking.

Youngsters, especially "slow to warm up" or "difficult" children, in the green zone may express considerable reluctance about starting a new grade, school, camp, or other undertaking. Their initial distress is a function of their wariness of the new experience rather than the fear of leaving home. They are able to specify, too, what it is they are concerned about—making friends at a new camp, getting along with the counselor, passing the swimming test.

Among normally functioning teenagers the distress accompanying leaving home and entering a new environment passes within a reasonable time, usually a few days to six weeks. A "reasonable" time span varies with the child's temperament, the degree of adjustment required by the new environment, and parental reactions to the youngster's discomfort.

In young people in the green zone reason is stronger than anxiety and governs their behavior. For example, though he may not like the prospect of it, a boy knows that he will benefit from, and may even enjoy, traveling to Paris for three weeks with his French class during spring break. So he swallows his apprehension and packs for the trip. Their

TABLE 5.1
Estimating the Severity of Transitional Anxiety

GREEN ZONE—Normal Adaptation

- Reluctance because of wariness of new experience
- Distress at separation passes
- Reason governing action
- Missing school for acceptable reasons
- Average school attendance

YELLOW ZONE—Temporary Adjustment Reactions

- Excessive tardiness/absences associated with reluctance to go to school
- Production of physical symptoms at pressure to leave home
- Failure to adjust to new situations
- Reason impaired by anxiety, inhibiting action

ORANGE ZONE—Neurotic Symptoms

- School phobia in absence of stress
- Persistent unwillingness to be away from home overnight
- Obsessive, unrealistic worry that harm will befall parents
- Failure to participate severely diminishing pleasure
- Parents at odds

RED ZONE—Severe Maladjustments

- Separation anxiety
- Parental collusion inhibiting independent behavior
- Ambivalent attachment

intellect also enables these youngsters to learn from experience and anticipate coping successfully with a new situation. A girl nervously awaiting the first day of high school might recall the same emotions she had when she started middle school. She recollects, perhaps with her parents' support, how anxious she was in the beginning and that it gradually waned. She also remembers how she went about coping with this transition and thinks she may use some of the same strategies this time.

Should the teenager miss school, it is for an acceptable reason. It may be to stay home with the flu or severe menstrual cramps, because the previous night was spent talking to a brokenhearted friend, or because the youngster needs a mental health day. An "acceptable" reason may be to cut classes and go to the beach with friends on the first really warm day in spring. In all instances, however, there is no reluctance to return to school following the time away.

In the green zone, school attendance is within average limits, presuming there are no lengthy illnesses or other events keep the adolescent away. This figure varies from year to year and from community to community. Among high schoolers in two Boston suburban communities the average number of students' absences in 1983–84 was eleven. Tardiness is a statistic that often provides the first clue to transitional anxiety. Every school has its own standards for what is considered excessive lateness to class, and normal adolescents don't exceed these limits.

By contrast, students in the *yellow* zone are much more frequently late for class—typically the first ones of the day—because of their disinclination to go to school. These youngsters dawdle around the house, miss their bus, and wind up being driven by a parent. Their absences also far exceed the average. As in Roger's case, Mondays and the first days following vacations contribute a large proportion of the total time away from school during the year. The "explanation" is that they don't "feel well": they have a sore throat, persistent cough, nausea, dizziness, the flu. Should real illness strike it takes them longer than their classmates to return to school.

If parents insist that these reluctant boys and girls in the yellow zone go to school, they produce an array of physical symptoms—commonly, stomachaches, diarrhea, and headaches—in order to stay home. Some will exhibit vomiting, heart palpitations, hyperventilation, and fainting. As soon as they are allowed to stay home their physical problems disappear. Occasionally these youngsters will soldier off to camp or boarding school without a whimper. But shortly after arriving they develop alarming physical symptoms that cause their parents to retrieve them and schedule intensive medical tests. These become unnecessary, however, because as soon as these teens arrive home, the ailments vanish.

The anxiety of young people in the yellow zone is related to recent unfamiliar and/or excessive stress. Prior to these unpleasant events these adolescents had a history of successfully managing difficult situations. Gloria's problems began with her parents' separation and were compounded by having to adjust to a new school environment.

In an adolescent who has handled new experiences successfully in the past, a yellow flag is the failure to adjust to an unfamiliar situation within a reasonable time. Roger's inability to continue in college because of unmanageable anxiety was in contrast to his history of coping with similar distress. When young people are away from home, an inverse relationship exists between their adjustment and how often they communicate with their parents. The happier they are the less often they write or call. A yellow-zone indicator is the boy at summer camp who sends his parents an undiminishing stream of letters chronicling his misery. Occasionally a gradual increase in contact with parents occurs: Gloria's phone calls to her mother escalated slowly during the first six weeks at boarding school.

Anxiety impairs reason and inhibits normal freedom of action. For instance, a boy becomes so focused on the inner discomfort the idea of leaving generates in him, he is unable to anticipate the advantages of going on a trip with his class. Teenagers will attribute their fears to specific aspects of the situation they wish to avoid: the boy's French is inadequate; the teachers directing the trip to Paris hate him; the other students are bullies or nerds. Anxiety also intermittently blocks the recollection of past success at coping with transitions. The girl about to enter high school can't remember how she went about managing new situations earlier in her life. Even if she can recall a successful coping experience, it seems ancient history, no longer relevant.

Transitional anxiety in the *orange* zone reveals itself most often in school phobia, a terror of going to school. It occurs in the absence of clear-cut stress. The youngsters in the orange zone make it very difficult for parents and teachers to get them to school. Many have had a long history of problems adjusting—Roger's discomfort at the beginning of every new academic year is an illustration. Their unwillingness is clothed in phantom illness or the conviction that school is a dangerous place. No

amount of reasoning counterbalances their anxiety sufficiently to motivate them to return to class. Lengthy periods of absence result.

Every day is a test of will between parents and these teenagers. If the
youngsters are forced to go to school a number of evasions occur: they
report to the school nurse with nausea or cramps; they may go only to
those classes where they feel most comfortable; or they spend their time
sitting in the cafeteria, shooting baskets in the gym, or hanging around
the school yard until it's time to go home. Even if they can be coaxed
into remaining in their classes for a week or two, no growing feeling of
comfort accompanies this accomplishment. The next Monday brings
back the same terror.

The persistent unwillingness to sleep away from home, unless accompanied by family, is an orange flag. For instance, Roger found excuses to
avoid sleeping over at friends' houses. He was, however, perfectly comfortable spending a month in Maine with his mother and sisters at their
summer place. Part of the reason orange-zone teens don't like sleeping
away from home is that many of them have trouble getting to sleep.
Roger needed to know that his mother was in the house before he could
sleep. From time to time he asked her to read in his room until he
dropped off.

Perhaps the most unique neurotic symptoms of these youngsters is
their irrational, unrelenting fear that the parents will be victims of a
calamity. Gloria became convinced her father would die in a plane crash.
When she knew her father was flying somewhere on business she listened to the radio in a near-panic expecting to hear of the crash. Roger's
obsessive worries were unspecified, but he couldn't shake the morbid
preoccupation that a tragedy would befall his parents when they went
out to a neighbor's party at night. These teens' convictions are intensified by reading of muggings in the paper, seeing the wreckage of a plane
crash on TV, or hearing of a neighbor being robbed.

Failure to attend school and participate in other normal teenage activities away from home greatly diminishes pleasure from all areas. Roger's
uneven class attendance resulted in his gradually falling behind in college. At first Roger borrowed other people's lecture notes but he stopped
because he grew embarrassed trying to "explain" why he wasn't in class.
Quickly he found he couldn't keep up by doing only the required reading.

Not infrequently, considerable disagreement exists between the
mother and father as to how much pressure to put on these children to

behave more independently. Moreover, as soon as the father attempts to force these youngsters to go to school, they break down weeping and complaining of stomach pains. The mothers can't stand to see them in distress and thrust themselves between the fathers and the children, permitting no more pressure for normal behavior. Frustrated, the fathers withdraw, and the problem worsens.

The hallmark of the *red* zone is separation anxiety, which is not limited to school phobia, but is an overpowering dread of being detached from parents, home, or other familiar surroundings for any reason. Teens in this zone shadow their mother in the house and become nervous if she is not within sight or sound. Because the thought of separation mobilizes such terror in them, they steadfastly refuse to leave home to attend school. Should these adolescents be pressured to go they strongly resist: jumping off the bus or out of the car taking them to school is not unknown; neither is hysterical screaming or punching at those who try to force them to leave home.

When apart from their mothers these adolescents often withdraw, seem sad and listless, and have trouble concentrating. Their schoolwork deteriorates and they lose interest in playful activities about which they were previously enthusiastic. When Roger went to college, he had enormous difficulty paying attention in class, and his mind wandered when he tried to study. Since he wasn't on the campus he missed opportunities to join social groups or work as a techie for the school theater. Eventually the only enjoyment he could count on was being with his mother.

In nearly every case, separation anxiety develops with the active—if unwitting—collusion of the parents. Typically, the father's contribution has been to give up and withdraw, condemning his child for being a baby and his spouse for causing the problem. For her part, the mother establishes a mutually dependent relationship. Many clinicians believe this intense mother-child attachment is rooted in mother's own unresolved dependencies. Subconsciously the mother discourages normal autonomous actions and reinforces the youngster's dependent behavior because the child's anxieties resonate with her own fears that the world outside her home is filled with potential harm.

Finally ambivalence characterizes the dependent attachment to the mother and father. Roger didn't mind his mother doing all those things for him—cooking his favorite foods, shopping for his clothes, being continually at his bidding. He also knew, however, that she was overcontrolling his life and limiting his normal growth. Because he was so depen-

dent upon her, Roger couldn't break away. The result is a continuing
stormy emotional climate. Roger was increasingly angry at his father,
too, because of his withdrawal, but he felt he couldn't vent his anger
directly toward his father because he might risk losing the little attention
he received.

Follow-up

GLORIA

*When Gloria refused to return to boarding school after Christmas, her
mother called her father and asked him to come immediately so they
could talk with her together. Gloria repeated the list of reasons she did not
want to go back to school: her friends were still in Cupertino; she liked
living at home, so why should she go away while her brother didn't have
to? At no time did Gloria talk about how anxious going away to school
made her.*

*Despite her increasing protests and distress, the parents insisted Gloria
return for the winter term. The drive down to school was a nightmare of
Gloria's cursing them for not loving her, hysterical sobbing, and threats to
run away. When they stopped for gasoline Gloria locked herself in the
ladies' room and yelled that she wouldn't budge unless they agreed to take
her home.*

*Eventually they arrived on campus. By now Gloria was disconsolate.
She sat in the car weeping while her parents carried her belongings to her
room. Feeling considerably upset themselves and unsure whether they
were doing the right thing, they talked with the dorm head and Gloria's
adviser. They all agreed that Gloria should stay, and together they in-
formed her that she was going to remain at school. In a rage Gloria
stormed into her room and would not speak to anyone. The drive home for
the parents seemed extraordinarily long and painful.*

*The winter was difficult for everyone. Gloria was nasty and sullen. Her
grades continued to be marginal. She avoided her classmates and seemed
depressed. Gloria parried the adviser's attempts to talk with her. She flatly
refused to consult with the school counselor, though she did strike up a
friendly relationship with the nurse whom she saw several times a month
for various physical complaints. The only thing she showed any interest in*

was writing poetry. Encouraged by the student editor, she submitted a poem to the school literary magazine which was accepted.

Gloria continued to call home frequently, occasionally telephoning both parents in the same day. The topic was always the same—her misery. Finally her mother and father agreed to limit Gloria to two calls a week. This resulted in her checking into the infirmary with severe stomach pains. Gradually these passed as she talked to the nurse about the unhappiness.

Bit by bit Gloria's adjustment to school improved in the winter term, partly because she was able to take a less demanding math course, partly because the editor of the literary journal asked her to join the staff. Perhaps most important was that she felt the nurse understood her problems and was sympathetic.

Her father and mother held their breath when it came time to take Gloria back to school for the spring term. Though Gloria said she didn't want to return, she packed willingly and was happy to see her dorm mates when they returned to school. In spite of the fact that her academic work remained uneven, Gloria's involvement with friends and activities grew. When her parents picked her up in June she hugged several of her classmates and her adviser. Weeping, she said how much she would miss them and couldn't wait to see them in the fall.

ROGER

During the year following Roger's leaving college his activities outside the home diminished. Though he went out with old friends if they called him, Roger never initiated contact. On rare occasions Roger dropped by the AV room at the high school or a local electronics store to hang around for a few hours. But mostly he stayed home. When asked by a chum what he did with all his free time, Roger replied it was a little like being retired —and few retired people ever complain that they are not busy enough.

A year later Roger was still at home and his activity outside the house was virtually nil. He seemed lethargic. The combination of a hearty appetite and little exercise resulted in Roger's gaining twenty-five pounds during the twelve months after he dropped out of college.

More and more his mother worried about Roger's physical and mental health; his father wondered if he would ever finish college. One evening after a long, hard day, and a few drinks, Roger's father laid into him, calling him "soft," "spineless," and "stupid," and said that he seriously doubted Roger'd ever amount to anything. Roger flared and for a moment it looked as though a brawl was inevitable. Crying hysterically, the mother separated them. She continued to weep while Roger went to his room and his father took a drive.

So shaken were all three by this event that they sought help from their family doctor. After a physical exam of Roger revealed no organic cause for his depression, the doctor referred them to a psychologist who specialized in work with adults and their families. After a diagnostic evaluation, a treatment program was planned which contained several ingredients: the therapist would meet with Roger weekly and his parents once a month; Roger and the psychologist would work on altering the pattern of his phobic behavior; and Roger would get in shape, find a job, and eventually return to college.

In the next six months Roger's self-esteem improved and his parents began to work together to support his efforts to be independent. The therapist taught Roger relaxation exercises to reduce his anxiety and then gradually accompanied him back to the college campus. Eventually Roger was able to sit in the student union and then audit classes by himself.

Two of the most significant events that changed the course of Roger's life were accidental. To get back in shape Roger began lifting weights at a nearby health club. There he met Katey, four years older, a divorcée with a child. She was attracted to him immediately and shortly they began an intense affair. Roger's parents were opposed to this relationship, though they acknowledged he was benefiting from it. A few weeks later the manager of the health club asked Roger to work part-time. Within a month Roger began full-time, enabling him to rent an apartment so he could spend more time together with Katey.

With everyone's support Roger took two part-time courses the next term and did well. The following year he returned as a full-time student.

Suggestions for Helping

What can parents do to prevent temporary apprehension from mushrooming into school phobia and separation anxiety? First, recognize the potential for the problem to develop. Normal young people are more susceptible to transitional anxiety whenever they confront an unfamiliar situation: a different unit of school such as junior high school, high school, or college; an altogether new school, camp, or travel experience; leaving home for the first time. Slow-to-warm-up or difficult children are far more disposed to become fearful than are others with different personalities. If you are aware of their vulnerability at these change points, you are in a better position to help them overcome their momentary fears and cope successfully.

INTERVENE IMMEDIATELY

Don't allow temporary anxiety to gain a foothold. As soon as you see yellow-zone indicators, act promptly and decisively. The quicker youngsters are returned to school the less likely a phobia will take root. If a girl wants to remain home Monday morning or prolongs an illness in order to avoid going back to school, her fears about school will worsen. Predictably this means hearing how much her stomach hurts, how miserable you are making her by forcing her to go to that awful place filled with people who hate her, and how little you care because you are forcing her to cope with such a ghastly situation. Our children are deadeyes for saying things that will stimulate maximal guilt, and we must control these emotions so that we can act promptly to help them.

Coordinated action agreed upon in advance by both parents is required. In the ideal world both the mother and father should be involved in returning a teenager to school. A single-parent mother usually can muster a male relative—uncle or grandfather, older cousin, nephew, or brother—to reinforce the commitment to returning to school. Experience suggests that fathers or other significant male adults are more effective in helping anxious young people get to and remain in school.

BE DECISIVE

Decisiveness is also critical. Once you make up your mind that a son *is* going on a trip to Paris with his class, stay with the decision in spite of his sobbing protests and attempts to reopen the issue. Continually reexamining the decision, changing your mind as you are buffeted by your teen's distress, creates greater rather than lesser nervousness on his part about the trip. Avoid false reassurance and be realistic. Telling the boy how much he's going to enjoy the trip when all he can feel is how unhappy he'll be doesn't work. Instead, empathize with his apprehension and confirm that he indeed may be miserable in the beginning. But it is also true that he has adapted successfully to these stresses in the past and there is no reason to imagine this situation will be different. Moreover, he might enjoy some aspects of the trip with his friends and it will certainly give them some interesting things to talk about when they return.

Peers and slightly older adolescents have a powerful influence on teenagers disinclined to try new experiences. One mother was able to get her reluctant son to a new school the first week of the ninth grade by arranging for two of his friends to stop by for him on the way. Earlier she had overcome his resistance to go to scout camp by asking older members of the troop whom he admired to encourage him to attend and spend time with him the first few days there.

Coordinated action, agreed upon in advance by the parents, helps young people overcome their fears. When his parents are unanimous that a boy has to go to camp or on a school trip, that show of unity both relieves anxiety and reinforces the reality that he has no alternative other than to go.

REEXAMINE CONTRIBUTING FACTORS

Recognizing the problem and acting promptly and decisively usually results in diminished anxiety and a rapid adaptation to the feared situation. But what if the adolescent doesn't adapt and the symptoms worsen rather than dissipate?

In these instances, reexamine the nature of the stress the teenagers must endure. From time to time we will find that we have misread just how bad a particular situation is: a tenth grader really is being scapegoated by a group and this has to be stopped if he or she is going to return to school. Or we have underestimated the impact of the combination of stress. For instance, sending a child away to boarding school following a separation may seem an excellent idea to the parents, but it often triggers severe transitional anxiety as well as other symptoms. Waiting until a youth begins the freshman year in college to split up has about the same emotional impact. When crises occur in a family— marital separation, illness, unemployment, someone new added—young people adjust better when they stay close to home. When things settle down they then can leave more comfortably.

If after these efforts the teenager remains just as reluctant to leave home, consider the possibility that family relationships are impeding the road to recovery. The vast majority of the teens whose momentary fears turn into school phobia or separation anxiety come from families with two recognizable features. The first is an unusually close attachment to the mother who may herself have a history of experiencing anxiety in unfamiliar situations and so reinforces her child's fears. The result is a mixed message to the young person: "Yes, Roger, you have to go to school; but, no, you shouldn't because it's dangerous and something awful may happen to you." The second feature is intense disagreement between the parents about how the adolescent's anxiety should be treated, resulting in inaction: Roger's mother identified with his nervousness and was reluctant to force him to return to college; his father, who wanted to press him to go back, felt blocked by his wife and withdrew from Roger in angry frustration.

Occasionally, recognizing these patterns leads to a change in family interactions that frees the parents to work together to help the boy or girl. More often, professional assistance is required because tangled mother-child dependencies and lack of parental unity block prompt and decisive actions.

LOOK FOR PROFESSIONAL HELP

If concerted action is impossible or doesn't work—the child is absent from school for three consecutive days because of paralyzing anxiety and parental collusion—seek outside help. A good place to begin is with a medical examination to rule out any physical cause of the stomachaches, headaches, depression, or other symptoms associated with the transitional anxiety.

When the boy or girl is found physically sound the next step is to contact a professional who can assist the youngster and the parents in overcoming their mutual problems standing in the way of the teenager's normal adjustment outside the home. Most ways of treating orange- and red-zone transitional anxiety involve a mix of approaches. All require the children to return to school as soon as possible as well as ongoing family therapy to help everyone understand the factors underlying the problems and cope with the stresses associated with overcoming the phobia.

Many times the therapist works through the father or a male relative who accompanies the teenager to school and the first classes of the day. Should it be impossible to use parents, same-sex surrogates are effective. A fourteen-year-old girl who missed fifty days of school in the first three months was able to return to the ninth grade when accompanied by a female college student. She devised her own strategies for helping the girl overcome her fears while in weekly supervision by a psychologist.

A multiple-therapeutic approach teaches teenagers anxiety-reduction techniques. These enable them to act upon themselves to minimize their distress when their stomachs begin to churn or they feel terrified at the thought of leaving home. Examples of these approaches are relaxation and meditation. Another method includes visualizing the feared event, experiencing the anxiety connected with it, and then using relaxation techniques to overcome the fears.

Once the adolescents master these skills in the therapist's office, they are put to the test in real life. The therapist may accompany the student out of the home to school. If the teenager becomes excessively nervous, he or she is encouraged to apply the relaxation procedure to control these emotions just as the student did in the therapist's office.

Another essential in these multiple-treatment methods consists of preparing the school faculty for these teens' reentry. Many a promising recovery has been halted by a teacher's sarcastic greeting or detailed questioning to returning pupils as to the reasons for being out of school. The teachers can help enormously by welcoming them back and weaving them into as much of the normal pattern of school as they can tolerate. Likewise, they should not send the students home at the first complaint of feeling woozy. This type of treatment program continues until the youngsters attend school full-time for six weeks. Afterward the teenager's family and teachers are warned to be especially wary of periods when the transitional anxiety are most likely to occur.

Ironically the biggest blockade to parents' prompt, decisive actions or seeking professional help for these youngsters is their closeness and empathy. The greater their attachment to their offspring, and the greater their feeling for their childrens' emotions, the harder it is for parents to face the intensification of the physical and mental distress that forcing their children into an anxiety-producing situation entails. These mothers and fathers feel damned if they do and damned if they don't. From the teenager's point of view, however, it is far better for them to be damned for doing.

6

"Thirteen Going on Twenty-one" Precocious Social and Sexual Interests

Precocious social and sexual interests do not "exist" as an entity in most textbooks about teenagers, but few forms of adolescent behavior attract more interest. Early puberty, the desire to be with, dress like, and participate in intimacies characteristic of youths three or more years older characterize this precocity.

Puberty is the term used to encompass the onset of menstruation in females, the capacity for ejaculation in males, and the appearance of secondary sexual characteristics. The age at which this process begins varies greatly. Though girls usually have their first period at around age twelve, some experience menarche prior to ten and many have still not menstruated at sixteen. In a group of fourteen-year-old boys, several may be mistaken for twelve while others could easily pass for college students. Earlier maturing girls and boys are more likely to find their contemporaries "juvenile" and have more in common with older teens. As a group they tend to become sexually active earlier than those with delayed physical maturation.

The peer group provides its own rules of appropriate social and sexual conduct. A girl's interest in being with members of the opposite sex is highly correlated with the desires of her friends. Friends usually liberalize the code set down by the older generation with respect to proper dress and makeup, when it's okay to go to mixed-sex parties, dating, petting, going steady, or coitus. For a youngster to retain his or her status within the peer group, considerable pressure can be experienced to conform to their level of social and sexual activity.

Sexual precocity may result in unwanted pregnancy or venereal disease, both at an all-time high in the United States. But many of the difficulties associated with this precocity are not sexual. By far the most severe problem is intergenerational conflict—as parents, made nervous by their early ripening fourteen year olds, blow up when these teenagers have a fit about not being allowed to go to a weekend college fraternity party at the beach. Other troubles connected with premature sexual behavior include lower self-esteem, poor academic performance, identity questions, and wariness about commitment.

DAWN

Midway through the year, Dawn told her father that she was tired of being a "goody-goody" and was going to start being "herself." Trying to make light of what she had said, he asked, "Are you going to start being a 'baddy-baddy'?" "Maybe," Dawn snapped, and slammed the door. The door had a large Keep Off the Grass sign taped to it.

At the time, Dawn was a seventh grader in a junior high school in Minneapolis. Her father was an attorney and her mother worked part-time in the high school library. She was also president of the junior high school's parent-teacher association.

When her parents talked to Dawn's teachers about her in April, her mother commented afterward that the most common phrase used to describe her daughter was "until recently." Until recently Dawn had been getting good grades, now she was slipping. Until recently Dawn was a leader, now she didn't want to be in student government because "you never really have any power anyway." Until recently Dawn was a promising athlete, now she was losing interest. Until recently Dawn's friends were the stars of the class, now they were definitely not. And until recently Dawn had not been interested in boys, but now she certainly was.

Dawn's parents were assured by a school psychologist that she was "just going through a phase." When they caught her smoking marijuana in her room the following September, they began to worry. When they "grounded her" for the high school junior prom—to which she was invited by a seventeen year old—Dawn climbed out her window, shinnied down a rope, and went anyway.

At the end of their own rope, they called the police to bring her home. One of the patrolmen suggested threatening her with a stubborn-child warrant to keep her under control. When they told Dawn, she laughed in their faces and said she'd prefer jail.

But it wasn't all bad. Dawn had moments of remorse and made tearful promises to "straighten myself out." Beginning ninth grade, Dawn got off to a fair start and her parents began to trust her again. They asked Dawn to baby-sit for her two younger sisters while they went to a twenty-fifth wedding anniversary for some friends. Partway through the evening, Dawn's father had to return home for a camera to photograph the proceedings. When he walked into the living room he found Dawn, partially unclothed, on the couch in the embrace of a high school student. The boy bolted for the door. When her father gasped, "What's going on here?" Dawn sat up with a challenging smile on her face and said, "Well, what do you think? You don't think I'm a virgin, do you?" Her father thought he was going to have a heart attack.

KEN

In the sixth grade Ken started to mature more rapidly than his classmates. By his thirteenth birthday he was heavier and stronger than his friends and could sing bass in the school chorus. But it embarrassed him that in the shower the other boys kidded him about his pubic hair and the size of his penis.

Girls were interested in Ken. As soon as he arrived home from school, the phone started ringing with calls from females, some a year or two older. Several pursued him—waiting around for him after the middle school chorus practiced or dropping by the family hardware store in Ladue, Missouri, where Ken helped his mother and father part-time. They tried to shoo them away, but the girls were persistent.

By the end of the eighth grade Ken had gone steady twice and rumors of his sexual prowess filtered through the community. In fact, Ken was still a virgin. Though he had engaged in heavy petting with one girl, he stopped short of intercourse because of his own uncertainty.

Because of his natural music ability Ken as a freshman was invited to join the high school chorus and was encouraged to try out for the winter musical. Before long he attracted Brenda's attention. She had the second lead in the musical, was pretty, had a car, and was said to be sexually experienced. Ken's mother and father were not pleased, but the more they tried to discourage him from seeing her, the more he wanted to be with her. They forbade him to ride in her car, but Brenda parked the automobile at his house so they could go for walks.

While he liked being with Brenda, Ken felt more and more isolated from his classmates. When his envious friends wondered jokingly whether he and Brenda "had tried any new positions lately," he felt the hostility in their remarks. He didn't fit in socially with Brenda's classmates either.

Ken and Brenda were together constantly. One winter afternoon they wound up at her house alone, eventually in her bed, and had sex. Ken was relieved finally to shed the burden of his virginity, but he didn't find intercourse anymore enjoyable than masturbation. For a while afterward Ken and Brenda regularly slept together.

Shortly after the end of the winter musical Ken failed to maintain an erection two afternoons in a row. From then on Ken avoided being alone with Brenda because he worried that he might be impotent. Feeling rejected herself, Brenda broke off their relationship in March and started seeing a college student. Ken was jealous and brokenhearted. He withdrew more and more, his grades at school fell dramatically, and he decided to drop out of the choral group. He brooded about why this relationship had fallen apart and concluded that it had been all his fault due to his declining interest in sex. "It must be that I couldn't get an erection with Brenda because there is something wrong with me," he thought. "I wonder if it's because I'm gay."

An affinity for older same-sex friends is the most common of the green-zone indicators. Because they are so much more physically advanced than their classmates who have yet to see puberty, precocious boys and girls are likely to find their contemporaries light-years behind them socially and physically. As in Ken's case, their friends may be boys a year or two older, but at the same level of physical development. Or they could be girls in the same class whose social interests are a grade or two ahead of their chronological age. Idealization of older teenagers occurs. Precocious youngsters want to be with and act like them. And they can't understand it when their parents won't grant them the same freedom to date, to come home after midnight, and to go to weekend beach parties as sixteen and seventeen year olds.

Marginal members of these older groups, the precocious teens are tolerated and often ignored. From time to time their elders exploit them. Dawn was allowed to exist on the fringe of a group of high school girls on the condition that she furnish them with liquor from her parents' supply for their parties.

Early heterosexual behavior characterizes these teens. Because they are physically precocious, they experience the increasingly intense sexual feelings. They press for release through interest in the opposite sex and through masturbation.

Sexual intercourse is another release for sexual tension. In the past two decades a growing percentage of high school students lose their virginity prior to graduation. In 1965 about 10 percent of female and 25 percent of male students reported they were sexually experienced. Recent research suggests the comparable figures for today's teenagers are about 30 percent and 50 percent, respectively. In college the shrinking pool of female virgins approximates that of males. Thus the biggest change in sexual activity among young people is among its female members.

In spite of their efforts to appear sexually sophisticated, the majority of advanced thirteen to fifteen year olds back away from intercourse, though nearly all have engaged in heavy petting. To some degree this may be due to the absence of opportunity as well as to apprehension about not being able to "do it" well—to be attractive, responsive, and fulfilling to their mate. This anxiety is often as strong a disincentive as pregnancy or venereal disease.

Though they would deny it at the time, a large proportion of younger adolescents don't find first coital experience especially satisfying. They discover, like Ken does, it doesn't equal the pleasure of masturbation. Moreover, many normal teens find themselves initially feeling guilty, confused, and anxious afterward. Though these emotions pass, and the great majority enjoy fulfilling sexual relations as they accumulate greater experience, these initial difficulties can be an unexpected source of stress for those adolescents who thought they had "no hang-ups about sex."

Romance is a component of teenage relationships whether or not the couple is sleeping together. North American youths, perhaps more than any other group of young people in the world, believe that love and sex go together. In spite of a far greater societal permissiveness, well over

TABLE 6.1
Estimating the Severity of Social and Sexual Precocity

GREEN ZONE—Normal Adaptation

- Mature same-sex friends
- Early heterosexual behavior
- Fidelity
- Secondary celibacy

YELLOW ZONE—Temporary Adjustment Reactions

- Oppositional, provocative precocity
- Uniformism
- Double-dare mentality
- Rush to physical intimacy
- Not playing for keeps

ORANGE ZONE—Neurotic Symptoms

- Overdriven, uncontrollable social/sexual interests
- Intellectualization inhibiting enjoyment
- Alien homosexual concerns
- Isolation from age-mates
- Associated school, drug problems

RED ZONE—Severe Maladjustments

- Delinquency, promiscuity
- Psychosexual disorders
- Sexual deviations
- Disaffection, withdrawal, depression

half of modern teenage males and two thirds of females lose their virginity with someone to whom they are emotionally attached.

Fidelity is characteristic of normal adolescents. This expresses itself as loyalty to the values and attitudes of intimates. Among sexually active teenagers fidelity replaces chastity as the prominent value. In this context fidelity doesn't imply the commitment, care, concern, and the sense of "we-ness" typical of adult couples, though it may include these. It does, however, entail an openness, exclusivity, and trust. With some young people the relationship is rightly called "going steady." With others it closely imitates the intimacy of marriage. In such a primary bond sexual intercourse is a natural part of the emotional involvement.

As a rule, however, such relationships are unstable—especially for younger teens. Even adolescent couples who say they are in love with each other when losing their virginity have a no higher probability of staying together over a two-year period than pairs whose first sex involved less romantic feelings.

It is not unusual for normal teenagers to become celibate after their initial sexual encounters. This secondary celibacy may confuse parents who have just gotten used to their son's or daughter's being sexually active. The reasons vary. One teenager will say it's fear of pregnancy and another will be overcome with retroactive moral guilt. A third doesn't like the isolation from same-sex peers that going steady inevitably entails. Still others are unwilling to make an exclusive commitment to a single lover. As one fifteen-year-old girl said, "I'm not ready to settle down yet, so I think I'll be a virgin again."

Oppositional provocative precocity marks the *yellow* zone of concern. Teenagers' advanced social and sexual interests seem intended to provoke a reaction from adults. For example, a girl has an excellent idea of how upset her parents will be when she wears an especially tight-fitting outfit or is asked to a weekend beach party. The provocative behavior isn't intended to cause maximal grief—though that's what it often does. Rather it is part of the effort of adolescents to try to take greater control over their lives by flaunting their social and physical maturity and opposing parental efforts to control it. This is *the* battleground upon which their war for independence is fought.

The same girl may walk the dog, carry out household chores, and visit a grandparent in a nursing home without complaint. But when her mother suggests that she does not need to talk to her friends on the telephone four hours a day, that she has to be home from weekend parties by 11 P.M., or that she can't attend a dance, it is World War III. It is a relatively safe bet that parents will not approve of their youngsters' intimates. From the adults' point of view these chums may be too "social," the wrong race, religion, or socioeconomic class, or—as in Dawn's case—too old. These adolescents are deadeyes for those peers who raise the anxiety of parents the most. And when they are confronted with the edict that they find "better" friends, they accuse their parents of prejudice and hypocrisy. Besides, they smilingly point out, the girl their parents think is a tramp gets straight As and the boy they believe to be a druggie is vice president of the junior class.

Among these youngsters' variety of self-protective responses one of their favorites is uniformism. In essence the youngster becomes part of a group of older adolescents who seem to have the credo: "Sooner, Faster, Bigger." They love to create the false impression of sophistication. They affect a free and easy attitude about sex: a ninth grade girl tells us that if she likes the boy well enough to kiss him, why not go all the way? If we protest, we are accused of being repressed, or probably guilty, about our own sexuality. In fact, these youngsters mute their anxiety about sexual intimacy by using group support. So long as their actions are codified as a part of standard peer behavior they can control their fears because everyone is doing it.

Uniformism encourages a double-dare mentality. This is a tendency to interpret parental warnings as a challenge. To tell a boy that riding on a motorcycle without a helmet is dangerous, that he should not smoke marijuana, or that he's too young to have sex is to goad him to try it. His father's cautioning Ken that continuing to see Brenda will ruin his life forever motivates Ken to feel he must prove him dead wrong. Magically these teens equate the reality of their fantasies with the reality of the external world. Like high wire performers, they imagine themselves to be able to glide above danger, without recourse to a safety net.

A rush to physical intimacy is a yellow flag. The younger adolescents view their virginity as a burden to be shed. Losing it brings them a feeling of relief because they have "done it," have jumped over a critical developmental hurdle. The experience often occurs with someone they care little about. There is much focus on "me," and very little upon "we," in this drive to become sexually experienced.

In the yellow zone they are not playing for keeps. When her mother breaks down sobbing because Dawn swears at her for making her stay at home on a school night rather than going to the mall to hang out with her friends, Dawn is shocked. She hadn't intended to hurt her. When the guidance counselor asks Dawn to meet with her Thursday afternoon to discuss the matter of her declining grades, surly attitude, and accumulating class cuts—and bring her parents with her—she is upset. She hadn't realized people were taking her behavior that seriously.

Overdriven, uncontrollable social and sexual interests are prominent features of the *orange* zone. A half century ago a prominent psychoanalyst found that a large number of adult women she treated reported dramatic personality changes coinciding with the onset of menstruation. One of the changes was to become "boy crazy" while at the same time losing interest in academic work. Like Dawn, some of the girls in the orange zone focus all of their energies on boys. These girls fall in love regularly but don't stay in love. Once they attract the interest of a young man, they drop him in favor of a fresh challenge.

Parents feel unable to regulate the social life of these teens. When they say, "You can't stop me!" parents acknowledge their own limitations and wonder about calling the police. Dawn's mother and father felt powerless to forbid her to go to a high school dance and to make it stick. "We can't guard her door and windows all night," her father said. "We have to get our sleep." Using force to stop a boy or girl from going out results in an angry confrontation. When his girlfriend came by to pick him up in a car and his father said no, Ken pushed him out of the way and went anyway. The disagreements are sometimes more bruising. Not a few of these mothers and daughters, and fathers and sons have traded punches.

Excessive intellectualization inhibits sexual enjoyment. Precocious adolescents love to talk "frankly" with anyone who will listen about sexual matters, frequently taking an ultraliberal position that it's all right to do whatever feels good anytime with anyone. This apparent openness is in fact a way of reducing their anxiety about sexual encounters. This process also has several downside features: when it comes time to have sex, these still relatively inexperienced youngsters may find their expectations frustrated because of the gap between what they think should happen and reality. Also they discover that so much thinking and talking about it robs relationships of the intensity and zest that characterize fulfilling sexual intimacy. Finally there is a tendency among some highly cerebral youths to play the role of both participant and observer. Dawn many times felt as though she were two people—one in the act of coitus with a boy and the other watching the process from a distance—and as a result experienced little sexual pleasure. Even when an orgasm is achieved, sexual intercourse is reduced to a mechanical act after which loneliness and despair follow.

Homosexual concerns are not uncommon. As the enjoyment of heterosexual relations diminishes, some young people wonder whether their "problem" is caused by their being latently homosexual. Like Ken, a boy may speculate that his impotence with women is based on his attraction to his own sex. Since all of us have natural bisexual urges—and these are strong in the teens—some young men and women may find themselves being attracted to a friend, roommate, or someone in the shower room. They may actively fantasize about a physical relationship and this causes considerable anxiety. As a way of coping with this inner confusion, some youngsters conclude prematurely that they are indeed gay and hurl themselves into a homosexual affair.

Deteriorating relationships at home are not the only interpersonal problems. Painful isolation from age-mates occurs. Research on sexually active high school students shows that the greater degree of experimentation the less popular the teenagers feel. Perhaps because of their compulsive rush toward older youths, perhaps because of their arrogance toward their less mature contemporaries, these adolescents forfeit their membership in their peer group: before long Ken no longer felt welcome at class social activities. Especially noticeable is the lack of same-sex friends: Dawn's boyfriends come at the expense of female confidantes— a major loss. Both discover that being fringe members of an older set doesn't compensate for being cut off from classmates.

The provocative, oppositional qualities of these young people result in other problems too. Poor schoolwork and drug use are most common. Dawn's dramatic decline during her middle school years illustrates the former problem. At first her teachers viewed Dawn's sagging grades, obvious lack of preparation, combativeness, and truancy as a "phase." They took heart when Dawn promised to improve and did—for a week or so. Perhaps a faculty member, sensing trouble, may make a student such as Dawn a special project, coaxing her along, accepting her nastiness, sympathizing with her inability to make herself do the sort of work she is capable of. If someone doesn't intervene, however, the avoidance of school and schoolwork will continue, as well as the antagonism if pressed about it.

Since an adolescent's self-esteem is positively correlated with making good grades, these teenagers have to cope with an increasingly negative picture of themselves. A way of managing this growing inner anxiety is to use drugs. We know that by the end of high school a growing number of high school students have abused alcohol and have tried illicit drugs. This group of provocative precocious youngsters is vulnerable to earlier and excessive use of multiple substances. Chronic substance abuse temporarily shields orange-zone adolescents from confronting the real problems in their lives. It delays the moment they can look at their difficulties squarely and feel their distress and begin the process of corrective action.

An intriguing characteristic of these precocious provocative youths is that they retain their ambition and desire to do well academically. No matter how little they study, how much they disparage school, or how poor their grades are, they will tell us they intend to go to "good" colleges and become professionals. Not infrequently they have strong service motives as well. These youngsters dream and talk of making the world a better place. Somehow, however, these fantasies never convert to action.

Delinquency and promiscuity are features of the *red* zone. These teenagers run with packs of other youths who are generally regarded by the community as the "bottom of the barrel." Together they are truant, misuse drugs, and steal. Since they attract the attention of the police they may find themselves in juvenile court. These adolescents will engage in sexual relations nonselectively. Girls will sleep with boys they hardly know, occasionally allowing several at a time to have intercourse with them, without much erotic desire or gratification involved. The benefits seem to be a momentary verification of their attractiveness and their capacity to control males. Some of these young women become prostitutes. The sexual activity of the boys seems intended to demonstrate their prowess to other males. For both sexes, however, a primary motive is to get physically close to another person—to cuddle, to feel warmth—if only for an instant.

Psychosexual disorders afflict teens in the red zone. These are problems with sexual functioning caused by psychological factors rather than by physical ones. Examples are persistent inhibited sexual appetite, little capacity for physical arousal, or the inability to achieve orgasm. Premature ejaculation and secondary impotence—an inability to maintain an erection—occur in males while females experience chronic failure of lubrication, vaginal tightness, or pain. Inevitably this produces fear of failure, sensitivity to the reactions of the partner, and increased self-examination. This in turn impairs physical performance and leads to avoidance of sexual activity.

Sexual deviations—technically called "paraphilias"—are red flags. The essential feature of these chronic disorders is that sexual excitement requires unusually bizarre fantasies or acts. The fantasies may be playful— for instance, talking "dirty" or dressing in a nun's habit with nothing on underneath—to stimulate sexual excitement. Or they can mimic danger, as when someone becomes aroused only when imagining being raped or in bondage. Unusual acts that some find erotic include dressing in the underwear or clothes of the opposite sex, intercourse with animals, voyeurism, or exhibiting oneself. Other youths find that sadistic or masochistic behavior is needed for a "turn-on." Sadistic teenagers find it necessary to inflict psychological or physical suffering upon their partners, who may be consenting or not, in order to become sexually excited. Masochists find themselves aroused upon being humiliated, bound, beaten, or otherwise made to suffer.

Red-zone markers are disaffection, withdrawal, and depression. We see extraordinary active, precocious fourteen year olds becoming not only celibate but also completely disinterested in sex at eighteen. A substantial number who move in together during the high school or college years lose most of their sexual desire. With sex seeming like more trouble than it's worth, and feeling cut off from their age-mates, these young people isolate themselves. In unguarded moments some youths come to recognize that it hasn't been sex they have been after all these years, but love. By then, however, they are so unpracticed at giving love they are rarely the recipients of the affection of others. Depression can be severe among these adolescents, especially if they have severed ties with their families.

Follow-up

DAWN

Dawn's father did not have a heart attack. He called his wife who came home by cab. Then the three of them yelled at one another: her parents called Dawn a tramp. She denied that she and the boy were doing anything and screamed they didn't trust her. This confrontation ended the way all the rest did—Dawn stomping off to her room, her mother sobbing, and her father pouring himself a drink.

Dawn's parents began to have marital problems. Her mother thought that her husband worked so hard that he didn't have enough time to spend with Dawn. He thought that if his wife were at home more and spent less time working as a volunteer at school, Dawn would straighten out. The strain between them resulted in their sleeping in separate bedrooms. Eventually they sought marital counseling. Before long it was obvious their problems were caused in large part by the difficulties with their daughter. The counselor suggested they bring Dawn for a family conference. Dawn came to the therapist's office but would not leave the waiting room. When he tried to talk with her she refused to look at or speak to him.

At the end of their rope, her parents decided to send Dawn to live in Tucson with a favorite aunt and uncle who had a girl Dawn's age. At first everything was fine. But then trouble started—grades sliding and bad attitude at school, unresponsiveness to her aunt and uncle, and withdrawal. "She has made no friends at all," her aunt told her mother at Christmas prior to sending her home. "All she does is sit in her room, smoke, and listen to her stereo." Weepingly, Dawn promised to straighten out if her parents would let her come home. They relented. Dawn returned to Minneapolis to finish her freshman year without incident but was increasingly moody and isolated. Her parents thought that she was smoking a great deal of pot but didn't try to catch her. Increasingly she came and went as she pleased.

In high school for the tenth grade, Dawn made her familiar good start but by Thanksgiving she was failing all of her courses. A science teacher took a special interest in Dawn and tried to talk her into using her obvious ability. When Dawn reacted by saying she really didn't care how she did, the teacher asked if Dawn had given up on school. The question made Dawn furious. She still planned to go to medical school.

Just before Christmas, still several months short of her sixteenth birthday, Dawn stopped going to school entirely. To pay for her increasing drug use and a motorcycle, Dawn got a job as an orderly in a nursing home. Ninety days later she moved into her own apartment with two other young women with the consent of her parents.

Shortly afterward Dawn met a twenty-five-year-old fellow who was working part-time as a guitarist and full-time as a drug dealer. They lived together off and on over the next four years. Dawn worked steadily most of the time. Periodically they left Minneapolis to travel—when the illicit drug sales were booming—but always returned. Twice the young man was jailed for selling drugs.

During this time Dawn lost contact with her old friends and saw her family infrequently. This was just as well because in the four-year span Dawn had an abortion, contracted VD once, broke a leg and fractured her skull in two separate motorcycle accidents, used drugs indiscriminately, and was briefly addicted to heroin.

A week before Easter Sunday four years after she had left home, Dawn called her mother and asked if she could go to church with them. Warily they agreed. Dawn appeared, appropriately dressed and pleasant. After the service Dawn said she and the young man had split. "Living with him was instant middle age" is how she put it. Dawn also said she was thinking of going back to high school and wondered if her parents would be willing to help her.

Over the next two years, Dawn went to night school and made up courses she missed so she could take a secondary school equivalency examination. When she passed, Dawn enrolled as a part-time student at the University of Minnesota while continuing to work. Eventually she planned to go into a full-time premed program.

KEN

Ken's worries that he was gay diminished after a month or so. In their place came listlessness, apathy, and withdrawal. His grades in school continued to be poor even though he was both going to class and apparently studying. "My mind doesn't focus on what I'm supposed to be doing," Ken told a friend after flunking an algebra test. "Last night I sat for two hours without turning a page." Intruding thoughts about Brenda—how much he missed her, whom she was seeing now, and how angry he was at her—made it hard to keep his mind on schoolwork.

Ken tried going out with other girls, but it wasn't the same. He couldn't make himself care about them. Two young women made it clear to Ken that they wanted to have sex with him. Fearful of impotence he awkwardly refused their invitations. In the corner of his mind he still wondered if there wasn't something wrong with him.

Though they were relieved that Ken was no longer seeing Brenda, his parents worried about his growing depression. Ken moped around the house, didn't return phone calls from friends, ate too much, and gained *weight. He would not talk to his mother and father about how miserable he was and refused their suggestion that he talk to a therapist. Convinced they had to do something to shake Ken out of his lethargy, they enrolled him in a six-week summer music camp in Upper Michigan.*

Predictably Ken didn't want to go. But his mother and father insisted, so he went along with the idea. To his surprise he loved the experience. His natural singing ability and maturity attracted the admiration of his contemporaries. His teachers were impressed with his talents and obvious leadership abilities. Ken blossomed. His confidence in his musical ability returned. He lost weight and felt physically good again.

In this program he met two people who were to make a difference in his life. The first was a fellow his own age who, like Ken, was physically and socially precocious. They spent long hours walking in the woods and talking about their similar experiences. Ken was enormously relieved to find someone else in the world who could understand what he had been through.

The second significant person was one of the young men serving as a counselor for the students. A classics major, he seemed to Ken to be one of the smartest people he had ever met. Ken listened avidly to the stories of ancient Greece. Still bothered about the possibility that he might be a latent homosexual, Ken one evening asked the college student if it were true that a large percentage of those early Greeks were gay. "Not that many," the college student replied. "Some boys experimented with it in their teens, but like beer, they gave it up for the straight world." Ken found that brief comment enormously reassuring.

In the fall Ken returned to singing with his natural enthusiasm and started seeing girls again—this time ones his own age. He also started rebuilding friendships with boys in his own class. For a short while he kept up a correspondence with those people who had meant so much to him in the summer program. A legacy of that summer was Ken's decision to study classics.

What Parents Can Do: Suggestions for Helping

Few teenagers bother parents more than those boys and girls with precocious social and sexual interests, partly because these youngsters demand greater control of their lives by confronting, challenging, and defying adult authority. Partly this also is because parental overreactions to older friends, provocative dress, or sexual innuendos worsen the intergenerational conflict.

RESPOND MODERATELY WITH REASON

Beware of intemperate outbursts. Though these adolescents are much more likely than other youths to ignite in us an explosive reaction, in fact just the opposite response works best. Speaking softly instead of shouting, employing a moderate rather than a four-letter-word vocabulary, using reason rather than threats, all raise the odds of getting through to the teen rather than creating greater belligerence.

A temperate response includes trying your best to avoid either-or situations. Finding alternatives to the "do it my way or get out" options requires the savvy of a Middle East negotiator. Constructing an acceptable solution to the impasse begins by acknowledging the reality with the teenager that no ideal choice exists. Try to appreciate the youngsters' emotions: Dawn's clothes are a crucial statement of her independence right now; being required to change clothes would be humiliating. Yet her attire greatly upsets her mother and father. The young person needs to know what the parents feel. Dawn's parents are not demanding that she dress more conservatively because they enjoy exerting their power over her, because they don't "understand," or because they don't love her. They just don't like the way she looks. This recognition that the two generations each have a responsibility for the others' emotions—and down deep care—is a significant step along the way to an acceptable compromise.

Then the trick is to discover an alternative that you and your teenager can live with. In the ideal world the two sides give a little until they reach a compromise both can tolerate. Rarely does this happen. Typically someone gives in for now with the understanding that it is "my turn" next: Dawn can wear those clothes today but something more modest tomorrow; Ken can't go to a party with Brenda and the rest of the senior class at somebody's house they don't know, but his parents will allow him to have a group of kids—including Brenda and older teenagers—to his house next weekend.

Be Wary of Overreactions

Be sensitive to the roller coaster emotions these youngsters arouse in you. Be especially sensitive to your needs and fantasies about them. Especially avoid hypercontrol, assuming the worst, and name-calling. Hypercontrol is an excessive resistance to a teenager's desire to govern a relatively unimportant area of his or her own life—for example, whether Dawn can wear a pair of tight-fitting jeans to school. The result is a quickly escalating scenario in which her mother finally screams to Dawn that she is forbidden to go to school in "that outfit" and Dawn slamming out of the house, wearing what she pleases.

This behavior results in hardened positions, impervious to reality or logic. Because she is so intent on opposing her mother, Dawn doesn't see that her garb is out of step with her friends. Thus she doesn't modify her dress to fit in with the tastes of her classmates and further isolates herself.

The need to hypercontrol blinds a parent to the actual nature of the problem. If Dawn's mother allows her to go to school in that outfit, what realistic danger is she in? Has Dawn learned from experience in the past when she has behaved flamboyantly and tempered her actions? All her mother can feel is that Dawn is defying her and flies into a rage.

At the root of hypercontrol is generally the feeling of helplessness. Some mothers or fathers feel they must have total control over their children or they have no control at all. Thus Ken's parents feel that if they permit him to go with Brenda in her car this will lead to other excesses. They worry that unless they can command his obedience about this behavior a catastrophe might occur. Some adults worry that if they give an inch they will be unable to prevent their offspring from running roughshod over them.

Assuming the worst is hard to avoid with these teenagers. There is a tendency to imagine that what we see is only the tip of the iceberg. If thirteen-year-old Dawn is dressing and acting seductively, then she and her boyfriend must be having sex regularly—though in fact they may be far from it. Then there is the conviction that episodes of deviant behavior will surely lead to unhappy and maybe tragic consequences. Unless Ken stops seeing Brenda and improves his grades, he'll never get into a good college and probably will wind up as a bum.

Name-calling is unfairly and incorrectly labeling a teenager as a special kind of bad person because of actions that offend the parents: when

Dawn disagrees about what to wear to school, her mother calls her a "slut." The purpose of the name-calling can be to warn the teenagers they are headed for trouble, that something terrible will happen to Dawn unless she changes her ways. Unfortunately this approach often backfires. Some teens interpret the accusation as an expectation. Others treat it as a "double-dare." At the least it communicates to the youngsters the worst fears of parents. Whenever Dawn is angry at her mother or father or both she knows exactly how to act to raise their blood pressure.

Excessive reactions of parents—especially assuming the worst and name-calling—resemble those who throw dynamite on oil well fires to blow them out: when performed by experts it sometimes works; when carried out by those who are not, it usually spreads the conflagration.

SHARE YOUR CONCERNS

If you find yourself automatically overreacting consistently to a particular teenager of this type, a strong likelihood exists that this pattern is caused by not fully conscious emotions. Talking to loved ones—a spouse, parents, relatives, friends—who have known you well, and for a long time, may uncover the underlying reasons for your overreactions. Doctors, pastors, and educators who are acquainted with the family serve the same purpose as do mental health specialists.

Remind yourself that these youngsters are not playing for keeps. They are trying out new behaviors as well as trying to gain greater control of their own lives. They do not set out to visit pain upon you. If you can see the intent of their defiance as nonmalevolent, you have greater flexibility in what you can do to help them keep their behavior within normal limits.

Adolescents need to know they have the power to hurt us. A mother, for instance, might tell a fourteen-year-old daughter who calls her "a fat bitch" that she bruised her feelings. Called an "overbearing asshole" by his middle school son for being told to get off the phone and onto his books, a father can let the boy know those are fighting words, and is that what he intended to start? If not, the teenager should expunge that kind of vocabulary when he's around his father. Confronting this nastiness early on gives adolescents a chance to modify their negativism, keeping it within tolerable limits and lessening the chance of massive parental retaliation and escalation of the combat.

Don't be afraid to provide useful information. Our children have a way of listening to us even if they may appear to be deaf to what we are saying and violently disagreeing. For instance, most young people need more knowledge about sexual matters than they let on. Overall they learn little of value from sex education classes. It's helpful to talk about the reasons a teen may want to become involved sexually, that is, to be liked, to become more adult, to be emancipated from parents. Since at least half of today's high schoolers are still virgins, it can be useful to discuss openly why some young people elect not to have intercourse. Talking about the relationships among romance, sex, and love is always illuminating. It is nearly always beneficial to discuss proper contraception for boys as well as girls.

STAY IN CONTACT

Prevent isolation from adults. One of the key factors that discriminates transient adjustment problems from more serious disorders is that those with the former are still in touch with their parents and other adults. As Dawn's case shows, it is better for the parents to stay in contact, even hostile contact, with her for as long as they can. A negative relationship is better than no relationship at all.

Sometimes we become so upset with our children during especially difficult periods, we withdraw to save our own sanity. At these moments ask relatives, family friends, or other adults to initiate contact so that these teenagers have grown-ups in their lives who feel reasonably positive about them and who will anchor them to reality.

Becoming detached from peers and isolated from age-appropriate activities are special vulnerabilities of boys and girls in the orange and red zones. Because these teens are often afraid of new experiences or don't know what to do, parents should step in and make suggestions to reconnect them with other youths. His parents sending Ken to a music camp is an example. Though adolescents will often react unenthusiastically to advice that they go away for the summer, join the church or temple youth group, consider scouting, or participate in a program at the Y, once involved they may benefit from the experience.

ENGAGE THEIR INTERESTS

Keep trying things that may engage one of their interests, connect them to other adolescents, settle them down, and restore normalcy. Musical, athletic, mechanical, artistic, or other talents are an avenue. Their social and service interests sometimes provide a "handle" to engage them. It is hard for some of them to resist an opportunity to help others. Dawn found working in a nursing home gratifying because of her need to be needed. Work nearly always improves the adjustment of these youngsters. Ideally the job should be paid but, for example, a demanding volunteer field position with the Audubon Society can be just as effective.

Adolescent groups that frequently attract boys and girls are organized around slightly exotic, challenging interests: outdoor survival programs, martial arts, filmmaking, computers, or collecting beer cans, old records, comic books. Traveling anywhere with other kids is almost always successful. As one fifteen-year-old girl put it after spending the summer working and traveling in Israel, "When I picked grapefruits on a kibbutz I saw Israeli kids my own age working during the day and standing guard duty at night. That sobered me up pretty fast." The qualities of the leader of a group are crucial in stimulating and maintaining the interest of these young people. Often it is the case that only a few have the enthusiasm and competence, and the personal gifts, necessary to relate consistently to precocious teenagers.

The time span in which these behaviors are most intense lasts from six months to three years, though mothers and fathers report it feels considerably longer. Since even the best psychotherapists have trouble managing their emotions in helping these precocious teenagers, it is not remarkable that parents have a good deal of difficulty with these progeny. If you can avoid intemperate responses, help your adolescents recognize that strong feelings exist on both sides, that nobody is intending to hurt the other, and that both have a stake in trying to locate a mutually acceptable option, this can create a spirit of collaboration which can keep the generations in contact through this stormy period.

7

"I Try, But . . ."
Underachievement
in School

Day to day, week to week, underachievement in school creates more intergenerational strife than does any other problem. It is a rare high school class in which the grades of one teenager in three is not thought to be sub-par. Rarer still is the adolescent who brings home a report card that doesn't elicit a comment from his or her mother or father that some improvement is needed.

Underachievement is a significant difference between potential and attainment. This difference can be judged statistically, for example, with a girl whose standardized test percentiles fall significantly below her measured IQ level. Or it can be based on a subjective impression, as with a boy who seems bright but takes home Cs and Ds. Many parents believe underachievement to be a function of how hard the youngster works: "I don't care what grades you get as long as you have good effort marks," a mother might tell her daughter.

For the purposes of this chapter, underachievement is defined as the perception of academic performance lower than reasonable expectations which is not directly caused by underlying physical, intellectual, or cultural factors. Rather the problem emerges out of teenagers' own reactions to the school experience and the responses of their parents to the level of achievement.

JONATHAN

Jonathan described himself as an "agate-type nut." What he meant was that every day during the school year he studied the small print in the sports section of the newspaper. This section contained box scores of the previous day's high school, college, and pro games, as well as team standings, the day's schedule, point spreads, and a detailed statistical breakdown of the athletes' performance. Jonathan concentrated on his favorite sports—football, basketball, and baseball—but also paid attention to tennis, swimming, track, gymnastics, fencing, and golf.

The reason Jonathan gave for his detailed scrutiny of the agate type was that he eventually wanted to be a sports reporter. Unfortunately it looked as though these interests might be short-circuited by flunking out of school. Things started to go really badly in the winter of his sophomore year. Just after New Year's the second term grades came in—C+ in English, C− in physiology, and Fs in French III, geometry, and history. All Jonathan's teachers commented on his indifference in class, poor preparation, missed assignments, and numerous class absences.

Jonathan attended a public school in a northern suburb of Atlanta. His father was a Georgia Tech professor of civil engineering and presided over a small, active consulting practice. His mother coordinated the consulting work and often accompanied him on trips. Two older sisters, now at Emory, were outstanding students.

Jonathan used to be a competent student too. Until the sixth grade he was capable in the classroom, a good athlete, and a natural leader. But biology played a nasty trick on him, delaying his own physical maturation while his age-mates grew rapidly during the middle school years. Though he tried just as hard, his decreasing size relative to the other athletes greatly reduced his status from being a star at age eleven to a reserve on the JV basketball team by fifteen.

His academic work followed the same trajectory. In seventh and eighth grades his report card showed Bs and Cs. By freshman year Cs replaced Bs, and he dropped to a lower level of French because of a D+. At a conference with his teachers at the end of the ninth grade, Jonathan's mother and father were told that he had an IQ in the ninety-fifth percentile. "Professional help" was suggested, a recommendation the parents ignored. Jonathan vowed to mend his ways and his parents were encouraged by this pledge.

Over the summer Jonathan worked as a CIT in an overnight camp in

Tennessee where he'd been for six summers. In contrast to his school behavior, at camp he was responsible, hardworking, and outgoing. Jonathan started his sophomore year well—midway through the first marking period he had mostly Bs. But then he started to find geometry boring and the teacher in history uninspiring. Increasingly he was unable to resist the agate type and sports programs. He told himself that he could concentrate perfectly well on his homework with the Falcons, Hawks, or Braves on the radio.

Now and then he sneaked home from school to watch sports on cable when he knew his parents weren't home. With growing frequency this absence occurred during geometry. Finally the teacher called his mother at work and asked if Jonathan were ill. When she recovered from the shock of hearing Jonathan was not in school, she realized he was probably at home. When she came in the house she found Jonathan watching Australian rules football on ESPN.

SALLY

Exams terrified Sally. Sometimes she'd become so nervous the questions looked like they were written in Sanscrit. Even when she could decipher the questions, she more than once looked at the heading of the test to be sure she was taking the right one because she had no idea what the correct answers might be. Gradually the panic dissipated and she could see that she knew the answers to some of the problems. Then she worked as fast as she could. Two or three times during a final exam she would hit a question that stymied her. Then Sally would sit paralyzed, convinced she couldn't possibly pass the test. Occasionally she would still be in this frozen state when time was up. If she recovered, it was not unusual for Sally to answer the remaining questions as rapidly as she could because what she wanted more than anything else was for the exam to be over.

Sally was an eleventh grader in a boarding school in Virginia. She came there from a suburb of Washington, D.C. when her father, who was in the diplomatic corps, was transferred to Belgrade. Her older brother was mentally retarded and a sister, two years younger, was a strong student.

From her teacher's comments in elementary school, Sally and her parents had reason to believe she was a capable student. But that was before end-of-term tests started in seventh grade. From then on Sally began to have trouble. The majority of her marks were As and Bs, but Cs came home too, usually because of poor exams. Neither her mother nor father was pleased with this lower performance and wondered if she were working hard enough.

Sally was more upset than her parents. She started putting in longer homework hours, which paid off in her day-to-day classroom work, but not for the end-of-term exams. She was so nervous that she performed poorly three quarters of the time. It didn't seem to matter how many hours she studied, the result was always the same. From ninth grade on her mother drilled her and tutors reviewed material with Sally the nights prior to the tests. They found that she knew the material cold. But this knowledge evaporated in the test situation.

Her teachers were aware of Sally's exam-taking problems and did their best to help. A woman who taught her social studies let her take as much time as needed. An English instructor tried allowing Sally to take tests orally. These efforts helped a little, but nothing stopped her increasing exam panic.

On a Saturday morning in November of Sally's junior year, it came time to take the PSATs. She had tried not to worry about this test the week before and thought she succeeded. But as Sally sat down the familiar anxiety returned. The letters forming the questions looked fuzzy and her mind felt sluggish. With two minutes left in the first section of the test, Sally realized she had answered only four of the multiple-choice questions.

Youngsters in the *green* zone share several qualities that result in grades conforming to their abilities. The first of these is setting clear, realistic, congenial goals. These teens start the year with a commitment to achieve measurable outcomes in their classes: a girl with strong ability wants to make the honor society while a boy with an average IQ sets his sights on three Cs and a B. The expected outcome is clearly in mind and positively stated. They don't say that they will do the best they can or tell us they hope to avoid last year's disaster. The goals are within their power to obtain without heroic effort. Moreover, these students feel the standards to be agreeable: the girl aspiring to high grades is working to please herself, though she knows her parents are likely to be happy too.

General goals divide into smaller doable units. The girl with honor society aspirations knows she will have to study three to four hours a night during the week as well as Sunday afternoons. She commits herself

TABLE 7.1
Estimating the Severity of Underachievement in School

GREEN ZONE—Normal Adaptation

- Clear, realistic, congenial goals set
- Selective attention
- Effective learning strategies
- Fate control
- Ability to work when not feeling like it

YELLOW ZONE—Temporary Adjustment Reactions

- More than 0.5 average grade decline
- Bad "fit" of cognitive style with more than one teacher
- Defensive channeling of energy away from schoolwork
- Unmotivated about school
- Performance contingent on external factors

ORANGE ZONE—Neurotic Symptoms

- Significant disparity between ability and achievement
- More than 1.0 average grade decline
- Passivity, inattention
- Low risk taking
- Aversion to owning academic performance

RED ZONE—Severe Maladjustments

- Failure to thrive
- Phobic, dropout
- Other major trouble

to attending all of her classes, especially math and science where she is less capable. She schedules time in the afternoon to go over her classroom notes to stay on top of the material as well as finding out what she doesn't know so she can ask the teacher about it the next day.

Normal students possess selective attention, the capacity to focus their awareness on a particular event while simultaneously shutting out numerous other distractions. An adolescent is able to follow the teacher's explanation of the mysteries of quadratic equations while keeping his mind off the pretty girl behind him; he can recall the principles doing his homework while suppressing his anxiety about the strange noises his stereo is starting to make; and he can direct his attention to the questions on a final exam instead of reacting to the hard, hot, sweaty chair, his growling stomach, and worry about how he will perform.

Green-zone adolescents employ effective strategies to help them get the grades they want. They sign up for courses they like or for which they have an aptitude. When they must fulfill requirements in areas difficult for them, they look for a friendly teacher or a generous grader. Knowing their capabilities, they set priorities. A girl knows she has a good chance for As in English and history but is destined for Bs in math and chemistry. She's also aware that French III could go either way. Therefore she makes a conscious decision to study French when she is the freshest and then do her English and history. Since no matter what she does she is unlikely to earn an A in math and science, she gives these the least attention and energy.

Adolescents in this zone all have favorite places to work which support their study efforts. For most their rooms are reasonably comfortable and quiet. Others study in the kitchen, dining room, or basement. Some regularly use the library. Electronic accompaniment is limited to their stereos. Telephone calls and TV watching are scheduled around study hours. Variation also exists in how long youngsters can work without a break. An eleventh grade girl may be able to study two hours straight while a ninth grade boy is lucky if he can go half an hour without a break. However, they all put in the necessary time to do their work. The average number of hours of studying at home Sunday through Thursday night for freshmen in a college preparatory curriculum is about ten, for sophomores fifteen, and for eleventh and twelfth graders fifteen to twenty.

Capable students participate in classroom discussions. This enables them to demonstrate their knowledge and clarify their thinking about what the teacher wants: when the teacher's frown begins forming when a boy starts to answer a question, he modifies his response to evoke a more positive reaction. That piece of knowledge will benefit him on the next exam. These youngsters also know that talking in class also combats boredom. Instead of drifting off into fantasyland during an especially dull period of British literature, entering into the discussion keeps the boy's attention on the subject. And, this makes it easier to study at night.

These youngsters believe their fate in school resides within their own control. A girl feels that her report card depends on her own ability and effort, not on luck, chance, or an act of God. The morning before a final exam in biology she doesn't consult her horoscope or read the back of a label on a teabag for an omen as to how she will do; she knows whether or not she is ready. After the test the girl probably has an accurate sense of how well she performed. Teens with high fate control take responsibility for negative as well as positive outcomes. The girl accepts that her D+ on the test was because she didn't study enough, not because of what her teacher had for breakfast before she graded the exams.

Normally functioning adolescents can do school-related work when they don't feel like it. They can harness themselves to their homework when they would much rather be outside shooting hoops or watching the Raiders in the second half of a Sunday TV doubleheader. They don't require that a course be fascinating or a teacher charismatic to do what's required. The ninth grader can memorize the parts of a tree in a course in which he has virtually no interest just as an eleventh grader will faithfully do the work for a French teacher who puts her to sleep.

Finally, green-zone students are skilled consumers of assistance. When a girl doesn't understand something in a language class, she tracks the teacher down before the next period for a clarification. A boy who has a terrible time in biology is not too proud to ask for a tutor. Both ask their parents to review material with them the night before exams. Another girl might form a study group with two other classmates to meet before term tests in English and history so they can go over material that is likely to be covered. An interested boy will ask last year's biology students what was on the final and try to find copies of old exams.

Report cards contain quantitative clues to the *yellow* zone of concern. The marks of the teenagers in this area will be .5 to 1.0 (on an A = 4.0 basis) lower than the previous two terms. An example is Jonathan's Bs and Cs in the seventh and eighth grades (a 2.5 grade point average) changing to three Cs and a D+ (a 1.75 average) in his freshman year.

This decline has to persist beyond one marking period to be significant because many students have transient problems adapting to new grades, subjects, or teachers, but they recover within a few months.

Within this declining picture may be substantial variations in performance among specific subjects and dramatic fluctuations from one grading period to the next. In the first term of his sophomore year Jonathan managed Bs in geometry and English but a D in Spanish and an F in history. On his next report card he brought his D in Spanish up to a C+ and passed history, but Cs in geometry and English replaced the honors grades of the previous term. Not infrequently these teens start every new year well. At the October parents' conference everyone is encouraged. But by February the youngsters have lost momentum and the deteriorating pattern continues.

In the yellow zone it's not unusual to find a bad "fit" between the learning style of the student and that of several teachers. Our learning style is the way we habitually understand and organize knowledge. Experts on the subject divide learning style into two groups which are called by various names: left brain and right brain, perceptual and conceptual, serialist and holist, or more colorfully—cower and buller.

In their purest form "cowers" are students who work hard to learn facts, master techniques, and understand logical sequences. They thrive on exam questions such as "When was America discovered?" or "What are the five steps in the scientific method?" Their awareness of information is often without awareness of the frame of reference or points of observation that determine the origin or meaning of data.

By contrast unadulterated "bullers" relate facts to a larger frame of reference, are interested in the origin of information and ideas, look for links to other concepts, and rely on intuitive judgment and reactions as well as on hard data. They crush essay examinations or questions beginning with "Compare and contrast . . ." They enjoy displaying the inaccuracy of facts ("By whose calendar was America discovered?") or showing the naïveté of the "right" answer ("Does any real scientist follow the five-step sequence of the scientific method?"). However, the buller is weak on information and logical problem-solving techniques.

Capable students are androgynous, containing both the cow and the bull, and can adapt their learning styles to the requirements of the course or teacher. A problem develops for some students when their anxiety or other reactions to the learning experience cause them to overdevelop a particular learning style. The more worried Sally became in a class, the harder she worked to memorize facts, the less able she was to see the big picture and was increasingly unable to synthesize information, generalize, or otherwise apply her knowledge. This situation occurred not with one but many teachers.

Defensive channeling of energy away from academic work into other activities is a yellow flag. These adolescents want to do well in school, but anxiety triggered by difficulty causes them to avoid rather than confront the problem. As soon as they receive a low grade, fail to come up with the correct answer when called on in class, or have difficulty with a teacher, they control their distress by directing their attention elsewhere. They feel the need to plan a party for the weekend, spend extra hours lifting weights, go shopping, or trying out a trendy new hairstyle. The result is a successful avoidance of anxiety but also of their schoolwork.

One intriguing manifestation is becoming "a-literate." These capable teenagers can read but choose not to. Instead they devote their time to passively watching TV and movies, or playing video games that require little energy from them. If they read at all, the material is usually comic book quality—short pieces with plenty of pictures and humor. Some teens, like Jonathan, turn to statistics and the agate type. They memorize the names of all the players on the teams and details of their athletic performance, but take no intellectual interest beyond these facts.

When they perform up to their capabilities in school, their work is contingent upon external factors. Little apparent capacity exists to motivate themselves. For Jonathan the history teacher has to be stimulating, otherwise he drifts off. Others require a subject be continually exciting in order to complete their homework. Not infrequently tutors are brought in to help them keep up in this or that subject. As long as the tutor is present these young people have no trouble learning the material, but no ignition occurs. Without these tutors their interest stalls out again.

Yellow-zone teens will often be described by adults as unmotivated about schoolwork. By "unmotivated" we mean a seeming indifference to their academic chores, a reluctance to start them, short attention span, and distractibility once they begin. It takes them enormous effort to drag themselves away from the TV or phone to begin their homework. They seem unable to sit still for more than a few moments without being overcome with the need to make a phone call, get something from the refrigerator, read the latest periodical, or play with the dog. Any new noise, smell, or event instantly absorbs their attention.

What is unique about these boys and girls is that these behaviors aren't apparent in other spheres of their life. For example, the scholastically unmotivated boy cheerfully works thirty hours a week for an office building cleaning firm, is never late, and thought by his bosses to be the most energetic employee in the organization. The girl with no ability to concentrate on her English has no problems working all Saturday sewing a new outfit.

A significant disparity between ability and achievement characterizes the *orange* zone. That is, the student's performance in the classroom or on standardized tests is substantially lower than might be expected on the basis of measured intelligence. Just what a "significant" difference is varies with the statistical characteristics of the class or test. A rule of thumb is the gap between ability and achievement has to be about thirty-five percentile points to be significant. For instance, Jonathan's ability compared with his classmates placed him in the top third, but his three Cs and a D ranked him in the bottom quarter of his freshman class. Students may demonstrate the same difference between IQ and SAT results.

A greater than 1.0 decline in grade point average for more than one year is a related orange flag. This pattern is often seen when a teenager changes schools. In this instance the B student (3.0 grade point average) in junior high comes up with Cs (a 2.0 average) in the tenth grade and remains in that rut through secondary school. Another youth experiences the same problem in college. Their substantially lower grades are not a function of freshman adjustment problems or the "sophomore slump." Rather they seem to start off on the wrong foot and never recover. Also, unlike the yellow-zone students, little variations exists in their grades. No As or Bs counterbalance the Cs and Ds.

The passivity and inattention of orange-zone teens is striking. When they do their homework they exhibit what has been termed a "superficial-passive" approach. Jonathan turns the pages of a history assignment, looking at the words, but doesn't think about what the author is saying. He completes math problems without asking himself whether he understands the principles involved. This behavior stands in contrast to the internal dialogue he has with a sports reporter when he reads his column about the origin of the Olympics, or his comprehension of the significance of the On-Base Percentage.

These adolescents feel helpless to control their attention. Unlike green-zone students who can selectively focus their minds, these boys and girls have overinclusive attention. They react to everything—the feel of their chairs, the acidity of their stomachs, the actions of classmates, the look on the teacher's face—which makes it extraordinarily difficult to concentrate on what the main point of the lecture is.

Exams present a special terror. Like Sally, many of these young people suffer from extreme exam panic due to their inner feeling of helplessness. They believe that what happens to them on a test is beyond their control, that it's more a matter of luck, and the fortune is more likely to be against them than on their side. In addition they attribute low test results to causes that are internal, constant, and unalterable. For instance, Sally will be certain that her poor SAT results are due to her low IQ rather than think the test was not a fair measure of her ability. She "knows" she will always do poorly on such tests instead of thinking she had a bad day. And she is convinced that her scores can never be improved rather than imagining that the results could be raised by her own better preparation or tutoring.

Low risk taking is a prominent neurotic symptom. With these youngsters the motivation to avoid failure is far greater than the desire for success. One result is the "nothing ventured nothing lost" mentality. In class they sit as far out of the teacher's vision as possible, seeking to blend into the background. Though apparently attentive they *never* volunteer an answer. Should they be called upon enormous anxiety develops. Some freeze and others blurt out any answer that comes to mind to bring their ordeal to an end.

Aversion to "owning" their academic performance characterizes these adolescents. Rarely do they examine a returned test or paper to see what they missed so they can improve the next time. They glance quickly at the grade and toss the papers in the trash. Were an uncle to ask an orange-zone nephew what his grades were the last term, he would not be able to recall. He might look quickly at his mother as though she, not he, should have that information.

Lack of ownership permeates the way these adolescents talk about their schoolwork. If we listen to them we will hear considerable third person and contingency statements.

Third Person

"The French grade is poor."
"The report card was disappointing."
"The studying isn't going well."
"The term paper isn't getting written."

Contingency Statements

"As long as I study for the exam I'll do okay."

"All I have to do is write one page a day this week and the paper will be done."

"If I do my reading for the course there'll be no problem."

"My report card will be fine this term provided I stay motivated."

Nowhere in these statements does the teenager tell us *"My* French grade was poor" or *"I'm* disappointed in my report card" or *"I* can't concentrate." Nor is there any kind of commitment to getting the academic work done, no statement like *"I* plan to do the reading for this course" or *"I* will study for the exam" or *"I* intend to write a page a day" or *"I* want to stay motivated."

Failure to thrive is the primary *red*-zone indicator. Borrowed from pediatrics, and applied to underachieving teenagers, this condition has a number of features. Apathy and disinterest make their appearance alongside the yellow- and orange-zone markers. When teens in this area go to school, it's clear they merely are going through the motions. No attempt is made to learn anything in class. At home their passivity and helplessness become paralysis, making it difficult for them to understand their homework. Studying the simplest material wears them out. They seem to require huge quantities of sleep and mope around exhausted when awake. Efforts to tutor them or provide special educational services at school bounce off their indifference. They have given up hope. Parents despair of their ever finishing school.

It is not surprising to find that adolescents in the red zone avoid school. Some become school phobic or develop the pathological separation anxiety described in Chapter 5. A large number make it to school but do not attend classes. They may show up for some where they like the teacher or are still surviving academically. But mostly they can be found hanging out in the cafeteria, gym, or on the fringes of the school grounds. In college they may never see the inside of a classroom. Instead they devote their days to routine chores or wasting time and their evenings to being with their friends. Since college professors rarely take attendance and often base the students' grades on final exams and papers, the fact that their youngsters have in fact been doing nothing for a term may not be apparent to parents for many months.

Out of school, cut off from the vast majority of their contemporaries, these adolescents are prime candidates for other major trouble. Much of the trouble is internal. They become disabled by anxiety attacks and depression. We will see red-zone indicators in other areas—feelings of emptiness and personal fragmentation, sexual deviations, and conduct disorders. While the majority of underachievers are not delinquents, a large proportion of teens in the United States and abroad who behave antisocially have had a long history of performing poorly in school. As a group they are more prone to drug abuse and sexual promiscuity than are those who perform satisfactorily.

Follow-up

JONATHAN

After his parents discovered Jonathan in front of the sports channel, they sat down with him to talk about what was happening. These evening discussions continued for the next week. His parents went over all the records and teacher comments going back to the elementary school years. Bit by bit they pieced together an understanding of the overall picture. Jonathan had been indeed the shining light of the sixth grade class. They saw that as his classmates began to pass him in physical stature and athletic ability Jonathan's academic decline started.

Jonathan admitted that his immersion in sports was not driven by the desire to be a sports reporter—he showed no interest in writing for the school newspaper—but rather by a dislike of school. As he talked to his mother, Jonathan acknowledged that he had on several occasions tried to improve his grades but lost his momentum in a few days.

His father suggested that Jonathan keep a record of the number of hours he spent each day watching or listening to athletic events and reading sports periodicals. At the end of the first month Jonathan discovered he totaled ninety-eight hours. This fact shocked Jonathan into recognizing how much of his life was being consumed by sports. As he and his father talked it over, Jonathan acknowledged that he didn't devote anywhere near the same amount of hours to watching and reading about athletics at summer camp. "There," his father thought out loud, "you play a lot of sports."

Everyone agreed that Jonathan would try his best to pull himself to-

gether during the remainder of the tenth grade. But he couldn't sustain his pledge to stay away from the agate type and the TV, so no significant improvement occurred in school. "I feel like a drunk who can't avoid the booze," he admitted.

After talking to several people, Jonathan's parents decided to send him to a small Tennessee boarding school. Of course Jonathan didn't want to go. He knew something had to be done, however, so he agreed to visit several with his mother and father. The first one he saw he liked. What particularly appealed to him was the structure: there was specific time allotted for classes and sports or other activities. A supervised study hall, known as the "Pit," was mandatory for all new students.

Eventually Jonathan was accepted and he reluctantly agreed to attend. His reluctance was enhanced when the school required that Jonathan enter as a repeating tenth grader. His parents were delighted because they had thought for some time his physical maturation was slow for his age.

The tight organization of the school forced Jonathan to keep his attention on his academic work, sustaining his own commitment to improve his record. Two hours in the Pit every night absorbed most of his leftover time. An unexpected factor that helped Jonathan a lot was repeating his sophomore year. The added twelve months of physical maturation, plus the smaller number of boys out for the teams, enabled him to play varsity football and basketball. Playing sports reduced his need to read about them, freeing him to concentrate on schoolwork.

SALLY

When she realized she had done so little on the first section of the PSATs, Sally felt panic exploding in her. From then on she raced through the other sections. If the answer wasn't immediately apparent to her she marked "A"—in the hope of maximizing probability—and moved to the next one. She completed the last section with plenty of time to spare.

Sally didn't tell anyone about her trouble. When the PSAT results arrived in the late fall, they were low: Verbal 340, Math 410.* Sally was embarrassed and frightened, but her parents wrote from Yugoslavia not to worry. They were sure her scores would be higher in the spring; after all,

* *Zeroes added for the sake of comparability to the SATs. The national average is about 430 and 470.*

her school gave a course on taking SATs. Unfortunately anxiety again savaged her performance. The results were Verbal 380 and Math 450.

Otherwise it hadn't been a bad spring. She was elected to one of the student leadership posts and would be the photographer for the yearbook. In May, Sally went to the college adviser who didn't know her very well. She looked at Sally's grades, which were slightly above the average for the class, and her SAT scores, which were among the lowest in school, and concluded Sally must be an "overachiever." She suggested Sally look at small four-year or junior colleges. These institutions would be less demanding, she assured Sally, and besides the chance of being accepted was much greater than that at the more selective schools.

Her parents were shocked at the recommended college list. They imagined Sally would apply to Duke, several Ivy League colleges, and the University of Maryland as a backup. When they called to ask the college adviser why "quality" schools were not on the list, the woman told them that quite frankly Sally was not up to that level of work—in the unlikely prospect she were accepted. Besides Sally was "high-strung" and would fare better in a less pressured atmosphere.

Sally's parents were not so sure. Her father called a psychiatrist working for the State Department in Vienna. After hearing the story the doctor recommended that a thorough evaluation of Sally be carried out to assay her ability as well as to determine whether emotional factors might be contributing to her exam problems. Her mother flew home and scheduled Sally for psychological tests at a clinic in suburban Washington.

The results confirmed that Sally indeed possessed a superior IQ and was relatively knowledgeable, but that she suffered debilitating panic attacks. A multimodal behavioral treatment program by a psychologist in the area was suggested.

The main element of this program was desensitizing Sally to testing situations. The therapist first taught her how to put herself in a relaxation state. Then Sally was asked to imagine moving closer and closer to taking the SATs in November. As soon as she felt the slightest twinge of anxiety she was instructed to evoke the relaxation state. Sally practiced this desensitization exercise twenty minutes each day. Within six weeks she was able to think about taking the SATs without overwhelming panic.

It worked. Sally's fall SAT scores were Verbal 560 and Math 640. She noticed a new respect in her college adviser's eyes, who now thought some of the higher-level colleges were not so untenable. Her scores, along with her leadership and photographic skills and two exceptionally strong inter-

views, were responsible for Sally's admission to Duke and Cornell as well as to the University of Maryland. In her freshman year in college she wrote her parents that she still hated exams the same way she didn't like bridges. But they didn't block her pathway anymore.

What Parents Can Do: Guidelines for Helping

Teenage boys and girls spend more hours in school and at related academic activities than any other enterprise. School is the primary work of this life stage. How much pleasure an adolescent derives from the school experience is to a large extent based on being able to perform satisfactorily. Here are several guidelines for lowering the probability of teenager underachievement.

RECOGNIZE PREDISPOSING FACTORS

Pay attention to developmental and constitutional forces that set the stage for underachievement. The most frequent reason for poor school performance is that the youngsters lag behind their age-mates in physical, emotional, or social maturation. In elementary school they are small for their age. They exhibit great variation in the development of their abilities: for example, a bright seven-year-old boy reads and spells well but is shaky in arithmetic; he has poor handwriting and fine motor control. Psychologically some children are unable to function independently in school. The interpersonal skills of others are so immature that they are isolated from other students, making going to school an unhappy experience.

Occasionally the psychological and social effects of lagging physical development occur as a result of delayed puberty. Jonathan's case illustrates this point. Suddenly in junior high school the other boys matured more rapidly which undermined his self-portrait as an athlete and a leader. In a case like this underachievement comes as a reaction to reduced status.

If you believe your youngster lags behind his or her contemporaries, think seriously with the teacher about having the child repeat the year. Follow-up studies on immature youngsters who have repeated a year have been overwhelmingly positive with few adverse effects noted. Often the negative impact of the change can be minimized by taking the year over in another school in the same community.

Some youngsters have constitutional weaknesses that impair learning. Most common among these are visual and hearing problems. Over one half of a group of struggling children seen by a diagnostic clinic in New Haven needed glasses. Other physical difficulties associated with under-achievement include hearing loss, mild neurological conditions, and in-adequate nutrition.

Then there are youngsters with attention-deficit disorders.* These boys and girls are impulsive and hyperactive. They have enormous diffi-culty concentrating on schoolwork or anything else demanding sustained attention, don't seem to listen, are easily distracted, and often fail to finish what they begin. Their impulsivity expresses itself in low frustra-tion tolerance—waiting their turns to be called on in class or to bat in a softball game is nearly impossible. They give up quickly, exhibit rapidly shifting attention, and have a penchant for becoming upset when things do not go their way. They are always on the go, have trouble sitting still, break things, and rebel against any type of discipline.

Finally, some youngsters have innate difficulty learning to read, spell-ing words correctly, writing legibly, or solving arithmetic problems. In secondary school, college, and beyond, these youths struggle with high-level math and science. Mastering a foreign language is a chore and their spelling remains unpredictable.

Early diagnosis of these constitutional factors that inhibit learning is crucial. If your child isn't learning properly, start with a medical exami-nation. Occasionally the exam will turn up a treatable condition which will help—glasses for a myopic girl or medication for a boy who can't sit still. At the very least, it rules out any obvious physical cause for learning difficulties.

If your child continues to exhibit a weakness in particular areas, re-quest a careful psycho-educational assessment. Such an assessment may pinpoint specific deficits so that remedial help can be started. Keep in mind that many children who have these difficulties *do not* go on to develop learning disabilities that compromise their educational future. Moreover, follow-up studies of overactive children into their young adulthood don't show significant differences between this group and

* This condition is also called "minimal brain dysfunction."

normals on employer ratings of performance, self-ratings of adjustment, or maladaptive behavior.

With tutorial help these youngsters can learn to read and spell reasonably well, write competently (or learn to type), and grasp the essentials of math. Be aware also that remedial help is a double-edged sword. When we offer tutoring to a child we also convey the opinion that something is wrong and needs to be fixed. Adolescents are especially vulnerable to having their self-esteem eroded by the requirement that they spend time in the high school resource room or receive extra help in geometry.

As teenagers they can be encouraged to learn what they can and can't do well. They take Latin, and unspoken, logical language which can be memorized, instead of French, replace chemistry and its mind-boggling symbols with physics for liberal arts majors, and schedule a required high-level math when they won't have other demanding courses and can secure outside assistance.

WATCH OUT FOR OVERREACTIONS

Monitor your reaction to your teenager's academic performance. Excessive parental responses to adolescents' schoolwork can cause their grades to fall rather than improve. Three types of parental overreactions often accompany underachievement.

The first is the overanxious parents who equate their offspring's academic success with being "happy." They assume that doing well in school leads to being accepted at a good college, which in turn results in getting a good job and accumulating money or success—all of which means their child will be happy. Like a pyramid resting on its point, everything is based on high grades.

As a result of this dubious theory—money and success do not necessarily guarantee happiness—these parents panic at Bs and Cs or worse. They threaten or bribe their youngsters to achieve better marks. They say bizarre things to motivate them: one father told his son the morning before his SATs that if he made a combined score of 1200 it would compensate for his four grandparents who were murdered in the Holocaust.

Upwardly mobile fathers, who themselves may not have been great students, are among the most anxious about their children's grades. It is enormously important to these men that their progeny be more successful in school than they were. For some it is a "make-up" need, having a child be successful in an area they were not. For others their child's entry into Stanford will validate their business success and new social status.

In response to their parents' excessive anxiety some young people like Sally worry too much about their academic work and experience exam panic. Others honestly don't believe doing well in school is as important as their parents make it, and so say. The result is a chronic low-level antagonism which drains energy away from classroom work.

Then there are anxious single-parents. Most often mothers, their concern stems from their belief that because their child "doesn't have a father" the youngster is vulnerable to problems in school. They constantly scan for signs of trouble. Report cards are examined minutely to be sure that academic effort marks are up to par. Even if the marks pass muster, these mothers greet the next report card with their hearts in their throats. At a teacher's conference a mother may hear that her son is a top student, president of the class, and will be the star of a musical. Not reassured, she asks why the boy is not involved in sports or whether he might be overachieving to compensate for his underlying lack of confidence.

A variation of this pattern is the parent who believes her youngster requires special handling. From the beginning of school it is made known to the teachers that her child's record should be marked "fragile." Tutoring or another form of special help is demanded at the faintest suggestion of trouble. As a result the youngster doesn't have the accumulated self-reliance to cope with a momentary problem learning math or with a teacher he or she doesn't like.

A second form of overreaction is being overly demanding without day-to-day contact and caring. When we exhort youngsters to work at a high level, the chances of their being successful are better when we remain in close proximity, are consistent, and are willing to hear their reactions to our demands. Too many busy parents believe they can yell over their shoulders as they leave for the railroad station in Greenwich, "I don't care how you do in school as long as you do your *best,*" and obtain the same results from a daughter as an underling in the city. Or a father thinks that a quick in-depth conversation will lift a daughter's sagging grades. After all, it's the quality that counts not the quantity.

It is a popular myth about child rearing that we can have quality time without quantity time with teenagers. Though this may be possible with children, parents need to put in an enormous amount of time with teens to obtain any quality at all. You may decide that you will have a talk with your daughter over the weekend about her sagging marks. Friday night she's out. Saturday morning she gets up late and doesn't want to talk. There is a game that evening, then afterward a dance. She will be ready to talk at midnight when she comes home, but you may have been asleep for an hour by then. (You could take a nap in the afternoon so you could be awake for a good talk at midnight.) Sunday morning she goes to church and then over to a friend's. During the afternoon and evening she is in her room studying or on the phone. An entire weekend can pass without a good opportunity to talk.

Finally, parental overenthusiasm can convert interest in a school subject or activity to passionate disinterest. For example, a tenth grade girl brings home an A in French. The next thing she knows, her parents have signed her up for a summer program in France. Two months later she's living on a farm in Provence, milking goats and wondering where she'd gone wrong. Or there's the thirteen-year-old boy with a minor talent in the flute. His father is so delighted he buys him an expensive instrument, signs him up for a year's worth of lessons twice a week, and encourages him to try out for the local youth orchestra. Instead of waiting to see whether the teen's interest will continue or the talent is deep enough to make a sustained commitment, these parents wholeheartedly pounce on the first flicker of interest. In many cases they quench that spark with their enthusiasm.

Be aware of a tendency to be overanxious, overdemanding, or overenthusiastic. Allow your teenagers to develop their own coping skills, set their own standards to work for, and develop a set of talents and interests of their own. By doing so, you raise the odds of their being open to your suggestions about how they might go about performing effectively.

ENCOURAGE EFFECTIVE STUDY HABITS

One of the most important ways you can help teens achieve acceptable marks in school is to tell them how to study effectively. A distillation of suggestions inspired by the Harvard Bureau of Study Counsel is contained in Table 7.2, which summarizes strategies used by successful students to help themselves stay organized, study, and take notes properly, and to overcome concentration problems and slumps.

TABLE 7.2
Hints for Studying Effectively

I. STAYING ORGANIZED
1. Set aside a consistent time and place to study
2. Know your daily assignments, when exams are scheduled, deadlines for papers and projects
3. Schedule studying a week at a time
   - Set priorities:
     - ·· Which material has the nearest deadline?
     - ·· Worry about one thing at a time
   - Break down papers and projects into doable, small chunks
   - Be ready to change time commitments
4. Don't overtax your mind and body
   - Eat and sleep properly
   - Schedule time for exercises, relaxation
   - Avoid cramming

II. STUDYING
1. Find a good study area with
   - A comfortable, but not too comfortable environment
   - Good lighting
   - Adequate air circulation
   - Freedom from distraction
   - Access to needed resources
2. Understand your optimal work style
   - Hours of peak efficiency
   - Length of concentration span
   - Ways of refreshing yourself
3. Cultivate a mental attitude conducive to studying
   - Separate "study time" from "free time"
   - Be ready to work when you sit down
   - Recognize the need for "warm-up" time
   - Read lighter material or do mindless work if you can't do what you plan to do

III. COMBATING CONCENTRATION PROBLEMS
1. Recognize that you are in charge
2. Establish your purpose for studying by asking yourself, "Why am I studying this?"

- "It's been assigned," "To pass the course," "To get a good grade," "To avoid feeling guilty"
- "Because I want to learn," "I want to understand," "I'm curious about it"

3. Ask yourself, "What do I already know about the subject?"
   - Reminds you that you are not starting from scratch
   - Helps you focus on new, unfamiliar material
4. Ask yourself, "What do I want to be able to do or say after I study this chapter or lesson assignment that I can't do now?"
5. Read the summary first
   - Read the first and last sentences of each paragraph to obtain a skeletal picture of the chapter
   - Picture what the author intends to say
6. If your mind wanders, ask yourself, "Why am I studying this?"
   - Review reasons
   - Make a choice: finish the assignment now, later, or not at all
7. With math, do simple problems and problem sets first—before reading the chapter
   - See how many you can answer with your present knowledge or by applying your ingenuity
   - When you get stuck, use the chapter to help you
8. After completing the chapter or assignment
   - Make notes, highlight, underline
   - Imagine talking to a friend about what you have learned
   - Think about the questions that might be on the examination from this material

IV. TAKING NOTES IN CLASS
   1. Try to read ahead because
      - Helps understand lectures
      - Gives time to understand more complicated ideas
   2. Organization
      - Date your notes
      - Develop your own shorthand
      - Take notes according to the structure of the lecture, not necessarily in outline form
      - Include graphs and tables if there are no handouts
      - Keep your notes in one place
   3. Recording notes
      - Use one side of the paper

- Listen to teacher's point of view to identify important points and unifying ideas
- Record material mentioned more than once
- Record material mentioned in the lecture also covered in the readings
- Record material mentioned in the lecture to which examples or anecdotes refer

V. ANTICIPATING SLUMPS
1. Recognize these occur every year
2. Triggers
   - Overload
   - Getting sick
   - Falling in love
   - Cramming for last term's finals
   - Problems with teacher/course
3. Don't give up
   - Attend all classes
   - Stay on a normal schedule
   - Try to do all the homework
   - Ask friends for help
   - Seek extra help from faculty
   - Find an incentive to keep you going

Don't assume that because your son knows what he's supposed to do, he will be able to follow these guidelines without help. He may need your aid in finding the best time to study or in setting priorities. Though he knows he should read the summary of a biology chapter first, he may forget and resume plodding cheerlessly through it. He may panic when the slump hits him in February. Be there to help your youngster recognize the problem and support constructive changes and positive thinking.

Support moderate risk taking. Encourage your daughter to enter into class discussions, thereby helping her discover the limits of her knowledge which may stimulate her to study the subject with greater interest. Many students become reluctant to admit they don't know something publicly. As a result they fall behind unnecessarily. Urge your youngsters to ask questions when they don't understand something. You may have to help them find a way to make their uncertainty known without undue embarrassment. Also encourage them to think about a teacher's point of view. If it's difficult to divine, suggest she ask students who took the same course last year what they think.

Reinforce learning from experience. Debrief teenagers after an exam, helping them recall what was in it, what seemed easy, and what was a mystery. When tests or papers are returned make sure your adolescent looks at the comments as well as the grade, not an especially pleasant task for the modest achievers because the teacher's remarks may be largely negative. The impulse is to place them in the circular file. If you can go over returned materials with your teen without being overly judgmental or otherwise upsetting the youngster, this effort can be helpful in determining what went right as well as what went wrong. Discuss how the preparation and performance might have been improved, and what this might imply for the next time.

PAY ATTENTION TO FIT

Watch out for the lack of "fit" between your teenager and the teacher. A predictable problem in high school is that the learning style of your adolescent and the teaching style of the instructor will not mesh. An example is your hardworking, rote-learning daughter taking an eleventh grade English class from someone whose cognitive style is highly conceptual. The teacher delights in expounding on the symbolic meaning of Milton's *Paradise Lost* but never tells the students how to identify and understand these underlying meanings. Since the faculty member seems to have only one way of explaining the material—and that is not the way by which your daughter easily learns—find a tutor who can teach your child in a way she can understand.

Also pay attention to the "fit" between your child and the academic setting. Knowing your youngster's temperament and the conditions that stimulate reasonable performance can make a considerable difference. Some temperamentally slow-to-warm-up or difficult adolescents learn more effectively in a structured, lower-pressure atmosphere than in an open or highly competitive environment. Others respond well to higher levels of demand and underachieve without it. Then there are students who thrive in smaller classes with considerable individual attention and there are those who perform better in the relative anonymity of larger classes.

Watch out for low teacher expectations which become a self-fulfilling prophecy. Some of the difference between a competent student and a low performer is how they are treated by their instructors. People tend to do what we expect of them and students are no exceptions. Research shows that if students with the same intellectual capability are described to teachers as either "promising" or "ordinary," the first group is more likely than the latter to achieve higher grades at the year's end. Moreover, measures of knowledge and even intelligence may be higher for the "promising" group.

Presently it is not altogether clear how this occurs. It is more than just a "halo effect," the children being given higher grades because the teacher believes them to be brighter. There is a whole range of subtle smiles, postures, closer physical contact, and longer interactions that communicate affection and encourage higher quality attainment.

It is wonderful for teenagers to be the beneficiaries of this type of pupil-teacher interaction. Unfortunately, they also can be the recipients of negative expectations: their very presence evokes a frown and nothing they can say or do is rewarded. When pupils are labeled by several faculty members as hopeless underachievers, these youngsters live down to expectations. In these situations the best course of action is to change instructors, drop the course, or find another school.

COMBAT UNDERACHIEVEMENT

If you have a teenager who gradually or suddenly exhibits the characteristics of the orange or red zones of underachievement, try to avoid the feelings of passivity and helplessness that infect the youngster. Rule out physical predisposing factors, your own overreactions, or lack of effective study habits that may be contributing to the school difficulties. Then look for obvious situational factors. Is your son who flourished in a small junior high school overwhelmed by the regional high school of five thousand with thirty students per class? The majority of young people perform at a higher level in smaller classes rather than in large ones, and better in large classes than in very large classes, because teachers can monitor the students' performance more closely, keep them at a task, and provide more frequent feedback.

Consider the faculty and school environment. The individual teacher is enormously important in preventing a high-risk child from developing learning problems. Your child could have a learning disability in one teacher's class and not in another's. In a study of children vulnerable to learning disabilities, half of those instructed by poor teachers failed. By contrast 77 percent of those in classrooms with teachers rated as "adequate" passed.

The milieu within which teachers operate impacts their effectiveness. Secondary schools which look very similar in terms of pupil population facilities and faculty experience produce graduates with markedly different behavior and achievement. The reasons for the difference include greater structure, stability and professionalism of faculty, an emphasis on academic matters, more time devoted to the subject and less to managing disruptions in class, more frequent engagement of the whole class in discussions, periods of supervised quiet work in class, the use of rewards and praise, and rapid checking of homework with feedback. It is the cumulative effect of these factors that creates an ethic—a set of values, attitudes, and behaviors—that characterizes higher quality schools.

If your adolescent is in a school setting that isn't working because of the size, quality of instruction, or the atmosphere, consider changing schools. As the example of Sally indicates, however, sending an underachieving teen to a private school is not always the answer. But if you feel that your youngster has made a reasonable effort in the present school for a year with no improvement, make a change. Every large city in North America has educational counselors who can advise you as to proper placement.

If you wonder whether the problem may reside within your teenager and not the school setting, seek an evaluation by a psychologist or a physician who has expertise and experience with this age group. A psychological evaluation may consist of interviews with the parents and child as well as of a long battery of tests. Some take one or two days. A physical or neurological consultation also may be recommended. The assessment should provide a fuller understanding of the causes of the underachievement as well as a recommended course of action. For instance, the assessment of Sally revealed mild underlying depressive feelings, a belief that she had to do well in school to make up for the retarded brother, and terrified feelings that she wouldn't make top grades on the term exams in order to qualify for a prestigious college.

The recommendations should be quite specific: in Sally's case, (1) physical exercise to improve mood and provide some arena for the demonstration of competence; and (2) a cognitive behavioral therapeutic program aimed at helping Sally replace self-defeating thoughts with positive ones.

Indeed, recommendations such as this are often helpful for a number of underachieving youths. It is not unreasonable to suggest physical fitness training for a poor student. A high proportion of students at the bottom of their classes in high school and college are also at the low end of physical fitness. Clinical experience with underachievers who have begun to lift weights, run, or do aerobics, regularly finds that they achieve higher grades at the year's end. We can speculate about the causes for this improvement, but surely two reasons are the improved mood, known to be associated with regular workouts, as well as a more positive self-concept.

A psychological approach where professional mental health workers employ a blend of cognitive and behavioral techniques frequently helps underachievers overcome their deeply ingrained feelings of anxiety, low fate control, and pessimism about school. With subjects with exam panic, such as Sally, a helpful technique involves learning to relax while imagining the stress-producing test. Youngsters who have trouble sitting down to study may be taught to visualize themselves doing their homework while in a relaxed state before they begin. Other elements of the treatment can involve reshaping a student's catastrophic thoughts.

Consider Sally who thinks that studying for a test is a hopeless proposition because she's sure to flunk anyway. She might be helped to recognize that it is her *thoughts* about the studying, not the studying itself, that are the problem. She is then trained to recognize these pessimistic thoughts and replace them with more realistic ones. Instead of thinking "What's the use of studying, I'll never pass these tests!" she is taught to think, "I've done all right in class" or "Others dumber than me pass these tests" or "Let's see what I already know" or "I can get help if I need it" or "I don't have to know it perfectly to pass." Eventually Sally comes to recognize that the mind that can make her nervous is also the mind that can calm her down.

Whenever possible, parents should be included in the treatment process. Had Sally's mother and father been in the country they might have been counseled to try to help Sally relieve some of the pressure on herself by helping her understand she didn't have to make up for the retarded brother. Parents with teens who underachieve for other reasons can help too. Youngsters with little self-discipline can be taught by establishing a reward system for appropriate study habits. Rewards can be a ball game with Dad, greater use of the car, throwing a party, or money. To obtain these rewards the teenagers must be able to show, for example, two hours of homework per night for a week and notes from all their teachers that they have been prepared for classes every day.

A careful diagnostic evaluation leading to an understanding of the reasons for underachievement, which points to a plan to help the teenager, is often successful. It is also true, however, that even the best diagnostic assessment is an inexact process, for it may not turn up the reasons for a learning problem or may emphasize secondary rather than primary factors. Yet doing something—even if it isn't a perfect match between diagnosis and intervention—often results in improved school performance.

PUMP UP SELF-ESTEEM

Imagine being trapped in a job you dislike but cannot leave, where, compared to your co-workers, you find the work very difficult to comprehend, where your boss makes it clear to you that you are marginal and details your inadequacies in written reports to your family a half dozen times a year. This is what it is like to be a low achiever in school. As a result, many young people develop neurotic symptoms—anxiety, withdrawal, avoidance, aggressiveness, and regressive behavior—which are as much a barrier to learning as physical immaturity, poor eyesight, or a reading disability.

Once you have gotten an expert evaluation of your low performer, are satisfied that the youngster is in the right school, and that proper tutoring is at hand, do not assume that things will be just fine. The reason so many young people fail to benefit from comprehensive evaluations, expertly crafted educational plans, extensive resource rooms, and skilled tutors is that the inner conviction of being stupid overwhelms them, causing so much distress that they shut down. Looking at a book engenders so much fear that they won't be able to understand what is on the page, that they cannot concentrate on the words. They go blank while trying to solve a simple math problem because they are certain that they will never be able to figure it out.

With these youngsters, do all you can to pump up their self-esteem. You can help them enormously by making it clear that you understand how difficult it is for them to confront daily a school situation that promises humiliation. Talk with them about what it is like. The fact that you comprehend some part of this painful experience and are sympathetic does a lot for the morale of these boys and girls. Let them know that you recognize how hard it is to do homework when it seems so incomprehensible. But encourage them to keep at it, engaging the material actively. Remind them of the long-term payoff (there are hundreds of colleges for low-achieving but motivated high school graduates). To the extent that you are able, go over the material with them. Reward their efforts even though their school marks may continue to be unimpressive.

Finally, don't view the underachieving teen only through the restrictive lens of the report card which may obscure more than it reveals. See the whole person. Is the girl who slides by in school an energetic fast-food clerk? How about the boy with marginal grades who is a solid camper or above average in Hebrew school? Acknowledge these other accomplishments of your children and be sure you care about them, no matter what their report card says.

Remember that your child is doing the very best he or she can do in school under the circumstances. Your son is not deliberately having trouble to frustrate you. Neither is your daughter acting out of a masochistic need to inflict pain on herself by underachieving. Remember, too, that the relationship between how we do in school and how we do in life is slight. Most of the successful men and women in North America were not academic stars and did not graduate from prestigious universities. Life makes very different demands on us, rewarding human qualities that are not easily graded on a report card. While you want to do all you can to help your child avoid difficulties associated with poor academic performance, make sure you don't allow your anxiety or frustration to distort the place of school in your youngster's life, and to fracture the bond between you.

8

"You Can't Make Me"
Oppositional Behavior

Rare are the teenagers who at one point or another don't see our request that they be home at midnight after a party as unreasonable and the basis for an argument. Equally unusual is the adolescent who promises to mow the lawn or empty the kitty litter and doesn't occasionally "forget," or become sullen when reminded once again to do it. Then there are those who pledge to get an early start on a term paper but procrastinate until the las† moment.

As these examples suggest, both direct and indirect resistance characterize the oppositional behavior of young people. Direct opposition includes open defiance, negativism, or disobedience in response to parents, teachers, and those in authority roles. They debate every rule, then provoke nasty confrontations by violating parental prohibitions. Temper tantrums occur when they are obliged to do things they don't feel like doing. Indirect opposition is often called passive-aggressive behavior. The essential feature is seeming compliance, when more assertive behavior is possible, followed by insidious resistance to adult demands. The resistance expresses itself in dawdling, forgetfulness, fatigue, and procrastination as well as sullenness, irritability, or tantrums when pressed.

As a group, oppositional youngsters feel unappreciated and misunderstood, are jealous and easily piqued by minor slights, and wear their emotions on their sleeves. Around them we feel edgy, as though we are walking on eggshells, waiting for them to blow up.

For most youngsters these episodes of oppositional behavior are both mild and brief. For a smaller group, however, these actions and attitudes become a habitual reaction to the desires of others, which undermines their satisfaction from living. Chronic wrangling characterizes their relationships with their loved ones. Erratic, moody, and disorganized, they underachieve in school. Typically these teens don't regard themselves as "oppositional" but see the problems arising from the unreasonable demands of their mothers and fathers.

HARLEY

For his fourteenth birthday, Harley put an earring in his left ear. That started yet another fight between Harley and his parents.

Harley is a seventh grader in a middle school in San Antonio. His mother works as a secretary in an insurance company and his stepfather is an Air Force pilot stationed at Randolph Air Force Base. Harley's natural father had been a pilot too but was killed in a landing accident when Harley was four. Harley describes his nine-year-old sister—the child of his mother and stepfather—as "Miss Perfection."

Harley is bummed out: he hates school and can't stand his parents. "School doesn't interest me," he says. "Why do I have to learn where Zimbabwe is anyway? And the teacher puts me right to sleep."

At home things are bad. "All we do is yell at each other," his mother says. "We have to walk on tiptoe around him." His stepfather adds, "I don't feel we have any control of him anymore. He comes and goes as he pleases." Harley complains, "All they ever do is pick on me."

Harley has never been much of a student. Early learning problems caused him difficulty learning to read and spell. Because of this problem he repeated the first grade. He also had special tutoring which brought his reading up to grade level, but Harley always hated the special help. "It made me feel like a retard," he said.

Through the sixth grade Harley was a pleasant, somewhat shy boy. Then he changed. A seventh grade teacher said, "Harley in no way resembles the youngster described by the elementary school." Harley was doing almost no studying. "When I feel like it, I make one pass and if it doesn't lock in, forget it" is what Harley says about his study habits. The only material Harley read regularly were the magazines Dirt Bike *and* Penthouse.

The day Harley had the earring installed, his stepfather was furious. He told him to take the earring out. Harley refused. His mother sided with her husband and told Harley to remove the earring. Harley shouted at his

*stepfather, "You can't make me, you're not my real father." His mother
then said, "Harley, either you do what we say or get out."*

Harley left.

MICHELLE

*Procrastination plagues Michelle's life. She is a senior at the University
of Toronto and has never been able to get anything done on time. Term
papers are a particular nemesis. Ever since her secondary school days in
Hamilton, Michelle has a terrible time getting things in by the deadline.
Unfailingly Michelle vowed to "start early" on every assigned paper. But
as the term wore on she found herself doing everything but working on the
writing project—reading magazines, rearranging the furniture in her apartment shared with two other girls, trying out new recipes, corresponding
with people she hadn't heard from in months.*

*Often the ways of avoiding the real work provided the illusion of prog-
ress toward completing the paper: organizing her desk, recopying her
notes, alphabetizing reference books, or creating a schedule for writing—
which needed to be continually updated because she never kept to it. In an
attempt to relieve the building pressure Michelle tried getting together
with friends, going to movies, or even spending a weekend in the mountains. But the unfinished work shadowed her wherever she went, undermining any enjoyment.*

*Finally with the deadline looming and whiplashed by the anxiety she
could no longer contain, Michelle usually finished the paper in a last-
minute sprint—handing it in, as often as not, after the deadline. The
quality of her writing generally was high enough so that her teachers still
were able to award her honors grades.*

*Michelle was a third and last child. Her father, a high school dropout,
ran a successful auto-leasing firm. Neither of her older brothers cared for
school and were happily working at blue-collar jobs. This lack of academic
interest was a blow to her mother, a bright woman who had not had the
money herself for higher education, who wanted her children to graduate
from university. Michelle was her last hope.*

*Michelle was about fourteen when her mother began to pressure her to
be an outstanding student. At first her marks in school improved under
her mother's relentless attention. But there was always something in Michelle's tests or teacher comments on papers that fell short of perfection.*

Her mother pounced on these flaws, ignoring what Michelle had done correctly.

By her last two years in high school, Michelle started to "forget" to bring home returned graded schoolwork. She also had problems getting down to writing papers. Predictably this behavior raised her mother's anxiety level. The relationship between them became increasingly strained. Though Michelle never openly opposed her mother, irritability and moodiness increasingly displaced the genial positive traits of her childhood. From time to time Michelle exploded in reaction to her mother's demands, but then became contrite, begged forgiveness, and promised to do her absolute best on the next school assignment.

At university the procrastination continued. Because she was not able to get her papers in by deadlines or prepare adequately for exams she had to take incompletes and go to summer school after her sophomore and junior years.

In two weeks Michelle's honors thesis is due. She has completed all the reading for the project and has a shoe box filled with notes. But she has yet to write one word of what promises to be a hundred-page manuscript.

A *green*-zone expression of oppositional behavior is comfortable assertiveness. The key element for teens in this zone is the belief that they have legitimate rights, that it is okay to express these openly, and that they need take responsibility only for the intent of their actions—not also the responses of others. For instance, a fourteen-year-old girl doesn't feel guilty at her father's becoming upset when she declines his offer to go to a movie in favor of spending the evening with girlfriends. As they move into adolescence these boys and girls feel secure enough in their relations with adults to believe they are entitled to certain things—being treated fairly or being given reasons for required behavior.

Normal young people believe they have a right to be heard. Not long after their age is recorded in two digits children begin to argue with their parents, especially around issues of fairness: Why does this eleven year old have to mow the lawn before going to a movie, when his sister who forgot to empty the dishwasher can go without doing her chores? By thirteen or fourteen most adolescents like to argue for the sake of arguing. Mostly they bait their mothers—engaging them in debates about rules, morals, religion, drug use—treating the discussions as practice fields for sharpening their skills.

At midadolescence it is no longer a game. Youngsters in the green

TABLE 8.1
Estimating the Severity of Oppositional Behavior

GREEN ZONE—Normal Adaptation

- Comfortable assertiveness
- Setting of apparently modest goals
- Absolutist thinking
- Goofing off

YELLOW ZONE—Temporary Adjustment Reactions

- Contrariness
- Subintentional inefficiency
- Brinkmanship
- Intense ambivalent relationships with adults

ORANGE ZONE—Neurotic Symptoms

- Chronic negativism
- Nothing-ventured nothing-lost mentality
- Setting of unrealistically high goals
- Crippling procrastination

RED ZONE—Severe Maladjustments

- Masochist manipulation
- Seriously impaired work performance and relationships
- Associated psychological problems

zone don't worry excessively about the reactions of parents when dis-agreement occurs. These teens argue to win a point: why can't they have an advance on their allowance, use the car, or go to an unchaperoned party at a friend's ski house? If the argument turns into a shouting match these adolescents often will feel that their mother's tears or father's threats are an overreaction. After all, it is the teen who is the victim.

Setting apparently modest goals in relation to ability can be a green-zone marker. These adolescents seem to want to keep their aspirations to themselves as well as covertly resisting parental standard setting for them. For instance, a bright and talented girl will be reluctant to say that she wants to be an A student and selected as a soloist for the school chorus. In fact, she will work hard for top grades and will practice long hours to be in top form for her singing audition. But she won't acknowl-edge openly to her parents the level or intensity of her desires.

Absolutist thinking is a green zone feature. Adolescents have a way of seeing people and the world around them in black-and-white terms. While they have periods of knowing that this radical division is artificial and that shades of gray exist, teens with oppositional tendencies find themselves unable to act in keeping with their awareness. We can wit-ness this tendency to polarization in their vocabulary: their peers are beautiful or ugly, brilliant or stupid, hot or cold, jocks or wimps. They characterize teachers as terrific or terrible, friendly or hostile, exciting or boring. Depending on their mood they see their parents as good or bad, totalitarian or libertarian, powerful or weak, giving or withholding, loving or hating. These youths generally don't publicly acknowledge gradations which might be suggested by describing someone as "fairly friendly," "not so friendly," or "unfriendly." Neither do they appear to recognize that a parent can be strict one time and not another, or that it is possible to give in and still be strong.

Absolutist thinking sets the stage for stereotyping the older genera-tion. For example, a boy's dealings with his mother may be based on his illusion that she is incredibly strict, tightfisted, and will never give an inch. When he asks her for permission to attend a midnight showing of *Purple Rain,* he is ready to do battle. He will interpret a momentary reluctance on her part as "no" and will immediately become argumenta-tive. In calmer moments normal young people sense the invalidity of this stereotyped thinking and will acknowledge it with a smile. This aware-ness, however, may not change their behavior.

Finally, goofing off in school is one of the most common oppositional activities among normal younger teenagers. The term "goofing off" embraces a variety of student behaviors whose aim—in their words—is to "bug the teacher." They come to class wearing a hat, sit in the wrong seat, whisper to another pupil while the teacher is talking, pass notes, pretend to be chewing gum, or move with exaggerated slowness when asked to work out a problem on the blackboard. When out of the teacher's line of sight, they shoot wads of paper across the room, burp, laugh, or crack a joke. When a teacher walks by a group of goofing-off teens in the hall, muffled humorous comments about the instructor's dress, gait, or personal habits may be heard.

Goofing off allows students who are in largely passive roles to express a form of indirect resistance without running the risk of serious retaliation from authority. It also is intended to have an amusing element much of the time, which provides diversion from school routine. Most faculty members understand this and tolerate a modest amount of these passive-aggressive actions.

Oppositional behavior of the *yellow* zone is directed at adults and is both active and passive. Much of the active opposition can be grouped under the heading "contrariness." Whatever parents are for, the teenagers are against and will be only too glad to argue their point. Rules set down by the older generation exist only to be broken in the minds of the youngsters: this girl who is forbidden to wear jeans to school leaves the house in a dress and changes into denims in the girls' room. That boy whose parents want him to study two hours a night will say, "Why do I have to? I can finish it in twenty minutes."

Provocation is a heavy weapon in the arsenal of contrariness. Yellow-zone youths possess a remarkable facility for knowing exactly what will get the biggest rise out of grown-ups. Harley's putting in an earring illustrates the point. Other teens know that chewing gum or using certain phrases or body postures will drive the parents to the brink. Some develop considerable skill at malicious caricaturing of adults.

Passive expressions can be lumped under the term "subintentional inefficiency," that is, complying with adult requests in a halfhearted manner. They carry out home chores with remarkable incompetence: they might fill the dishwasher with dishes and silverware caked with melted cheese, mashed potatoes, and egg yolks. The five books they were supposed to read over the summer are skimmed and sketchy reports written a few days before classes begin. The reasons they fabricate to explain inept work are often as inventive as they are unbelievable.

Another passive form of opposition is "forgetting"—to feed the dog, attend confirmation class, the time to be home from a date, what the homework assignment might be, or the rule against hanging around a certain part of town. Apathy breaks out. They lose interest in adult-valued tasks. Adolescents in this zone don't see the point of church attendance, continuing their membership in the scouts or 4-H, or doing well in school. On Saturday afternoons a fifteen year old might slump, transfixed and apparently exhausted, in front of the TV, watching cartoons designed for third graders, causing his mother to wonder if he should be checked for mono. Then a phone call comes from a friend inviting him to come over and the boy is out of the house like a shot.

Brinkmanship is a yellow flag. This is the practice of putting things off until the last moment, then using the tide of rising anxiety to provide the impetus to complete the task. Throughout high school Michelle inevitably could not study for final exams or write term papers in advance. As the deadlines came closer and closer she became increasingly tense, restless, and frantic. Finally, in a last second rush, she pulled a series of all-nighters, cramming for finals and finishing her papers.

Friends and parents (when they get used to it) often find this brinkmanship amusing. But for Michelle, and others like her, the process is nerve-racking and exhausting. And, paradoxically, these teens learn the wrong lessons from this experience. Instead of the memory of how difficult it was to cram all of their work into the last few days of the term propelling them to begin earlier, recollection of the painful process causes them to avoid it for an even longer time the next semester.

Intense, ambivalent, adult relationships characterize oppositional teenagers in the yellow zone. Like the little girl who "when she was good she was very good, and when she was bad she was horrid," these young people can be close and affectionate one moment and withdrawn, hostile, and resistant the next. They can't maintain a comfortable interpersonal distance with grown-ups. One day a fifteen-year-old girl may confide everything to her mother and solicit her advice about the most intimate subjects. Twenty-four hours later she won't communicate in anything but monosyllables and tells her mother its "none of your business" when she asks the girl what she is planning to do after school. The capacity to give and receive affection vacillates wildly. This instant a girl charms her father out of his socks and cuddles in his lap; the next she's irritable and freezes at his touch. Today, she readily agrees to take care of her younger brother and sister while her parents take a long weekend in the mountains, but tomorrow the girl has a screaming fit when asked to pick up her sneakers in the family room.

Not infrequently explosions are followed by tearful self-condemnation, remorse, pleas for forgiveness, and pledges for improvement, leading to passionate reconciliations. After the fiftieth or hundredth time this cycle occurs parents may begin to feel that they are being manipulated by the emotional storms and the contrition coming afterward.

In the *orange* zone active resistance is expressed in chronic negativism. The tantrums, sulking, provocations, argumentativeness, and stubborn resistance no longer appear as brief outbursts but take up permanent residence. Yet these teenagers don't see themselves as negativistic. They perceive their actions as legitimate responses to the unreasonable demands of grown-ups. They feel misunderstood, unappreciated, and the recipients of the short end of the stick. In Harley's mind if only his parents knew him, valued what he could do, ceased hassling him about his schoolwork, and stopped favoring his sister, everything would be just fine.

Negativistic behavior compromises relationships with peers. These adolescents behave erratically with their friends too. One morning they can be pleasant, cheerful, enthusiastic, and cooperative; but that afternoon they are spiteful, sullen, quarrelsome, and demanding that everyone do things their way. They don't hold up their end: Michelle "forgets" when it's her time to clean the bathroom in the apartment. Though she agreed with her friends to volunteer to work on a candidate's political campaign, she is a no-show at the first envelope-stuffing session on a Saturday morning. The acquaintances of these youngsters tire of making all the accommodations and feeling on edge. Eventually they open the distance between them.

A nothing-ventured nothing-lost mentality is a neurotic symptom. These teens make it clear to everyone that they are *not* giving their best effort. Harley boasts to his friends that he hasn't cracked a book in English class all year and is conspicuously present at the video arcade the night before finals. After the freshman football coach tells Harley he could be a good linebacker if he'd work at it, Harley makes a point of missing practices.

The behavior pattern has two purposes. First, it is a form of opposing adult demands. Second, it covers over fears of being unsuccessful by creating the image that they could do well if they tried. Because they are so obviously not making an effort they can't be held accountable for their underachieving performance.

An orange-zone indicator is setting unrealistically high goals and then failing to reach them. This maneuver on the part of adolescents works to pacify adults in their lives who may be becoming testy at their continuing low performance, and it also enables them to deny that they have a problem. It's as though saying it will make it happen. For example, after a bitter night of wrangling with his mother about his attitude at home and his poor grades at school, Harley promises to turn over a new leaf. "From now on," he says tearfully, "I'm going to be nicer to everyone and get all As." Unfortunately the first time Harley and his sister disagree over whose turn it is to use the telephone and their mother sides with her, he has a fit. Later when he has trouble comprehending quadratic equations he gives up and reverts to his old bravado about scraping through tests without studying.

Some high goal setters find themselves struck down by fatigue—which is their "explanation" for not doing better. These youths view themselves as ambitious and highly competitive, but they wind up making poor grades because they are tired all the time. Though they take fewer classes and get as much sleep as their contemporaries, they suffer from chronic exhaustion. These same youths will complain they are too tired to go to parties, hold down a part-time job, or participate in intramural activities.

Finally, crippling procrastination is a neurotic symptom. Unlike the "brinkmen" of the yellow zone who typically finish their work in the last minute, the youths in the orange zone fall short. "Incomplete," "Withdraw," and "No Credit" accumulate on their transcripts because they fail to hand in necessary papers or prepare for finals. One reason they put off doing the required work is that they worry that the outcome will not be as outstanding as they desire. Scratch a procrastinator and we usually find a perfectionist.

Another motive for procrastination is discomfort dodging. As the name suggests, this phrase means putting off starting a project because of the unpleasant sensations associated with it. Michelle knows that writing a paper requires considerable effort—lots of frustrating hours digesting her notes, organizing the material, and struggling to express her thoughts well. She recalls the disagreeable physical sensations too: the heavy perspiration under her arms that occurs when she writes; the crick in her neck from being hunched over her desk; the unpleasant touch and smell of typing paper; and the low-level tension she must live with through the whole ordeal. Like someone contemplating diving into a cold ocean off the Maine coast, Michelle is reluctant to endure the pain.

Masochistic manipulation of others marks the *red* zone. This behavior is the tendency to demand the affection of adults by the suffering adolescents bring upon themselves through their oppositional behavior. They say in effect, "Love me because I'm so miserable." Michelle's mother should feel sorry for her because of her paralyzing procrastination. Because these teens refuse to recognize their wounds as self-inflicted, they take no responsibility for their indirect or direct resistance. Rather they portray themselves as helpless victims of circumstance. Therefore Michelle's mother is not allowed to lower the boom on her when another cycle of procrastination begins.

Another aspect of the masochistic manipulation is to convey to parents that only *they* can make things well—and then to frustrate their best efforts. In high school Michelle made her mother feel that unless she stayed up all night with her, making tea and toast, copy editing and typing, she could not finish a term paper. Michelle also caused her English and history teachers to feel she needed special handling: Unless they allowed her to hand in papers late, it would be their fault if she didn't survive.

But it doesn't matter what these parents and teachers do, there's no helping these youngsters. Partly, this is based on the conviction of these teens that nothing will help. Also, it comes from their subconscious resentment toward adults for keeping them so weak and dependent. An indirect means of expressing their hostility is to make others who try to assist them go through the same experience of helplessness they endure by frustrating their efforts.

Seriously impaired performance at school or work and in relationships with others because of chronic passive-aggressive behavior is a red flag. A long-standing inability to prepare for exams or produce papers on time causes students to skim along the bottom of their classes or drop out. On the job their bosses don't promote them into positions for which they possess the qualifications because they are late, forget assignments, lose things, or take forever to finish tasks. Or they are fired because of their constant insolence, complaining, and criticizing.

Parents tire of being continually opposed. Mothers and fathers tire of their constant demands for affection while the youngsters' behavior makes it nearly impossible to love them. They tire of never being able to help or please these boys and girls. They tire of their pathological jealousy. Any flicker of parental praise for his sister's straight A report card drives Harley into a frenzy. Eventually parents start to avoid contact. The social world of these youths becomes increasingly depopulated too. Even though they can turn on considerable charm when the mood strikes them, friends tire of their me-first orientation, unreliability, and sulks.

Young people with severe oppositional difficulties develop psychological problems in other areas. Most common are anxiety attacks around new experiences, such as beginning a school year. These teens become school phobic as described in Chapter 5. Vague physical complaints develop. Nausea, blurred vision, erratic heartbeat, or general weakness occur with no medical diagnosis. Depression and characteristics of the borderline personality organization portrayed in Chapter 13 appear. The function of some or all of these symptoms originally was to manipulate parents or other adults into attending to their needs. But as time goes on these behaviors harden and become problems themselves.

Follow-up

HARLEY

When Harley left he went to a friend's house. His mother liked Harley and didn't mind his staying with them for brief periods. They spent long hours talking and she listened to Harley's distorted version of what went on between his parents and himself. Harley often wished he were her son. But as the household had three other youngsters living in the small house, Harley went home.

As usual there was a tearful reconciliation, and Harley promised to improve. On the advice of their dentist Harley's parents decided to become involved in a local parent program to set limits for their youngsters. But they couldn't stand the guilt that taking a stand required, so they dropped out. At the suggestion of a friend at a dinner party, they sent Harley to a military school in southern Texas, hoping the structure and strict enforcement of rules would straighten him out.

It didn't. He rapidly accumulated demerits for sloppiness and refused to follow orders from upper classmen. In October, when he was assigned to a weekend work detail because of his large number of demerits, Harley left school and went to his friend's house. After two days he came home. Waiting for Harley was a letter expelling him from the military school.

Desperate for help, his parents took Harley to a local psychiatrist who specialized in adolescents. Harley refused to leave the car to meet with him. The parents felt some relief talking to him. At this point his parents were numb and lost whatever remaining confidence they had in their capacity to help Harley. "We coexist" is how his mother described their relationship with him. "We've just about given up trying to help him. He comes and goes as he chooses. We're trying to save ourselves." They continued to talk with the psychiatrist who helped them cope with Harley's oppositional conduct.

During the summer that Harley turned sixteen, his ear became infected so the earring had to come out. When he started school in the fall, Harley met with a guidance counselor to plan his courses. Harley frankly said he hated school but he didn't know what else to do so he thought he had to stay. Noting his earlier learning problems as well as his disastrous middle school years, the guidance counselor made two suggestions: (1) that Harley go on a work-study program, completing his classes in the morning and getting a job twenty hours a week after school; and (2) that he receive tutoring via the resource room in math and science, the courses hardest for him.

Though his parents were opposed to his working half time ("When will he study?" they asked themselves), Harley got a job at a Mexican fast-food restaurant. To his parents' amazement, Harley was not fired at the end of the first week. On the contrary, he was thought to be reliable, hardworking, and popular with the customers. By the first of the year he was made night manager. Pleased, but a little stunned, his mother and stepfather asked him on one of his rare days off why he was doing so well at work. Harley summed it up, saying, "I'm doing this myself."

School was still a struggle and Harley continued to loathe it. With the help of a resource teacher he managed to make passing grades through the remaining years of high school. After graduation Harley decided to join the Navy and train to be a submariner. As he left for boot camp, Harley answered his mother and stepfather's unspoken question. "Enough Air Force people in this family," he said in a voice flavored with a smile.

MICHELLE

Michelle did not finish her thesis and therefore did not graduate with her class. Humiliated, she decided to remain in the apartment in Toronto with one of her other roommates and complete the writing.

Struggling through the hot summer trying to write the first chapter, Michelle was not pleased with what she produced. "I've started the introduction a hundred times, I've filled wastebaskets full of horrible first pages, and I can't get beyond it," she told a friend. With all the difficulties she had starting the thesis, the prospect of completing it seemed as unlikely as flying to Pluto.

Her mother sent her a book on overcoming procrastination which she did not read. At the end of the summer Michelle hadn't put a word on paper. In the fall she started working as a salesperson in a computer store. As the next academic year moved on, the thought that she would never finish her thesis tormented Michelle.

Help came from an unexpected direction. During Christmas dinner at her grandmother's, Michelle sat next to an older female cousin who wrote advertising copy for an agency in Toronto. Eventually Michelle told her she hadn't graduated because she hadn't finished her thesis and began to weep. Then when Michelle looked up she noticed tears in her cousin's eyes. She told Michelle she had had the same problems in college and never earned her degree. The cousin told Michelle that she would do all she could do to help her overcome this problem.

Together they planned a strategy. Both read the book Michelle's mother had sent her about procrastination. That gave them some general ideas. They decided that part of her problem was that Michelle could only visualize the effort to write the entire thesis. They agreed Michelle would break the project down into smaller, doable units. She would divide each chapter into sections and work on them one at a time. She elected to start with the review of the literature chapter which would be the easiest one to write rather than the introduction.

Originally Michelle planned to write four hours a day after work. By February, however, she had made no progress. Michelle commiserated with her cousin who recalled her own problems of being too ambitious. She suggested Michelle limit her writing to fifteen minutes a night. Though Michelle calculated that if she worked only a quarter of an hour each evening it would take her until the end of the decade to complete her thesis, she instinctively felt it was the right move.

Michelle could handle fifteen minutes a night without becoming anxious over excessively high expectations. In time she found she could spend up to fifteen hours a week writing. Though she told no one else about it, Michelle showed her cousin what she completed each Sunday afternoon.

By April, Michelle finished her thesis and was graduated the next month. That summer she began a new position writing user-friendly manuals for the computer store customers.

What Parents Can Do: Guidelines for Helping

Less is known about the origins of oppositional behavior and successful ways of overcoming it than most other difficulties afflicting adolescents. Yet parents can find these attitudes and actions among the most upsetting in the adolescent repertoire. Here are several guidelines to help reduce the negative impact of oppositional behavior.

WATCH OUT FOR OVERREACTIONS

Should oppositional behavior become a fixture in your adolescent's personality, consider the possibility that your reactions to that youngster may be perpetuating the pattern. To what extent is your boy's need for independence clashing with your need to dominate and control? Are your own uncertainties or disagreements with your spouse creating a highly inconsistent child-rearing atmosphere? Has another sibling absorbed affection previously bestowed on the teenage child? Discussing these possibilities with close friends or relatives, or with mental health professionals, often illuminates your feelings and will enable you to make changes in your relationship with that child.

The reactions of the older generation play a role in sustaining adolescents' negative conduct. In many families a predictable scenario plays like a continuous filmstrip. The plot may be framed slightly differently from time to time but the sequence is always the same. Feeling displaced by his sister and pressured to conform, Harley puts on an earring. His parents explode, Harley leaves. Eventually everyone calms down—until the next time. The plot lines of games adolescents play to indirectly thwart their mothers and fathers are suggested by the titles psychiatrist

Eric Berne gives them: "Look How Hard I've Tried," "Schlemiel," and "Why Don't You—Yes But."

If you recognize that you can be locked into an endless soap opera in which you play a supporting role in continuing your teen's oppositional behavior, try rewriting your lines. In Michelle's case her mother could have given up trying to help her daughter and acknowledged that she was powerless. This ploy could have broken the cycle of indirect resistance and forced Michelle to consider other means of overcoming the problem.

INTERVENE EARLY AND CONSISTENTLY

The problems of living with a teenager exhibiting oppositional behavior is a lot like inhabiting the same dwelling as a delayed-action bomb. You know it's going to blow up but not when. Trying to lead a semblance of a normal life while holding your breath is not easy.

Ideally you could summon a mental health expert to defuse your youngsters' explosiveness. Unfortunately oppositional teenagers vex mental health specialists almost as much as they do their parents. Treatment is complex and lengthy, and the results of various types of psychotherapy with this group are not impressive. Professional counselors, however, are often useful as consultants to the parents of these youngsters.

Oppositional teenagers often experience massive inconsistency in parental affection, attitudes, and expectations. Everyone experiences some variation in love and demands emanating from the older generation, but these youngsters are exposed to far more than their share. Mothers and fathers may differ hugely with one another whether it's important to dress conservatively or make good grades. Parents themselves behave inconsistently. One moment Harley's mother tells him he must wear a dress shirt and chinos to school and the next she smiles when he heads for class in his superpunk outfit. Occasionally parents beam simultaneously conflicting signals: "I love you for being you," her mother communicates to Michelle, along with the message that her affection rests upon Michelle's doing well academically.

These inconsistencies produce the same type of behavior in their offspring. The boys and girls don't learn which behavior patterns will be rewarded and therefore should be continued. They internalize the mixed messages they receive about their self-worth. Being unable to anticipate how their parents will respond to what they do, they are constantly keyed up, primed to react unpredictably.

You can reduce the likelihood of oppositional behavior taking root by being authoritative, consistent, and reasonable. Don't be afraid to establish rules for your offspring and expect them to obey. When you establish a rule, state it specifically and give the reason: "Please be home by eleven because I worry if you are late and can't sleep." Expect obedience every time, but tolerate grumbling. Allowing your son to complain that he's being treated like an infant conveys to him that you take his feelings seriously and allows for ventilation.

If a rule is broken, consistently apply brief penalties. These should be related to the offense. For every fifteen minutes a boy exceeds the curfew, he loses a night of going out. Be open to explanations why your youngster arrives home at midnight instead of eleven, but the "reason" should be unusually creative to avoid a penalty. Be open to negotiation as to changes in unduly restrictive rules.

Watch for oppositional behavior at transition points when the new environment makes greater or different demands than the old one. The first year of many fast-track middle schools requires mastering of a foreign language as well as a bustling, unfamiliar social environment. Ninth grade brings sectioning into faster-paced math and science courses along with more impersonal relationships with teachers. In college it's nearly impossible to do all the reading in all the courses, especially living in a coed dormitory. Your having graduated with a Phi Beta Kappa key matters not to the boss on the first full-time job who only seems to care about your exceeding last year's sales figures.

Fresh external stresses can precipitate in the twelve or fourteen year old a sudden breaking out of irritability, obstinacy, or feelings of incompetence. In the eighteen or twenty-two year old these new events may reactivate old oppositional patterns—intolerance of authority, forgetting deadlines, and moodiness—along with doubt and disillusionment.

In ninety-nine out of a hundred cases these regressions pass rapidly. You can help the process of adjustment along by underreacting to this negativism. Providing emotional and physical support—a hug accompanied by a sandwich and a glass of chocolate milk at 9 P.M. does wonders for the overwhelmed eleventh grader. Listen for underlying fears and resentment and be slow to reassure. Few comments offered an anxious, sullen, frustrated college freshman are more unwelcome than "Don't worry, you'll do fine!" or "I know you can do it." Gently recall past periods of life when the same feelings occurred and show how the teenager met the challenge then. Help the child to see the relationship between what he or she is doing now and a desirable future goal. If this can be laced with humor so much the better.

Encourage assertive behavior. Children need to learn that it's all right to have feelings that run counter to those of adults and that it is legitimate to express them. This encouragement lowers the probability that a teenager's resistance to the demands of the older generation will be channeled into aggravating, self-defeating forms.

Fostering assertive behavior begins with helping adolescents recognize that they may be unhappy with the demands made by their parents: A boy resents having to conform to his father's image of what a teenager should look like. If your adolescent responds to your dress code for him by sullen half compliance, talk to him and help him put into words what he feels. Remember that it is hard for any of us to display anger when the circumstances are sure to make it difficult or unpleasant. Remember, too, that a child's becoming angry doesn't normally lead to aggressive acts. The youngster's being able to vent these emotions will actually strengthen your relationship. It also will put you in a position to negotiate—the boy may agree to your dress requirements on even days if you let him put on his other clothes on the odd ones.

COMBAT PROCRASTINATION

Avoid precipitating a power struggle when trying to help teenage procrastination. Don't be afraid to acknowledge your own powerlessness. This recognition allows you to be supportive in a general sense and help your child find someone else to provide technical assistance. As Michelle's case illustrates, this may be another adult with empathy for the problems. Her example also suggests particular strategies that often benefit youths with writing blocks due to procrastination.

1. Divide the large intimidating project into baby steps, taking the easiest part first.
2. Focus on writing—*not* on note-taking, outlining, composing a writing schedule, putting together secondary tables, or other subtle ways of evading that central task.
3. Set aside two bearable periods of time per day to write. For

larks it may be 6 to 8 A.M. and 10 A.M. to noon. For owls it may be 8 to 10 P.M. and midnight to 2 A.M.

4. Within these periods try writing for brief tolerable time spans—as little as five or ten minutes—followed by a nondistracting break such as a short walk alone before another short period of writing.

5. Write on one side of the paper, using every other line. This makes an empty page less intimating; it also gives a more rapid feeling of progress and makes it easier to make corrections without interrupting word flow.

6. Avoid copying over, rewriting, and editing until the first draft is complete. These activities disrupt the writing flow.

7. Show the daily production to a sympathetic adult or friend who is not exerting great pressure to produce, and who can make suggestions to help the process. Occasionally writing in the same room with these people is productive.

8. Build in daily relaxation, exercise, or breaks away from the writing task in time equal or greater to the amount devoted to working. Ideally this time should be spent on one's own.

9. Be prepared to suffer. Writing a long paper is frustrating and exhausting. Periods of anxiety, depression, and fury can be expected. Find ways to relieve them.

10. Recognize that people who write have good and bad days —like everyone else at whatever he or she does.

11. Let something else go. Don't try to do everything else you normally do *and* write a long paper too. Go off your diet, allow yourself to forgo volunteer work, find someone else to cover for you on the job, skip classes where the consequences will not be lethal.

These suggestions work reasonably well for a youth with writing blocks and many of these suggestions apply to other types of procrastination as well.

Oppositional teenagers don't begin each day with the conscious intention of making parents miserable. Rather they see themselves as victims of unjust or stressful circumstances over which they have little control. In their minds they have no choice but to react the way they do. They have long periods of believing parents don't like them. Moreover, they cause for themselves considerable anguish through their negativism and inefficiency. As you struggle to control the cascading emotions your children arouse in you, recognize their pain, and be gentle.

9

"I'm So Miserable"
Moodiness

Inexplicable moodiness invades the personalities of teenage boys and girls. Last spring a thirteen-year-old boy was in tears one minute but laughing the next. This fall he slides into a morose funk which lasts for days. He cannot say why he is so miserable. By contrast his sister, two years senior, is disconsolate and knows the reasons. She bewails a friend's failure to return a phone call, a B+ on her report card, and her mother's saying "no" to a request to have her lovely auburn hair streaked magenta, pink, and violet. If we try to raise her spirits by pointing out how much she has to be happy about, she is furious at our lack of sympathy.

Though most adolescents describe themselves as pretty happy most of the time, about 30 percent will tell us they are sad right now. For all but a few, this melancholy state of mind passes rapidly. For approximately one teen in ten this dysphoria continues combining with other symptoms to form a clinical depression sufficiently severe to warrant treatment.

It is well established that adult females suffer from depression at a rate twice that of males. On the other hand, among individuals without a history of depression, the percentages of men and women becoming depressed for the first time may be nearly equal. As a number of these will be young people, we should not be surprised to find low spirits about as common in our sons as our daughters.

CARTER

Carter is heartbroken. He can't get his mind off Jennifer who broke up with him over a year ago. Jennifer told him just after Thanksgiving that she wanted to "de-escalate" their relationship because she thought Carter was too serious. They were both too young to exclude other relationships. This didn't mean, Jennifer told Carter, that they couldn't still be friends.

Carter is sixteen and a junior at a local private school. He is the third of four children in a family living in Haverford, Pennsylvania. Both parents commute to Philadelphia every day. His mother is a TV producer and his father works as an executive in a large department store. They've always been close to their kids. Neither can understand why Carter continues to be upset. Carter's father tells him to forget about Jennifer and that there are other fish in the sea. His mother laughingly recalls her own first fractured love affair and says not to worry because he'll get over it before long. These comments convince Carter that they have no idea of the agony he lives with.

It's late January, fourteen months later, and the pain of Jennifer's loss is just as excruciating now as the first day. Constantly Carter thinks about how much he loves her and how desolate his life is without Jennifer. Sadly recalling their wonderful times together, Carter is sure he will never know happiness again—unless she changes her mind and comes back to him. Since they both go to the same school, Carter continues to see her several times each day. If she ignores him, his whole day is ruined. If Jennifer casts a friendly glance his way, Carter interprets this as a sign she might be interested in restarting their relationship. Without fail, however, when Carter calls her, Jennifer refuses to be anything but friends. Finally she suggests that Carter stop calling her.

Carter's parents begin to worry. He continually mopes around the house, plays certain songs over and over on his stereo, and shows little interest in anything. They suggest to him that it might be useful to talk to someone but Carter refuses, saying that he doesn't need a shrink. He needs Jennifer.

Several months after their breakup Jennifer begins seeing a boy from a local college. Knowing that someone else is with Jennifer nearly pushes Carter to the brink. He drives by her house weekend nights to see if she's home from her date yet. Unable to sleep, he takes to calling Jennifer in the middle of the night. He rages against her for leaving him and ruining his life. Then he pleads piteously for her to return.

Alarmed at Carter's mounting instability, Jennifer tells him that she thinks professional counseling might help him to feel better. Carter agrees —if Jennifer comes to the first meeting with him.

WANDA

Wanda's family lives in Melbourne, Florida. Her father is an executive at Disney World. Though she's been thinking about "doing something other than being a volunteer" for the last decade, her mother doesn't work for money. Wanda is an only child.

Wanda was a capable student in high school, especially in languages, and played the cello. Though introverted, she seemed happy. She had a few close friends and a steady boyfriend. But she enjoyed spending time by herself in her room reading or practicing her instrument.

After high school Wanda entered the University of Florida. Soon after beginning college, she became more and more depressed. Wanda wrote her parents that she was down in the dumps and tired. She had made some new acquaintances but found the courses boring. The food was lousy. Though Wanda slept at least twelve hours a day, she was constantly exhausted. Playing the cello seemed more trouble than it was worth, so she gave it up.

A visit by her parents in the fall cheered her up for awhile. Then after the first of the year things started to go badly again. Having been always thin anyway, she lost weight. Because her sleep was of such poor quality she spent two thirds of her day in bed. She cut off communication with her parents because she didn't want to worry them any further. Alarmed at Wanda's deteriorating condition, her roommate asked her if she shouldn't go to the health service and see a doctor. Wanda replied, "I just don't have the energy."

By February, Wanda stopped going to classes. She couldn't make herself read the assignments. She told her roommate she didn't enjoy anything and saw no hope for feeling better. Her thoughts were slow and confused, frequently interrupted by the conviction that she deserved to flunk out of college.

Alarmed at Wanda's state of mind, her roommate called her parents and suggested that they come and talk with her. When they arrived and saw Wanda, they were shocked. She looked terrible, had lost a great deal of weight, and was unkempt. She moved and talked extremely slowly.

It was clear that she needed help. They arranged with a dean for Wanda to take a leave of absence. The next day they took her to the family doctor, who had known Wanda all of her life. He too was shocked by her appearance and was struck by her sluggish movements and speech. When he asked her if she had ever thought of killing herself, Wanda broke down and started to cry. "I think it's too late," she said. "I have already begun to die."

Moodiness associated with the recognition of tragedy and of the calendar occurs in the *green* zone. Tragedy compels the attention of early adolescents. They break down weeping watching *Love Story, Madam Butterfly,* or an updated version of *Romeo and Juliet* and are not the same for a weekend. They brood about real-life tragedies—three high school students killed by running their car into a tree, a classmate drowned in a boating accident, or a professional basketball player dying of leukemia. Though none of these individuals may have been known intimately to them, these teens experience the calamities as if they had befallen a family member.

One reason misfortunes hit them so hard is because youths in the green zone recognize clearly for the first time at this developmental stage that disasters can and do happen unpredictably. Their own households are no less vulnerable than any others. For some youngsters these recognitions come with the unsettling force of sonic boom and require several months of melancholic rumination to diminish.

Another reason is that tragedies befalling others remind them of their own mortality. One girl described her reactions to an uncle's heart attack: "For weeks I was unbelievably upset. Eventually I realized it was because his close call made me see that my life is finite." A boy graduating from eighth grade became downcast at the realization that he was finished with half of his education and that he would not be a child forever.

A number of normal teenagers have a penchant for worrying. What they worry about are potential problems. A ninth grade girl's mental "worry list" contains the following items: her grandfather's declining health; a falling apart winter coat which may not last the season; her increasingly shaky comprehension of biology; and a friend's mental health now that her parents are splitting up. She also has global worries. Without much prompting she can become fixated about chemical wastes polluting the world or the escalating arms race. The worrying contains

TABLE 9.1
Estimating the Severity of Moodiness

GREEN ZONE—Normal Adaptation

- Sense of tragedy, mortality
- Worrying
- Loneliness
- Pessimistic personality style

YELLOW ZONE—Temporary Adjustment Reactions

- Sudden transient depressions
- Grief reactions
- Helplessness
- Temporary masked depressions

ORANGE ZONE—Neurotic Symptoms

- Chronic depressed mood
- Prolonged bereavement
- Distorted negative thinking
- Associated conduct, physical problems
- Recurring suicidal thoughts and talk

RED ZONE—Severe Maladjustments

- Major depression
- Anhedonia
- Slowed mental, physical functions
- Suicidal preoccupation

anxiety that is experienced physically. When she broods about something, the young woman can feel the back of her neck tighten and her stomach turn queasy. Once begun, the worrying seems to possess a life of its own, persisting for several hours. Worry doesn't interfere for long, though, with the ability of a green-zone teen to enjoy life and cope with other day-to-day stresses.

A psychological event punctuating the end of childhood is the experience of loneliness. Gradually for some, suddenly for other teens, the recognition emerges that they are—at a fundamental level—all by themselves in this world. However warmly cherished by family and friends, they will live, pleasure, suffer, and die as a unique and separate entity. The awareness of the basic solitary nature of existence terrifies many adolescents. Not a few teenagers go through periods of feeling disconsolate following this awareness. Few of us as adults can recall how painfully these emotions were experienced when we were youngsters.

Normal teenage moodiness may be expressed in a pessimistic personality style. Pessimistic individuals dwell on the inescapable sufferings, limitations, and paradoxes which seems to them to afflict everyone. These youths have a well-developed tendency to focus on the hole, not the doughnut. To them life resembles a Greek tragedy: they see the potential for failure in any achievement, pain in every pleasure, loss in every choice, and reversible fortune hovering over those who are momentarily happy and successful.

Because actual and potential heartbreak attract their attention, these adolescents will seem withdrawn, introverted, and melancholy from time to time. Normally functioning pessimists, however, don't mind tackling new challenges such as learning to play the saxaphone or mastering a computer language. But they do so prepared for the worst and they are pleasantly surprised if things work out well. Since they are always prepared for and respect it, failure doesn't especially upset them. Indeed, examining how a good plan went wrong often amuses them.

Sudden transient depressions are a prominent feature of *yellow*-zone teens. The brilliant, self-confident boy of yesterday abruptly turns spiritless today. Grave doubts supplant former certainties about himself, self-abasement runs rampant, and moods collapse. The disparity between the ideal and actual self usually causes this unhappiness. The boy dreams of being urbane, witty, and admired. Instead he finds himself socially clumsy, inarticulate, and ignored. Feeling humiliated and ashamed, a failure for not realizing his dreams, he is inundated with despair.

Many times these sudden depressions occur at transition points such as attending a new school, camp, or grade; moving to another neighborhood; or a first job. One of the reasons these depressions are so painful is because the adolescents have had relatively little experience with them. It can be terrifying for a youngster to be in the grips of a dysphoric mood that seems both bottomless and endless. That fact alone lengthens the state.

The great bulk of adolescents find their way out of these transient depressions on their own. Instinctively they talk to their parents, seek out friends, throw themselves into their work, turn to prayer, or pursue activities that bring solace and a renewed sense of self-worth.

A grief reaction to severe stress is the most common of the yellow-zone indicators. The stressor may be the loss of someone or something of great value. These reactions commonly follow the death of a parent, relative, or close friend, or—in Carter's case—the breaking up of a romantic relationship. They also can occur with teens when the family moves to a new city just before a boy's sophomore year or when a girl doesn't get accepted at the colleges she wanted to attend. One young woman grieved for several months when her mother and father sold the house in a small Upstate New York town and moved to Arizona. When asked by a friend why she was so upset, the girl replied, "So many wonderful memories always used to come back to me when I went home and now they're lost to me forever."

The key features in the grief reaction are the apparent inability to find a substitute and also despair. In the midst of his unhappiness Carter is sure that no one will ever take the place of Jennifer who has just dropped him. No amount of logic will turn his thinking around. Bereaved adolescents exhibit many signs of a full-blown depression. Especially noticeable psychological features are crying, anger, guilt, loss of interest in things that used to bring happiness, lethargy, and mild-to-moderate mental inefficiency. Though these young people are not suicidal, a number believe they would be better off if they could just disappear. Certain physical symptoms associate themselves with bereavement—almost always insomnia and diminished appetite, along with light-headedness, shaking, nervous disorders, and GI problems. Even though the depressive feelings weigh heavily on these youngsters during their grief, they regard themselves as essentially normal—unlike teens in the orange and red zones who know that they are not.

Not all bereavement starts the instant the loss occurs. Some teens don't begin until as long as three months after the fact. The duration of grief reactions varies considerably because of individual and cultural differences. Most young people negotiate the process within two to six months.

All of us have built-in predictable psychological reflexes to loss, trauma, threat, or frustration. For one person, it may be fear; for another, anger. Moody youngsters in the yellow zone are prone to react to stress with a flood of helplessness. Young people prone to answer life problems with helplessness believe that they are responsible for their difficulties, and that their problems will continue because they can do nothing about them.

Consider Carter. When Jennifer broke up with him, his immediate response was to be sure that it was his fault, instead of entertaining the idea that she wasn't ready for a long-term relationship. He thought that he would never ever be able to find another girl to love, as opposed to noticing that many of his friends had had the same experience and were able to find someone else to care about. And he was convinced that his behavior that "caused" the separation was unalterable, rather than analyzing his deficiencies as a boyfriend and making necessary changes.

Not every depressed teenager looks depressed. Many boys and girls in the yellow zone exhibit temporary masked depressions. Though a careful interview or psychological testing will reveal the same underlying morose spirits as their contemporaries who are obviously down in the dumps, these adolescents don't show their depressive feelings or helplessness directly. Rather they are cloaked in behaviors not normally associated with melancholy—excessive activity, seeking fresh stimulation, misconduct, and experimenting with drugs.

Many of these boys and girls ward off their inner bleakness by staying constantly in motion. In class they can't sit still, at home they pace restlessly and finally jump on their bikes or in their cars to go somewhere. One seventeen year old couldn't stand hanging around and "doing nothing." One Friday at about 8:30 P.M. he convinced a friend to drive with him from hometown Cleveland, Ohio, to Niagara Falls. They spent about twenty minutes looking at it, then they grabbed a fast-food burger and a soda and headed home. As long as he was on the road he felt relaxed, but as soon as he arrived back at home he began to feel edgy.

A variation of this pattern is frantically seeking fresh stimulation. Teens in the yellow zone not only are excessively active, but also require a continuing diet of new external input to combat their dysphoric state.

They have to see every new movie, not miss any of the concerts, be there for the happenings at school, and visit all of the car, sports, and fashion shows. When they hear of a store or an eating place opening, they must try it out. It's as though they receive a transfusion of energy from these events. A weekend without continuing external stimulation precipitates a decline.

Less severe misconduct and drug experimentation also revive low spirits. Cutting classes, staying out late without permission, regular weekend partying, intemperate drug use, and leaving home for brief periods—with the parents knowing where the youngster is—exemplify this misbehavior.

In the yellow zone these activities pass within a few weeks. The melancholy moods lift or the youngsters decide that the ways they are coping with their unhappiness cause them too much trouble and abandon them for better alternatives.

Chronic depressed mood is a major characteristic of the *orange* zone. Teenagers in this area have long periods—the better part of a year—of feeling blue, worthless, disconsolate, and sorry for themselves. Tearfulness and crying, brooding about past tragedies, pessimism about the future regularly accompany these states. As Wanda's case illustrates, convictions of inadequacy flourish. Concentrating, remembering, and making decisions come hard. Even though they may function capably in school or work, with others or in a specific activity, everything requires enormous effort.

Praise or rewards spark no response in them, except perhaps incredulity. If loved ones persist in encouraging them to look on the brighter side of things their efforts may be repaid with a blast of anger for failing to understand how miserable they are and how rotten the future is. Like Wanda, they lose interest in people and activities that formerly gave them pleasure.

During these episodes these adolescents feel slowed down. Their appetites fluctuate. Some don't feel much like eating. Others gorge themselves. Insomnia or feeling the need to sleep all the time infects them. Rarely do they awaken refreshed. Numerous physical symptoms attend these depressed periods—fatigue, weakness, hot and cold spells, dizziness, numbness, upset stomachs, and constipation.

Anxiety troubles many with these depressions. These adolescents often feel agitated, jumpy and restless, or suddenly frightened for no reason. They may begin to be uncomfortable in subways, crowds, driving any distance, or walking across an empty school yard. Phobias take root: suddenly crossing a certain bridge is impossible as is taking an elevator, sitting by the window, or being alone in the house.

Unlike yellow-zone depressions, these can't be linked to a specific cause. They may emerge suddenly or grow gradually without an obvious stressor. The depressive symptoms may be continuous or occur in episodes separated by normal moods lasting from several days to weeks at a time.

Prolonged bereavement is a neurotic symptom. This is a grief reaction persisting well beyond a year. For teenagers like Carter, the pain of his girlfriend's leaving him is just as excruciating eighteen months later as it was the first day. Also, the sadness, lethargy, insomnia, mental disorganization, and impaired school or work and relations with others continue at the same level with no end in sight.

What causes young people to remain resolutely mired in chronic grief rather than putting the loss behind them and getting on with the business of living? One factor is the unwillingness to give up what has been lost to them. The girl who can't recover from the distress associated with her parents' divorce three years ago still cherishes the notion that her mother and father will get back together and restore her happiness. With teens whose prolonged grief was precipitated by an unrectifiable loss—the death of a parent or friend—mourning continues because they would rather grieve than face life without those who meant so much to them.

Another source of prolonged bereavement is ambivalence. It is not only our love for someone who is lost to us that causes us to be unable to let go, it is our anger too that keeps us locked in mourning. In Carter's case, the admixture of rage at Jennifer for breaking up with him, along with the desperate need for her affection, kept him bound to her in grief.

Distorted negative thinking is an orange flag. Unrealistic but perpetual low evaluations of the self, the world, and the future, generalizing from a single negative event to a conclusion of overall incompetence, and feeling guilt-ridden for causing their own unhappiness works to maintain a depressive mentality in these adolescents. They will believe they have no control over crucial life events and simultaneously hold the incompatible conviction that they are totally responsible for whatever misfortunes befall them.

What is often so striking about these youths is how evenhandedly they can judge someone else: they can see that a girlfriend's difficulty on a test doesn't mean that she is stupid, or recognize that another person is not the cause of a boyfriend's breaking up with her. But they do not have the same insight into themselves.

As her depression deepened, Wanda found less and less in herself to be pleased with. Though others thought her to be attractive, Wanda couldn't stand looking at herself in the mirror because she believed her calves were too heavy. When she received an A— on a paper with a dozen positive comments and one critical one, she could recall only the negative remarks an hour later. The failure of a boyfriend to call on a Thursday night at 9 P.M. as he promised precipitated in Wanda the certainty that he disliked her because he recognized inner tragic flaws over which she had no control. Wanda was sure that he would never care about her again, that no one would ever love her, and that she was doomed to a life of desolation. The fact that he was busy and didn't call until the next morning did not reassure her. Finally there is the certainty that all her problems are due to some moral failure in herself. She feels that somehow if she were a better person her life would be happier.

Depressed teens frequently exhibit school misconduct, drug and physical problems which we might not assume "go with" a dysphoric mental state. These are not behaviors that mask underlying depressions, but rather they co-exist with the low moods. If we are not careful we may overlook the underlying depression because these other symptoms are so compelling.

Inability to concentrate because of excessive anxiety and restlessness, impulsive activity to discharge tension, and truancy combine to create school problems. Misconduct—especially stealing, joyriding, fighting, and running away from home—regularly occur. These adolescents will attempt to anesthetize themselves through alcohol and drugs. The most frequent physical symptoms associated with orange-zone depression include tenacious headaches, abdominal pain, eating disorders, and insomnia. These problems worsen the underlying mental state.

Recurring suicidal thoughts and talk occur among a large proportion of these teenagers. The frequency and lethality of their thinking about taking their lives differs substantially from normal or temporarily distressed adolescents. If we should ask green- or yellow-zone youngsters if they have entertained self-destructive notions, one in three will reply in the affirmative. But they will also tell us that this was a momentary fantasy. While they want to be rid of their pain or "disappear," they don't want to die. And they have compelling reasons for staying alive.

By contrast, thoughts of killing themselves compel the attention of orange-zone youth. When depressed, they find themselves thinking they would be better off dead and fantasize about how they might do it. While the reality of taking their life frightens them, many of these teens play with the idea of a suicidal act. Some inflict physical harm on themselves—a few more aspirin than necessary, scratching an arm with a knife, leaning out through an open window from the top of a twenty-story building, or driving too fast. Often these actions occur when the adolescents are isolated and/or have been using alcohol or drugs. The intent of these actions is not to seriously hurt themselves but to signal their pain.

Orange-zone youngsters like to talk about suicide. Their discussions feature intense ambivalence. Books and movies, newspaper articles and magazine stories about people who have brought about their own deaths both appall and fascinate them. They have no trouble debating the morality and legitimacy—from their perspective—of suicide. But the act of killing themselves is still alien.

Major depressions set the *red* zone apart from other forms of moodiness. Most all of the features of the orange zone are present in more painful and lasting forms, along with massive impairment of interest in others or carrying out work in school or elsewhere. Highly exaggerated convictions of personal guilt and worthlessness torment the teens in this zone. Not only was Wanda unable to communicate with her parents, do any of her college work, or even care for herself, but she was sure it was somehow her fault. When in the grips of these major depressions the self-ruminations of these teens are so at odds with reality as to be delusional. Unlike the chronic depressions of the orange zone which allow for periods of relief, these dysphoric states weigh on the adolescent without respite for months.

One of the more persistent features of this state of mind is anhedonia —an overall diminished capacity for pleasure of any sort. A global dulling of interest subtracts enthusiasm from everything red-zone teens formerly enjoyed. For instance, Wanda no longer found playing the cello gratifying. Sharply reduced appetite commonly occurs. Two out of three severely depressed youths exhibit symptoms of anorexic behavior. Other young people turn away from sports, stamp collecting, TV, and friends. Even having sex takes too much effort.

One of the most dramatic qualities of the red zone is the slowing of mental and physical functions. Youngsters in this zone experience mark-

edly less energy. Walking up and down a small flight of stairs brings on
debilitating fatigue. Sluggish thoughts as well as difficulty concentrating
convert the slightest calculation or reading assignment into a Herculean
task. The rate of speech drops and periods of silence increase. The pace
of bodily processes falls well below normal. The time necessary for diges-
tion and elimination lengthens dramatically, one of the reasons Wanda
rarely felt hungry when she felt depressed. People in this condition may
not defecate for days.

Because youths in the red zone feel severely depressed, experience no
pleasure in their lives, and note alarming mental and physical changes in
themselves, it is a small wonder that many welcome the idea of suicide.
Suicidal behavior is a premier red flag. This year about five thousand
young people will take their lives. As many as two hundred thousand will
make an attempt. Females make about 80 percent of the suicide tries,
but four out of five adolescents who actually kill themselves are male.

Since 1965 the suicide rate among American young people has tripled.
Presently it is the third leading cause of death among people fifteen to
twenty-four. The statistics on teenage suicide underestimate the actual
figures. Many "accidental" deaths—cars driven into telephone poles,
alcohol, drugs ingested in a lethal combination—are in fact self-inflicted.

No one has been able to put a finger on exactly the factors that result
in a suicidal attempt. Two feelings most often associated with teenagers'
efforts to take their lives are hopelessness and desperation. For example,
a girl whose boyfriend breaks up with her may be so miserable she
believes she can't go on without him. The emotional desolation she feels
is like falling down a dark, bottomless mine shaft. Nothing she can
imagine happening will bring the boy back or assuage her overwhelming
despair. Out of hope and desperate to end her suffering, she overdoses.

Suicidal acts can be intentional, subintentional, or contraintentional.
Those who kill themselves intentionally have a clear purpose in mind
and try to carry it out efficiently. One boy bent on ending his life scouted
out various tall buildings until he found one with the door to the roof
unlocked. The next day he wrote a note, gave away his stereo, tidied up
his things, drank a pint of vodka for courage, walked to the building roof,
and jumped.

Like Russian roulette, subintentional acts leave room for survival. A
depressed sixteen year old might take all the pills in the family medicine
chest, not knowing whether the amount or mixture will turn out to be
deadly.

Adolescents making contraintentional suicidal acts don't expect to die, only to signal their misery. Unfortunately many of these result in accidental death. This student doesn't know a hundred aspirin will kill her. Another plans just to nick her wrists, cuts too deeply, and bleeds to death. A third throws a rope over the rafter of the ceiling in his college dormitory, fastens the noose around his neck, stands on a chair, and kicks it out from under him when he hears his roommate coming down the hall. Unhappily, the roommate abruptly decides to check the mail. When he returns to the room the boy is dead.

Follow-up

CARTER

Carter went to a pastoral counselor he and Jennifer knew and trusted. Though he tried counseling for six months, it didn't work because Carter couldn't let go of his angry feelings. He remained desolate and furious. Finally he stopped treatment. His grades worsened since he couldn't concentrate on his classwork and exams.

By this time his parents were frantic because of his agitation and continued grief. They talked to the pastoral counselor who suggested a consultation with a behaviorally oriented specialist in Philadelphia who might be able to help Carter relax. This therapist taught Carter to control his anger by evoking the memory of Jennifer and then finding a way to diminish his distress. First he thought of how much he needed her and wanted her back and then how angry he was at her. Then he found a way to control these emotions. For example, he imagined her body being carved in the trunk of a tree and then that succeeding years of growth of the tree would gradually obscure her outline—and his distressing feelings. Or he imagined Jennifer at the bottom of a huge hourglass. He found that when the image of her bothered him he would gradually see her being covered by sand which muffled his emotions.

Within three months of this combined treatment Carter felt the melancholia lifting. At the end of his counseling Carter saw that it was his rage at her for leaving him that prevented him from being able to put Jennifer behind him. Also he recognized that he went into counseling only to please Jennifer, not to help himself. As soon as he was able to control these feelings and understand how he himself could benefit from therapy he could go on with the process of living.

WANDA

When the doctor asked her what she meant when she said she'd already begun to die, Wanda said, "I'm poisoning myself . . . I . . . haven't . . . had a bowel movement . . . in a week!" Relieved that Wanda had not tried actively to commit suicide, the doctor reassured her that the slowing down of the digestive system was something that happens when people are depressed.

Then he arranged for Wanda to be seen by a psychiatrist in a community hospital. Because Wanda was not actively in danger of harming herself, the doctor elected to see her twice a week and started her on antidepressant medication. During the next three months Wanda felt no better. She had no interest in anything because everything seemed so futile and pointless. She refused to talk to her friends because they "want more than I can give." The slightest activity—brushing her teeth—seemed to require an incredible effort. Most of the time she stayed in her room. In therapy she continually said she felt worthless, apologized to the doctor for "taking up her time," and said she felt guilty for being such a burden on everyone. It seemed incomprehensible to her that she would ever feel herself again.

Though Wanda wasn't eating correctly, she began to drink alcohol in greater amounts than before. At first it was joining her parents for drinks at night, but then the alcohol intake increased. Though the doctor warned her about drinking when she was taking medication for her depression, Wanda continued because the alcohol made her feel a little better. During a particularly low period of feeling hopeless, however, Wanda consumed several bourbons and took all of her remaining medication in a suicide attempt. Fortunately she was found by her parents and rushed to the hospital where she recovered.

When her psychiatrist asked her why she had done it, Wanda said she had finally felt strong enough to make a suicide try, but not well enough to have any hope of getting any better. She added that she would not have had the courage to try to kill herself had she not gotten drunk first.

Wanda was transferred to a mental hospital for inpatient treatment. There she received a mix of therapies. In addition to medication she received individual and group treatment. Along with others Wanda recognized that one of the reasons she got depressed was because of a tendency to feel both helpless and responsible for bad things that happened to her. Gradually Wanda began to see that she could recognize some of the thoughts that had started her on the road to feeling depressed. Eventually, with the help of her therapists, she learned to change some of the ways she thought about these stressful events.

Bit by bit Wanda began to feel better. After two months in the hospital, she started playing the cello again. Thirty days later she left the hospital for a part-time job. Fourteen months later she returned to college for full-time study.

What Parents Can Do: Guidelines for Helping

Few conditions are as painful to bear, or as difficult to watch our children endure, as a depressed mental state. They feel so wretchedly miserable and there seems to be so little we can do to comfort them. Here are several guidelines that can lower the probability of adolescent moodiness deteriorating into a severe depression and shorten the period this melancholy must be endured.

PAY ATTENTION TO FAMILY HISTORY

Children whose parents or close relatives have been afflicted with depression have a slightly greater tendency to respond similarly to stress than the offspring of nondepressed adults. At present the reasons for this effect are not fully understood. Current speculation is that biochemical effects along with impaired parent-child relationships and modeling of depressive behavior by the older generation all contribute to teenage depression.

Suppose you find yourself in a situation in which either you or your spouse is, or has been, depressed. What might you do to lessen the vulnerability of your offspring to these same debilitating emotions? Begin by reminding yourself that the overwhelming majority of boys and girls with depressed progenitors don't suffer the same ailment. A mother—in spite of her melancholy spells—is still able to love her child, remain sensitive to the youngster's feelings and thoughts, and provide emotional support much of the time.

If you can't give the love and attention yourself, find a close relative or friend to do so. This substitute produces two positive results. First, another loving person partially fills the void left by the parent's emotional disability. Second, it allays your anxiety. Knowing someone is there to give your child essential care helps to relieve the guilt and allows you to focus your attention on getting well.

DON'T BE IN A HURRY TO MAKE IT WELL

Teenagers with depressive tendencies may bring out several reactions in their parents which often do more harm than good. The first is the universal desire to make them well—to raise their spirits, to cause them to feel better about themselves, the world around them, and the future. We talk to a morose daughter about all of her positive qualities which many envy, about her friends, the things she loves doing, and about how much she has to look forward to. To her we seem to be saying, "Cheer up! You have no reason to be depressed."

If the youngster doesn't respond to "reason," we may find ourselves becoming frustrated, especially those of us with strong needs to control the inner as well as the outer experience of our teens. In an effort to relieve our own growing upset and to help our daughter, we may hear ourselves exhorting her to stop feeling sorry for herself. Compared to the starving Africans or a friend who is mugged in a park and paralyzed, she has nothing to be sad about. "Buck up, dammit!" we may be heard to say. "You have no right to be unhappy because you have so much going for you."

If you have ever been depressed, you know just how worthless are logic and exhortation in helping you feel better. In fact having someone tell you that no earthly reason exists for your despair, or that it is illegitimate, creates even greater depression. In this unhappy state we can no more talk ourselves out of it than we can convince ourselves to overcome the winter flu by willpower alone.

Far more helpful to young people down in the dumps is to acknowledge the reality of their emotions. When they are obviously moody, ask them to tell you how they feel and give what comfort you can. They need to know that someone appreciates how miserable they are. Be willing to provide brief supports in the form of your physical presence, their favorite food, and allowing regressive behavior (many adolescents find solace in an old teddy bear, dolls, cartoons for eight year olds, sucking their thumbs, even blankets). Let them take a mental health day from school or work. Acknowledge that it may be some time before they feel better. That in the case of a severe loss it may be a year. Even then there may be occasional tears.

Don't assume every young person who is depressed can tell you why. Occasionally teens know the reason they're blue but just as often they don't. Either they have no idea why they feel so disconsolate or the cause doesn't seem nearly severe enough to result in so much distress. For those of us with a need to know "the answer" this behavior can be especially frustrating.

Finally, don't be in a hurry to reassure teenagers whose depression stems from severe loss. Often this impulse to reassure comes from our inability to tolerate seeing our children unhappy. It also may derive from our discomfort with the feelings of unhappiness these youngsters' depression triggers in us. Also don't rush to point out that good things come from trauma or that other options exist for happiness. While these facts are certainly true, it is also a fact that when someone is depressed, it seems incomprehensible that anything but continuing pain will result from the loss.

HELP TEENS RELIEVE MOODINESS

Almost every teenager's moody spells lift spontaneously without parental or professional help. There are several steps you can take to hasten the return of normal spirits. Most of these were known intuitively by our grandmothers' generation and have been validated by recent psychological research.

Encourage physical activity. Regular moderate exercise is associated with improved mood, better self-concept, and more effective intellectual functioning. Even depressed patients discover their spirits lifted by aerobic dancing, jogging, weight lifting, bike riding, or swimming. The exercise need not involve a sport. The same positive mental effect results from scrubbing the floor, washing windows, raking lawns, painting rooms, or cleaning attics.

Stimulate positive thinking. Youngsters with a tendency to become depressed think negatively. They obsess about what's wrong with their lives, overestimate their flaws and underestimate their positive attributes, believe they can't do anything about them, and think that everyone is as focused on their imperfections as they are. A boy might dwell on his acne and skinny physique, certain that these are the reasons he's so miserable in high school. To him these features seem as unalterable as gravity, so he sees no end to his unhappiness. He pays no attention to his good grades, holding down a responsible job, and a talent with the French horn. When he walks past a group of classmates and they don't seem to notice him, he believes it is because of his appearance. He suspects them of making nasty comments about his pimples and frail constitution behind his back. This type of thinking sustains his low spirits.

Try breaking this boy's mental pattern. Invite him to keep a log of the positive events occurring over the course of a week—a pleasant talk with a friend who doesn't ignore him, good grades on an exam, a kind word from a boss, listening to a favorite tape, playing with his dog. The total positive experiences over the week may be surprising and cause him to recognize that he's been overlooking the pluses in his life in favor of the minuses.

Help him find the resolve to tackle *one* of his problems. He doesn't have to do everything right away. For instance, encourage him to carry out bodybuilding in a health club or study one of the martial arts. Not only will the exercise improve his mood, but his sense of self will be enhanced by greater physical competence. Be sure that his goals are positively stated, small, and doable. Vague, overly ambitious aspirations —not to be "weak," to be able to stack the bench press—set the stage for failure.

A number of upset, disconsolate youths have been shocked back into a normal mental state by someone pointing out to them that most people have never heard of them or their acne. A comment such as this has the effect of cold water in the face. It can cause this boy to restructure his thinking and can bring to his attention that everyone is not as concerned about him as he is. His classmates don't go to bed each night with derisive remarks about him on their lips. They have their own troubles to worry about. Realizing this will help him become less focused on his weaknesses.

Do all you can to move a broody youngster out of the house into other social environments, especially on weekends. Weekends can seem endless to an isolated, lonely boy. Get him to do something out of the house each day of the weekend: a movie or basketball game on Friday night, shopping at the mall Saturday afternoon, and church Sunday morning. Take him yourself if you have to. These periods of activity bring temporary relief for him from thinking about how lousy his life is. They also raise the odds of finding pleasurable experiences—such as being with his peers—which counterbalance the depressed mood.

Drugs and depression don't mix. Actively discourage alcohol, marijuana, or other self-medications when your youngsters feel down. These substances will make them feel a whole lot worse. Eliminate caffeine too. Coffee and other caffeinated drinks increase depression as well as anxiety and hostility.

OBTAIN PROFESSIONAL HELP

As a rule teenagers with orange- or red-zone depressions don't respond to physical activity or parental attempts to motivate them to think positively. They require professional attention. Start with a medical checkup. Trouble has a way of coming in bunches. A boy whose extended despair surely seems related to a romantic breakup also can develop mononucleosis or a thyroid imbalance which also maintains his spirits at a low level. Ruling out a physical disorder, or treating it if one is found, frees you to get on with the business of helping to relieve the melancholy. Your doctor, pastor, or friends usually can locate a professional with experience working with depressed adolescents. If not, contact a community clinic or hospital.

Mental health specialists today use many different approaches to treating depression. By far the most typical outpatient technique is to blend antidepressant medication with psychotherapy. All of these drugs have minor unpleasant side effects, but those for whom the medications bring relief from depression are usually glad to tolerate them. Psychotherapy should accompany pharmacological treatment. As drugs improve the underlying moods, the reasons for the despondency can be explored, maladaptive patterns examined, and efforts to make necessary changes supported.

By itself psychological treatment works well with individuals in the yellow zone or those locked into prolonged bereavement. But as Carter's example suggests, a need may arise to bring in other treatment approaches to manage the emotions that slow the course of psychotherapy.

An influential group of therapists believes that depression results from a negative mental set. Boys or girls this is typical of live within a "worst case" mentality. Treatment focuses on teaching these individuals to realign their negative view of the world in keeping with reality. Psychologists at the University of Oregon teach a "coping with depression" course. Consisting of twelve two-hour classroom sessions over an eight-week period under the direction of psychologists, the program employs largely cognitive and behavioral strategies. The participants learn how their thinking maintains their despondent state, and they alter these depression-producing cognitions. They master techniques to relax and improve their social skills. They become aware of the value of pleasurable activities and inject these into their lives. And they learn how to use these new insights and behaviors in day-to-day life. Each session involves a pep talk by the therapists, practicing more effective ways of coping with unhappiness, reviewing past learnings and homework assignments. The results of this program have been promising. Versions of this approach have been carried out with success in several large cities, including Philadelphia, New York City, Houston, Minneapolis, and Toronto.

All of these means of treatment work effectively with the majority of depressed young people. Try not to second-guess therapists as to what procedure will work best. Give mental health practitioners space and time to employ the techniques they have found to be most effective. It's possible that modifications will be made during the course of therapy. Within six months recovery from adolescent depression usually begins. If at the end of that period no progress is made, you may want to confer with the specialist to discuss other alternatives.

Pay attention to the potential for suicidal acts. Severe depression along with feelings of hopelessness and desperation are usually present. Also the youngster may believe there is no one to turn to for relief because of continuing family strife and lack of supportive relationships. Alienation from religion and moral values, fractured dreams of ever being successful and happy, a history of impulsive behavior, and fascination with the death through suicide of a close friend, relative, or public figure occur with great frequency among individuals who try to take their lives. Alcohol and drug use, as well as giving away prized possessions in an apparently cheerful mood, are frequently associated with suicide attempts.

These factors provide a context in which teens contemplate ending their lives. If you sense that your child may be thinking about suicide, here are a sequence of questions, which can be rephrased according to your style of communication with your youngster, that provide a rough guide for telling how worried to be:

1. Almost everyone has thought of killing himself at one time or another. Have you?
2. Have you ever thought about how you might do it?
3. Do you have the means (pills, gun, rope, building, or razor) at your disposal and have you been tempted to use them?
4. How close have you come to doing it (counted out a lethal dose of pills, put a loaded gun in your mouth, cut your wrists, leaned out of a window on the tenth floor)?
5. Have you made an attempt?

Young people who have thought about how they might end their lives, and don't negate the thought by saying they wouldn't kill themselves, should be talked to by loved ones about why they think they would be better off bringing an end to their life. Then they should see a mental health specialist for a consultation. Teens who have thought a good deal about how they would kill themselves, have been tempted to make a gesture, or have come close to it require professional help.

Don't ever assume that youngsters who talk about suicide or make halfhearted attempts to end their lives—even when these appear contraintentional—are merely "looking for attention." People with suicide on their minds need to be taken seriously, to be assured others care about them and, if necessary, to be protected from their lethal impulses by involuntary hospitalization. Though minor disadvantages accrue from overreacting to a youth's suicidal threat, a far greater danger is not taking the person seriously. When confronted with a seemingly hopeless and desperate situation from which self-inflicted death seems the only exit, the indifference of a loved one to suicidal preoccupations is often the final proof that no one cares and dying is the only reasonable alternative.

Occasionally an adolescent's condition doesn't respond to outpatient treatment, or the depression leads to a suicide attempt. These teens who can no longer function in their world or who are a danger to themselves require hospitalization. Though most of us have an instinctive aversion to the thought of ourselves or someone we care about being committed to a mental hospital, it provides an important sanctuary for troubled individuals. In a hospital setting they receive protection from harming themselves, from embarrassing themselves in front of their friends, as well as basic physical care and treatment. The average stay in a mental hospital as an inpatient is about thirty days and declining.

It's hard for anyone who has been depressed to imagine feeling good again and enjoying the semblance of a normal existence. Our youngsters' pessimism may be infectious, causing us to adopt the same negative outlook and retarding our efforts to help them lift their spirits.

It may be helpful to recognize that throughout history many of the most productive minds were tormented by periods of melancholy. The Old Testament tells of King Saul's recurring despondency. One of ancient Greece's greatest philosophers, Heraclitis, was periodically laid low by despair. The eighteenth-century Prime Minister of England, William Pitt, suffered from periodic despair as did his contemporary, Samuel Johnson, one of the most prolific writers of all time. In America, Abraham Lincoln, William James, and Thomas Edison were subject to long spells of melancholy. Today, the media regularly inform us of depression among politicians, astronauts, scientists, athletes, business people, and artists.

Clearly these individuals did not accomplish much while in the grasp of depression. Their remarkable achievements came after they escaped their dysphoria. It is possible to rebound from periods of gloom and take pleasure in a productive life.

To our despondent teenagers, of course, this idea will seem the crudest fiction. But, whether or not they believe it, it's helpful to us, their parents, to remind ourselves that when a melancholy spell passes the usual opportunities for happiness remain available. Knowledge of this reality will support us in our efforts to lighten their gloom.

10

"Bad Actor"
Conduct Problems

Conduct problems often accompany in the second decade of life. Partly because of hormonal changes associated with puberty, this previously agreeable boy might develop a growing temper and taste for physical combat to go along with his deepening voice, larger physical stature, and increasing strength. That affluent, well-mannered girl takes up shoplifting not long after entering junior high school.

Since 1960 juvenile misconduct has more than doubled. Boys committing illegal acts outnumber girls about five to one, though the ratio favoring males has declined from about ten to one since the mid-1950s. Aggressive acts, vandalism, and car theft occur with far greater frequency among young males. Shoplifting continues to be a traditional female crime.

By age sixteen or seventeen these forms of misbehavior normally subside. A tiny fraction continues a pattern of explosive outbursts while others go on committing delinquent acts.* Most antisocial behaviors happen in the company of others. A very few teenagers act up on their own. Within this population there are many adolescents tormented by guilt but some who experience little remorse.

---

* The terms "delinquent" and "antisocial" will be used as approximate synonyms meaning regular violation of societal norms and the rights of others. These are not pranks or ordinary mischief.

STEPHANIE

Her heart pounded. Stephanie was certain that the clerk had seen her put the music tapes in her raincoat pocket. As she strolled to the exit Stephanie waited for a challenge, but it didn't come. She left the store and walked into the fall Seattle mist. Once again Stephanie had successfully shoplifted.

Stephanie was a freshman at the University of Washington. The envy of many of her classmates, she was smart, attractive, wealthy, and athletic. At high school in Edmonds, Washington, Stephanie's career had been one success after another: honor society, captain of the volleyball team, and editor of the school newspaper. Her classmates voted her most likely to succeed and the faculty unanimously agreed she was the best all-around senior.

Stephanie was raised in comfortable circumstances. Her father was a successful real estate developer and her mother ran a prospering interior decorating firm. A younger brother also was a strong performer. Stephanie admired her father enormously but didn't see much of him. He worked long hours and liked to sail or play tennis in his free time. Her mother was intense, perfectionistic, and hard to please, though she and Stephanie got along all right. They had a full-time live-in housekeeper.

Stephanie started shoplifting with some of her friends in eighth grade. Large supermarkets and drugstores, where merchandise seemed displayed for the purpose of taking, were their targets. Afterward they excitedly compared what they had taken—chewing gum, candy, cosmetics, pencils, and pens. All had the money to purchase these items.

In high school Stephanie drifted away from these friends, but her stealing continued. The difference was that she now shoplifted on her own. These were not regular events. Rather the urge to take something without paying for it gradually intensified until it was irresistible. Though always nervous when she shoplifted, as soon as she stole an item from a store Stephanie began to experience relief. There followed a period of not thinking about it for several weeks. But then the tension would start to grow once more.

In college Stephanie made varsity volleyball. On road trips to play other schools, they often had a few hours on their own before the game. It was then that Stephanie stole merchandise—often popular music tapes—from stores in these cities. A teammate she roomed with on these trips noticed

*Stephanie's penchant for acquiring new tapes. "Why do you keep coming
back with tapes you don't need," she joked. "You're not a klepto are you?"*

RICK

With tires squealing, Rick tore out of the school parking lot. Because
he hadn't seen him, Rick narrowly missed running down the chairman of
the math department with his sudden departure. "This is the last straw,"
the faculty member thought. "This boy is a menace. He has to go." He
headed for the principal's office.

Rick was renowned for his explosive outbursts in the suburban Denver
high school he attended. In ninth grade Rick had a running battle with
the same math teacher about where he would sit. Rick wanted to know
why he had to sit in alphabetical order. He was large even then and
wanted his seat at the end of a row where he'd be more comfortable. The
teacher insisted and Rick blew up, saying that he had the right to sit
where he wanted. The teacher threw Rick out of class and demanded that
the principal remove him permanently. Rick was incensed, believing himself to be victimized by the teacher's narrow-mindedness. The principal
transferred Rick to another teacher.

An only child, Rick lived with his mother who supported them by
managing a fitness center. She had divorced his father—an unsuccessful
professional baseball player—when Rick was an infant. Where he was no
one knew.

Sophomore year he had a run in with the football and track coaches. By
then Rick was 6'3" and 210 pounds of solid muscle. The football coach
wanted him to play tackle but Rick wanted to try out for quarterback.
Neither would give in so Rick wound up sitting on the bench. He quit
before the last game. In track he threw the shot put and discus, but he did
it his way because the coach gave in. Though Rick placed in every meet,
with better form he might have won all of them.

In the fall of his junior year Rick was in several fights after football
games with students from other schools. A parent whose son Rick had
beaten up badly filed assault and battery charges against him. Rick denied
it was his fault, saying the other boy had started it. He received a year's
probation and was mandated to receive psychological help.

Psychotherapy failed. At first Rick wouldn't go. When his probation
officer finally forced him to see a psychologist, Rick continually chal-

lenged, belittled, and provoked him. Except for the therapist's blood pressure rising, no significant change occurred. Eventually the doctor discharged Rick with the statement to the probation officer that he was an "incorrigible psychopath." The probation, however, was effective in keeping Rick's behavior in line.

At home his mother worried constantly that she could do nothing to control his outbursts. He was still difficult to live with. "You never know when he's going to blow," his mother told a sister who lived nearby. Twice he put his fist through the wall when he was frustrated—one time because of a telephone busy signal. At school his grades remained above average, particularly in math and science. He did appear at the junior prom drunk, looking for a fight, but no one turned him in out of compassion for his mother.

But the high school faculty came to the end of its rope in December of Rick's senior year when the teacher reported the details of nearly being run down by him. They voted to expel him. When the news came his mother broke down weeping. Rick said, "Those SOBs have it in for me!"

Rugged individualism characterizes *green*-zone youngsters of this type. They project an image of independent thinking, vigorous self-reliance, and dominance. Often this is an exaggerated means of breaking their bond of dependence on the older generation. They insist on the rightness of incorrect or bizarre views and become nasty if grown-ups don't instantly agree with them.

Authority figures or being outnumbered doesn't daunt them. In class or large meetings these adolescents have the courage to say things others feel but don't articulate. At his best Rick could put his finger on flaws in a teacher's reasoning or point out inconsistencies in the school's code of conduct.

As a rule these youths hold up well under stressful conditions. Whether it's working a double shift on a weekend job because the rest of the staff has the flu, managing the house during a grandparent's terminal illness, or struggling to win a game against a superior opponent, these teens usually give their best. And they are resilient. Losing motivates them to try harder next time.

Anger is their most predictable response to any stress. It matters not whether he has a difficult test in English tomorrow, has just had a girlfriend break up with him, or his car won't start, a boy might become furious. Among normally functioning adolescents, however, anger usually

TABLE 10.1
Estimating the Severity of Conduct Difficulties

GREEN ZONE—Normal Adaptation

- Rugged individualism
- Anger as stress reaction
- Occasional petty lawbreaking
- Sense of humor

YELLOW ZONE—Temporary Adjustment Reactions

- Intermittent explosive outbursts
- Manipulative
- Occasional running away
- Organized, continuing delinquent behavior

ORANGE ZONE—Neurotic Symptoms

- Recurring aggressive eruptions
- Unforgiving or remorseful
- Individual antisocial acts
- Associated family, school, legal problems
- Brief intense depression, anxiety

RED ZONE—Severe Maladjustments

- Conduct disorders
- Absence of morality, remorse
- Externalization of responsibility
- Intimidation of parents into defensive behavior
- Throwaways, pushouts

doesn't lead to aggressiveness. Rather, youths in this zone control it in a number of ways. If the source of their stress is a person, most often they respond assertively, talking over the problem with the instigator. If that's not possible, or the outcome is unsatisfactory, they will talk out their irritations with friends. When they're upset the language of both sexes can be extraordinarily salty. Frequently they ventilate their aggressive feelings physically by splitting wood or pounding a piano. Almost as frequently they sublimate this emotion—channeling energy from their anger into competitiveness or displacing it by taking out their frustrations on a younger sibling.

Because they are readier to believe themselves to have been unjustly treated, adolescents in this frame of mind can be vindictive. Many are unusually perceptive about the foibles and sensitivities of adults who have frustrated them and "retaliate." These are not Halloween pranks but indirect assaults. One teenager may trash the lawn of a perfectionistic neighbor who told him to keep his dog from defecating on his property. Another might write obscenities with lipstick on the car of a teacher who told her to stop talking in class.

Occasional petty lawbreaking occurs in the green zone. Nine out of ten teens admit to having stolen, cheated, vandalized, or committed some other illegal act at least once in the last year. There is no relationship between what sorts of grades students make and whether they shoplift, or between the number of activities they participate in and whether they bring a crib sheet into an exam.

In general disorderly conduct happens in a group: four fourteen year olds conspire to have a party at one of the girl's houses while her parents are away for the weekend. Each one furnishes alcohol by robbing the family liquor supply. Three fifteen-year-old boys hot-wire a car and go joyriding. A youthful gang in the city get into a fight with another group of young people after a concert. These behaviors may occur in a spree of several months—or until the adolescents are caught by authorities. Then they diminish.

A sense of humor is a feature in the normal adaptation of us all. With these aggressively reactive teenagers, however, the ability to laugh at themselves is an important green flag. Seeing something amusing in their feelings or behavior plays a vital role in allowing the discharge of their emotions without doing violence to others or themselves. For the most part the sense of humor comes into play after the fact—though more than one teenager has broken out laughing in the middle of an altercation with his mother because the whole thing suddenly seems funny to him.

Intermittent, explosive outbursts mark entry into the *yellow* zone. Typically these outbursts occur unpredictably when the teens believe they are being undeservedly persecuted, manipulated, humiliated, or dominated. What distinguishes these emotional storms is that their intensity far exceeds the degree of provocation. Whether it's a request by his mother to mow the lawn, a smart comment from another student after a football game, or a teacher who insists on alphabetical order, Rick's temper flares and he is ready to fight. Adolescents in this zone will turn red, yell and swear, tremble, drip perspiration, and may become physically assaultive. Once begun, these eruptions run a predictable course. Teenagers can no more stop them midway through than they can interrupt a sneeze.

The explosive episodes clear the air. No general aggressiveness characterizes these adolescents' behavior between episodes. Genuine regret or self-reproach because of the consequences of their actions follows.

Not all young people in this zone are explosive. Many exhibit remarkable manipulative skills. Some, like Stephanie, become leaders because they are charming, attentive to the feelings of others, and even inspirational. They use these skills to accumulate and retain power. In her campaign to become editor of the school paper she was unusually nice to the faculty adviser and key upper-class people who would have a vote in the selection. No job was too trivial for her to volunteer for. She looked for, and eventually partly fabricated, an "exposé" of the poor food in the school cafeteria.

These teenagers are ruthless competitors in their quest for power or honor. Unable to resist an exposed jugular, they exploit weaknesses of their opponents. Stephanie contrived to have a boy with no musical interests, who also aspired to be editor of the paper, assigned to cover a tour of the school orchestra and chorus. At one point she saw his notes for a story lying unattended. She ripped them into shreds and flushed them down the toilet. To herself she justified her conduct by thinking that it's a dog-eat-dog world and he probably would do the same thing to her if he had the chance.

Occasional running away is a yellow flag. Each year about one million teens leave home without permission. They come from every social class, race, and region. These youngsters storm out of the house following an altercation with their parents. Typically they stay with a friend close by for a day or two, perhaps as long as a week. Though they never tell their parents directly where they are going, it doesn't take long to discover the youngsters' whereabouts because they stay in school and connected to their peer group. When they cool off, they return.

Organized, continuing delinquent behavior occurs in the yellow zone. No longer do teenagers in this area violate laws on a whimsical, occasional basis. A gang of girls systematically plan how to loot panty hose from a discount store. Four boys in an eastern prep school make connections in Lima to bring back cocaine following spring vacation so they can resell it at a small profit. Four hackers figure out how to alter their grades on the high school computer and punch in the changes. Personal gain motivates these adolescents less than demonstrating that they can beat the system and so dazzle their peers with their daring-do. They have the money for the panty hose, can find all the drugs they desire, and their grades are already fine.

How long organized delinquent behavior continues varies enormously. Six months to a year is most common. Some youths persist through an entire unit of the school experience—junior high school, high school, or college. Very few of these teens ever come to the attention of the police. Should they be arrested this event usually terminates their acting up.

Recurring aggressive eruptions demarcate the *orange* zone. The hostile explosions, whether oral or physical, become a permanent feature in the teenager's psychological makeup. People who know these youngsters no longer are surprised when they blow up. They also learn to stay out of the way until they cool off.

Many adolescents experience their physical violence as preemptory retaliation. That is, they hit back first. In his mind, Rick believed several faculty members were out to embarrass or dominate him, though in fact this was a projection of his own hostility. Therefore he felt completely justified in landing a first strike when the math teacher innocently asked him to take his assigned seat. Keenly attuned to the slightest trace of competitiveness among their peers, they are quick to challenge and to fight. Rick had no compunction about knocking down a boy in the hall without warning whom he had seen talking to his girlfriend.

Unlike normal teens who have trouble recalling afterward what it was that caused them to blow up, orange-zone youngsters remain unforgiving of the people or situations that trigger their outbursts. Discharging his angry feelings doesn't alter Rick's perception that had the football coach let him play the correct position he would have been a star and it would have been a cinch to win an athletic scholarship to college. The fact that his old Chevrolet was a reluctant starter in the cold Denver mornings caused him to sell it and condemn forever all cars of that make.

An intriguing quality these youngsters share is that the memory of having been treated badly will arouse almost the same emotions as were originally experienced at nearly the same level of intensity. Years later Rick will flush, feel the surge of humiliation and fury, and pound the table as he tells a friend what happened to him in that ninth grade math class.

Not all chronically aggressive adolescents find their outbursts congenial. Some know well the meaning of Longfellow's line, "Whom the Gods would destroy they first make mad," and feel their violence as alien, uncontrollable, and a form of mental disorder. Like the alcoholic who pledges "never again" after a binge, they experience massive remorse after a blowup and swear to mend their ways. But they know in their hearts that they are helpless once the rage begins to build.

Similarly tormented are large numbers of adolescents who commit individual antisocial acts. When they steal or vandalize, these youngsters are without the emotional protection provided by group support. Alone, they find themselves experiencing extreme guilt.

Unfortunately these distressing feelings don't influence their conduct. As Stephanie's case shows, their antisocial actions occur in a predictable sequence: the impulse to shoplift grows to the point of becoming irresistible; stealing purges the desire; and a period of relief from the urge follows. These same phases characterize other forms of lawbreaking—fire setting, breaking and entering, obscene phone calling, pathological spending or gambling.

In the orange zone numerous problems associated with chronic misconduct become visible. A high correlation exists between delinquent behavior and poor school achievement. Antisocial adolescents have a higher percentage of learning problems and verbal deficits than do their normally functioning classmates. These problems make school a more difficult and frustrating experience for them. Antisocial teenagers tend to respond to their school difficulties by increased combativeness, vandalism, and truancy—being absent from school more than thirty days a year. While they are loosely connected to school they exhibit an increased frequency of lawbreaking.

Things at home are strained. Family disagreements, usually over how much freedom a teenager should have, don't get resolved. And so they fester. The friction can be so intense that the generations cannot tolerate being in the same room with one another. One girl did not talk to her father for over two years due to the hostility between them.

Feeling rejected and alienated from the home environment, these teens run away three or more times. They stay away for longer periods—more than a week. Typically their parents have no idea of where they have gone, usually because the young people have no particular place in mind when they leave. For example, they may hitchhike south or take the first bus west. Alone on the highway or in a city, many are easy prey for thieves, pimps, drug pushers, and the other violent inhabitants of the urban underbelly. Other suburban youngsters adapt with amazing speed to the ways of the street, subsisting by nomadic employment, panhandling, stealing, check forging, and dealing in illicit substances. Nine out of ten young people return home—or are located by police and returned —home within a month. Experts disagree as to how many teens disappear each year.

Running away also serves to relieve periods of intense depression and anxiety that beset youths in the orange zone. Contrary to the tough, independent exterior these teens project, they are vulnerable to fits of melancholy, loneliness, and sadness, as well as chronic tension. What separates them from adolescents with other problems is that they possess little tolerance for these emotions. Instead of examining the origins of the discomfort, they use the coping device of motility—staying on the move—in order to ward the feelings off.

A tiny number of teenagers exhibit the chronic conduct disorders of the *red* zone. They display several forms of repetitive antisocial acts. Experts identify four subtypes and examples of their behavior, depending upon whether the misconduct occurs alone or with others, and whether overt aggression accompanies the act.

Undersocialized, aggressive:
These youths are loners with little interest in, or caring for, others, who exhibit physical violence toward people or property. Examples are chronic individual bullies and fire setters.
Undersocialized, nonaggressive:
These teens are socially isolated; their misconduct is not violent but violates important societal norms. Examples are constant stealing and cheating.

Socialized, aggressive:

These youngsters belong to a peer group and together they regularly assault people and property. Examples are persistent mugging and vandalism.

Socialized, nonaggressive:

In the company of friends, these adolescents habitually misbehave in ways that infringe upon the rights of others or break laws without doing them direct harm. Examples are continuing computer fraud and breaking and entering.

Many boys and girls will show characteristics of more than one of these subgroups: they steal from their parents as well as with their buddies from the local open-all-night store. Or they beat up a smaller classmate in the morning and hot-wire a car for a joyride that night.

Teenagers in all four subtypes of conduct disorders share many of the yellow- and orange-zone qualities already enumerated. They are manipulative, mistrustful, and given to seeing others as the cause of their misbehavior. Difficulties at home, in school, and the community abound. Drug abuse, emotionally barren sexual activity, and physical recklessness leading to injury regularly make up part of this pattern.

The absence of an inner sense of morality and remorse is a large red flag. Adolescents in this zone behave according to what will benefit them most at the moment: a boy caught red-handed stealing a purse from an eighty-year-old woman by a policeman in front of a dozen witnesses will deny he did it. In court he will affect an air of total innocence and assure the judge he is being falsely accused.

If that boy happened to beat the woman senseless while stealing her purse, he is unlikely to feel remorse. "It's the fortunes of war," he may think. "What did the old woman think would happen to her if she held on to her purse when I grabbed it?" These youths assume that everyone would have acted as they did.

A large number of these red-zone adolescents externalize the responsibility for their delinquent actions by experiencing the impulse as irresistible. They rationalize their behavior by saying in effect, "I didn't want to do it, but I couldn't control myself." When Stephanie feels the desire to steal growing, she knows that it is just a question of time before she shoplifts. Control is out of her hands. For others the impulse comes on very quickly, giving no time for deliberation. For example, before a sixteen-year-old boy has a chance to weigh the pros and cons, he writes another bad check. He "knows better" but his thinking is short-circuited by desire.

Intimidating parents into defensive behavior is a red-zone indicator. These red-zone youngsters cause the older generation to feel seriously threatened by, and unable to control, the aberrant behavior of their offspring. As a result they move into a self-protective posture. After Rick had his license suspended for speeding, his mother was unable by saying no to prevent him from taking her car. Eventually she had a kill switch installed in her ignition system and she kept the only key. Other mothers and fathers lock their liquor cabinets, put in wall safes to protect their money and jewelry, and bar their children's entry into the house unless a parent is in attendance. Whatever trust once existed is long gone.

Not a few discover that their teenagers who used to be controlled by spanking or slapping now hit back hard when a hand is laid on them. Nose bloodied or ribs broken, and suddenly terrified, parents call in the law. They summon the police with a "stubborn child" complaint because the adolescent refuses to obey parental demands to attend school, come home at a reasonable hour, or desist drug abuse.

Eventually some of these young people become family throwaways or school pushouts. Unlike the runaway who leaves home as a temporary solution to family strife and returns when the atmosphere calms down, the throwaway's relationship with parents becomes so unbearable that the teen has no alternative but to leave. Intergenerational disagreement and discord give way to violence and bitterness which so poisons the atmosphere that no feeling of affection can flourish for long. Eventually one of the times the adolescent runs away he or she doesn't return. For the parents the feeling of relief outweighs regret.

Being a school pushout is a red flag. In suburban communities 3 to 5 percent of the teenagers intellectually capable of graduating leave school without a diploma. These youngsters have not dropped out of high school voluntarily. Rather the administration finally has had enough of their continuing acting up and votes to suspend them—for a week, a month, or in Rick's case, the remainder of the term. These youngsters accumulate three to six suspensions during their academic career. Eventually they don't return to school from one of them. The odds of this occurring are greater when their friends reinforce the idea of leaving school.

Follow-up

STEPHANIE

"No," Stephanie heard herself saying. "I'm not a kleptomaniac, if that's what you mean. I always do my Christmas shopping during the year, rather than waiting until December. These tapes are for my friends."

This event shocked Stephanie into recognizing how much she disliked this behavior in herself. She made a pledge to herself to stop. For nearly six months this inner commitment held off periodic impulses to steal. Stephanie thought she had the problem licked. Then during Christmas vacation she stole some more tapes as well as a scarf from a department store in a shopping mall. Just as she reached the door, a voice behind Stephanie said, "May I see the sales slip for those goods, miss?"

The plainclothes detective took her to the store manager. Talking to the thoroughly shaken and contrite Stephanie, hearing her deny she had done this before, noting her obvious intelligence and promise, and knowing her to be from a socially prominent family, the manager decided to let her off with a caution. Should Stephanie be caught again shoplifting, he warned, the store would prosecute her in court.

Confronting the reality that her stealing was beyond her control, she sought counseling at the student mental health service. She first saw a social worker once a week into the spring. During this period Stephanie began to realize several family factors associated with the desire to steal. Among these were Stephanie's feeling that her mother and father expressed relatively little affection toward her though they were proud of her accomplishments. Neither parent was there very much emotionally when she needed to talk. Finally she reinterpreted the freedom her mother and father gave her as a form of neglect rather than independence training. A good bit of her treatment from then on consisted of expressing her resentment toward her parents as well as seeing how this hostility might have been a factor in her shoplifting.

Again Stephanie believed she had overcome it—until she went on a stealing binge on the last weekend in April. She was mortified and her therapist was upset too. Both agreed that something else was needed to help her control this alien behavior.

The social worker referred her to a colleague who employed a mix of behavioral and cognitive techniques to assist Stephanie in overcoming the shoplifting. The first step of the treatment was to help her recognize early the impulse to steal. Then she was taught to identify irrational thought associated with this desire: "I've got to have those tapes!" and "There's no way I can stop my urge to steal them." The psychologist helped Stephanie challenge the belief that having another tape was essential to her survival and to replace this thought with others—that she could live without the new music. Then he showed her forms of relaxation to deflate the impulse to shoplift. Finally she was taught gratifying ways of rewarding herself for not stealing. Eventually she imagined herself in the music section of a local store and attempted to arouse the desire to steal. As she felt the impulse she was able to control it.

The final test for Stephanie was actually going into a store and handling the tapes while trying to arouse the impulse to take them. She found she had success in controlling the shoplifting desire in reality just as she had done in the therapist's office.

From then on shopping became a much more enjoyable event for Stephanie.

RICK

Being thrown out of school shook Rick more than he let on. Periodically in the next month he had moments when he was extremely agitated and depressed. Driving around helped, but the relief was temporary. For a while Rick hung around the fringe of the high school but his friends were all caught up in the excitement of senior year. Not being able to share it, he drifted away. He complained to her constantly about the unjust treatment by the high school and the favoritism shown other students whose sins were a hundred times greater. When his mother suggested he obtain a job, Rick told her to mind her own business. When she suggested he join the Marines, he wondered if she'd lost her mind.

His mother couldn't seem to do anything right—from Rick's point of view anyway. He constantly criticized her: she was a lousy housekeeper, a poor cook, didn't make enough money, and had the wrong values. When his mother didn't agree with him instantly, he yelled at her, saying that she was on "their" side. "I hope you're satisfied with what they've done to me" is how he put his feelings.

One Saturday afternoon Rick wanted to use the car and his mother didn't let him because she was going out for dinner with two female friends. Incensed beyond reason, Rick threatened to take the car keys away from her if she didn't give them to him. His mother relented and let Rick take the car.

When he left she cried for a long time. Then she decided to call her women friends—who also were single-parent mothers—for emotional support. They came right over and listened sympathetically to her problems with Rick. Neither had an answer, but one of them attended a self-help group for single parents at a local church. She invited Rick's mother to come to the next meeting.

Hearing other mothers struggle with the problems of their teenagers was reassuring to Rick's mother. Moreover, it made her realize that Rick's behavior was harder to manage than most. Using the group as a forum for thinking out loud about how she might deal with her son, she evolved a strategy. Then she rehearsed what she might say in front of the group and they role-played a variety of possible responses from Rick.

The next Sunday afternoon, when his mother knew he was usually in a good mood, she sat down with Rick to talk to him about the future. She told Rick that she thought it was hurting him to live with her and that she wanted him to move out within thirty days and live on his own. She would pay the rent for up to three months while he located a job and would provide financial assistance so he could eat. As long as he behaved himself he could visit his home when he wanted to.

Rick hit the ceiling. How could she do this to him? She had no right! He would leave in his own sweet time and that was it!

That was not it. Calmly his mother told him that she hoped he would be willing to leave by the month's end. But if not, she would do what she could to ensure that he would go. Two weeks later when Rick came home he was greeted by his mother's brother and his wife from Boulder, along with the Congregational minister. They were waiting along with Rick's mother to talk to him. Together they made it clear what was expected while also stressing the fact that they continued to care about him and that he was welcome to call on them for help.

It took him until a week after the deadline, but Rick left. By then he had found a job as a security guard working the 11 P.M. to 7 A.M. shift in an office building. Shortly afterward he located a cheap sublet near the University of Denver. After six months Rick began to study for his high school equivalency and passed the test.

In the next year Rick was fired three times because he had trouble getting along with his bosses. But because the security business was grow-

ing, and he was experienced, he had no trouble locating another position. He also excelled at the para-police training he was given. In the second year after he received his high school equivalency, he began to take courses at the University of Denver's evening program. Gradually he began to visualize what career line he would pursue: after all the security field was booming.

What Parents Can Do: Guidelines for Helping

Most teens with conduct difficulties do not go on to become violent adults or criminals. It's also true, however, that aggressive behavior in young people has a higher rate of persistence than other adolescent behavior problems. Let's look at ways parents can lower the odds of teenage misconduct developing into real trouble.

RECOGNIZE PREDISPOSING FACTORS

Be aware that genetic, academic, and family patterns contribute to more severe forms of antisocial behavior. Parents bringing overly aggressive teens for treatment often say they have "always" been that way. Closer questioning brings out that their not being fed or having a diaper changed at the instant they wanted it triggered a tantrum. Once they started walking they exhibited an energy and boldness difficult to contain, flashed a hot temper if controlled by others, and were undaunted by punishment.

Mothers and fathers will say an aggressive boy is a lot like his father was at the same age, or is his uncle Harry reborn. The fact that these behavior patterns are shared among family members suggests a genetic predisposition.

Pay attention to academic performance and do all you can to make school a tolerable undertaking. As a group, children prone to antisocial behavior have lower academic aptitude, especially verbal facility, than do their classmates. School attendance brings with it little gratification and an opportunity to feel constantly stigmatized. Poor students with a history of acting up engage in less misconduct if they drop out of school. The reason may be that they no longer feel frustrated by their chronic lack of success and therefore have less need to act out their unhappiness on the society around them.

BE CONSISTENT, PRESENT, AND CARING

Being unclear as to what is acceptable and unacceptable demeanor, overlooking antisocial actions one time and applying high-scale punishment the next, create a family atmosphere that encourages acting up. Large numbers of juvenile delinquents receive little supervision at home. No one seems to know—or care—where they are going, whom they are going with, what they are doing, or when they will return. Not infrequently the mothers and fathers of these adolescents rationalize their negligence as a carefully constructed plan to foster autonomy. "We've always given her a lot of independence," Stephanie's parents tell their friends, "and she certainly doesn't abuse it."

Home atmospheres with consistent discipline, accountability, and caring minimize the frequency and severity of misconduct. When behavioral standards are clearly stated and fairly enforced and when teens know their parents pay attention to where and with whom they are going, what they will be doing, and will be there to greet them when they return, that serves to reinforce their own developing conscience. One girl was deterred from continuing to steal because she knew her father would soon find out. A boy suffering from his friends' ridicule because his mother would not let him hang around the arcade on weekends finally said in exasperation, "At least she cares enough to say no!"

WATCH OUT FOR YOUR OWN REACTIONS

Teenagers prone to misconduct arouse powerful emotions of the older generation. The aggressive core of their behavior just plain scares us. Their seemingly random delinquent acts threaten to undermine the order and trust, not to mention the laws, that permit a free society to exist. We may find ourselves wanting to react to our fear of their explosive outbursts with physical punishment. Or those of us with strong needs to control our youngsters may find their tantrums will propel us in the direction of exactly the same violent, intemperate actions we are trying to prevent in our youngsters.

Try to manage these emotions by recognizing that aggression begets

aggression. Extreme parental hostility—vicious criticism, harsh discipline, or physical assault—produces high rates of belligerence and misconduct in adolescents, ironically, the very behavior the parents are trying to prevent. Children tend to copy the actions of their parents. If they
see adults they love screaming and punching when they are upset, the
youngsters are likely to follow suit.

If your son has an explosive outburst, try to check your instinct to
respond in kind and make an effort to underreact. Talk in a soft voice
rather than trying to match him decibel for decibel. Don't try to reason
with an adolescent in the middle of a tantrum. Wait until afterward to
talk about what triggered the blowup and how it might be minimized
the next time.

If you are being bullied by a larger teen, call for help from relatives,
friends, or the police. As Rick's case suggests, this precaution can be a
useful way to take control of the situation for the youngster's benefit.

Avoid double messages. More than one boy's violent outbursts have
been subtly reinforced by a father who responds with conflicting statements: "How awful that you blew up at a teacher who made fun of your
new haircut in class. But you can't let people walk all over you!" Nine
times out of ten these are parents who themselves have considerable
ambivalence about their own aggressive urges.

Confront antisocial acts and respond appropriately. Overlooking obvious aberrant conduct stimulates rather than discourages the acts. An
example is Stephanie's mother. Coming upon a drawer full of music
tapes that her daughter obviously didn't purchase, she quickly closed it
and walked out of the room. She decided that talking to Stephanie
might make a potential problem worse.

If you discover goods that are obviously stolen, express your disapproval of the child's actions, discuss motives, plan restitution, and monitor conduct for a period of several months afterward. Remember to
disapprove of a youngster's behavior and not of her essence. Saying "I
don't like it that you have stolen these tapes" works better than calling
Stephanie "a despicable thief." Also helpful is to avoid making dire
predictions based on adolescent misconduct—for example, "This means
you are headed for a life of crime and will never amount to anything."
Try to understand why teenagers steal. Often they can tell you; just as
frequently they cannot. In the latter case recommend professional counseling to help them clarify how and why the acting up occurs.

Help the youngster find a way to compensate the store or individual from whom she has stolen. If, as in Stephanie's case, this is not possible, calculate the value, then ask her to work until she's made that amount of money and donate the funds to a charity. Since a bond of trust has been broken, try to monitor the adolescent's actions for a period of time afterward. If Stephanie knew that her room was open to inspection and that her rights to privacy would be suspended temporarily she would have been less likely to steal.

HELP THEM FIND WAYS TO CONTAIN MISCONDUCT

Since the preponderance of young people exhibiting difficulties gradually stop by their twenties, parents can practice what might be called vigilant nonintervention. Unless the provocation or the crime is undeniable, organize an environment that reduces frustration and promotes behavioral control. Make school a tolerable experience by securing a tutor or placing the child in special classes to reduce frustration. Encourage teens to work or engage in sports that absorb excessive energy and teach discipline. For older youths who continue to find school failure demoralizing and infuriating, consider suggesting that they drop out and find a job. Later they can be persuaded to take a high school equivalency examination when they see the value of further education.

Do all you can to help them learn assertive behavior and empathy. The essentials of assertion—rather than aggression—are described on page 155. Helping your teen develop assertion skills gives him or her an alternative to violence when feeling provoked. Empathy, the capacity to understand how others are feeling and thinking, is remarkably deficient in delinquents. Think about ways to arouse in your adolescent an emotional understanding of how the misconduct might affect the victims of it. Some parents ask their children to recall their own reactions when similarly treated.

Teach your youngsters high-level means of discharging their anger. Start early. Begin by examining your own ways of relieving hostility. Since you are their first and most influential role model, you may wish to make some modifications in how you react to people and situations that arouse your ire. Or you may wish to explain that at times you don't handle aggressive feelings especially well, and you'd like to see if you can improve the next generation.

Some young people benefit from talking out their feelings. Other teens use physical outlets, and a few find their own unique ways for relief. Specifically it often helps a youngster whose friend has betrayed him or her to find someone—often a parent or family member—to talk to. Others find a long walk, solitary swim, cleaning the basement, or yard work brings relief. One inspired mother taught her youngster to go into the backyard and squeeze a small green apple as hard as he could to see if he could crush it when he was angry. If not, he was instructed to hurl it full force against a tree in the backyard. She later recounted that her son went through several bushels of apples during the early teenage years but continued to function normally.

Participation in sports helps control aggressive instincts in two ways. Along with improving self-esteem and altering mood, vigorous physical activity gives everyone an acceptable channel to vent frustrations and tensions. Also by playing sports young people learn to control fighting behavior when aroused, keeping it within the rules.

A story is told of a new dean at a New York college who happened to walk by one of the dormitories on a Saturday night and was appalled to see windows being broken and students fighting with one another. When he asked a colleague why this was tolerated he was told this was the "Animal House," the dorm for the football, hockey, and lacrosse players. "What can you expect from them?" his fellow faculty member commented. "Far better control than that," he thought to himself. The next morning he had a meeting of those rowdy students. He pointed out to them that since they were athletes, they were trained to control their violent behavior. Therefore he would expect more disciplined behavior from them, not rowdiness. He ended by telling them that any further antisocial behavior would be treated severely. His warnings brought to an end the Saturday night chaos in that dormitory.

The process of dissipating rage need not be vigorous. Some boys and girls listen to music, watch a movie, or read. One college student wandered by accident into a museum displaying Renaissance art after getting a D+ on a chemistry exam. He found that being around art from five hundred years ago put his problems in perspective and he relaxed. Afterward he always sought a museum when he found himself under cruel and unusual stress.

If a child is perpetually out of control and running away, look for an alternative. It may be that an aunt's house in Biloxi or a structured boarding school will be effective. Most communities have temporary shelters for youngsters where they can stay for several weeks or months until things calm down at home. Often if we move a teen out of an unstable family environment into a caring and controlled setting, antisocial conduct abates.

When moving the teenager out of the home environment is not possible, consider using a big brother or big sister organization. These seem especially helpful for early adolescent boys. A group of young males being raised by single-parent mothers who met with a big brother once a week for two years showed significantly less aggressive behavior and better marks in school than boys who were on the waiting list. Research with big-little sister pairs also showed positive results.

SEEK PROFESSIONAL HELP

When you've exhausted your repertoire of ways to help control your youngster's conduct problems, seek professional help. Individual antisocial behavior such as stealing and explosive outbursts respond reasonably well to therapies employing both cognitive and behavioral elements. In red-zone cases there may be a need for placement outside the home while a comprehensive treatment program is employed.

Stephanie's treatment illustrates one form of cognitive-behavioral therapy that is used successfully to treat misconduct, ranging from theft to obscene phone calls. It may be conducted individually or in groups and may include family members. Recent promising developments in techniques to help adolescents combat explosive anger contain many similar elements. The approach is often called stress inoculation training. If Rick had had the benefit of this treatment, it would have proceeded approximately this way: (1) he would have been encouraged to recognize those situations in the past that aroused hostile responses—for example, a classmate's snide comments; (2) he would be taught to recognize the physical and mental signs associated with being about to blow up— physical agitation, nausea, and the feeling of wanting to slam something, as well as thoughts of being humiliated, embarrassed, and in danger; (3) he would be trained in muscle relaxation; (4) in a role-playing situation which in the past provoked his aggression Rick would be shown how to stay in control through relaxation, reinterpretation, and calming statements, such as "He's probably jealous of me," "Stay cool," and "I'm not going to give them the satisfaction of reacting"; (5) he would practice assertive alternatives to explosive reactions, such as talking to the classmate privately about how much he disliked the sarcastic comments, asking him to stop; and (6) he would be taught positive self-reinforcement for staying in control—doing something nice for himself.

If individual counseling isn't effective, place the youngster in a residential treatment setting. The most effective programs combine a caring and containing physical environment with appropriate therapy, clearly stated rewards and punishments, small group discussions, meetings with family and small classes. Some of these can be found in halfway programs, some in special schools, some in mental hospitals. These residential programs significantly lower the rate of delinquency in acting out adolescents. Most rejoin their families and few exhibit further antisocial behavior.

Youngsters who experienced conduct difficulties in their teens, and were able to overcome them, are often found among the most talented and productive adults. Not infrequently this outcome happens because they were finally able to put their independent spirit and energy to good use in a profession or their own organization.

As grown-ups many are extraordinarily loyal to the educational institutions they continually fought during their adolescence. Indeed their names often grace the libraries, laboratories, dormitories, and other facilities that sustain the intellectual pursuits of American universities.

Whatever we as adults can do to reduce the odds of juvenile misconduct from deteriorating into an irreversible antisocial character keeps the door open for positive growth in the adult years. No single approach is guaranteed, but these ideas allow us to do something to help adolescents help themselves during this stormy teenage period.

11

"Bingeing, Purging, and Starving"
Eating Problems

In every decade a fresh teenage problem compels our attention. Identity crises dominated the 1950s and youthful rebellion was the centerpiece of the 1960s. The narcissistic preoccupations of the "me" generation fascinated us in the 1970s. The explosion of professional and popular interest in adolescent eating problems suggests this is the main event of the 1980s.

Like that of their parents, the eating behavior of teenagers fluctuates. During any calendar year they typically overeat in the winter and diet to take off unwanted pounds in the spring. They will load up on carbohydrates when stressed—or lose their appetite entirely—and reverse the pattern during tranquil periods. Nearly all devise methods to regulate their weight: they "pig out" on weekends and eat sparingly Monday through Friday; they diet, fast, or increase exercise following periods of indulgence. Recognizing these fluctuations, they acknowledge they "don't eat right" and, unless they are unusually spindly, say they would look better if they lost an inch or two around the waist or thighs.

On occasion young people misuse food as a means of coping with tensions or they become so obsessed with thinking about eating that problems develop. These irregularities occur on a continuum from temporary and mild to unrelenting and severe. Two types of serious eating disorders are bulimia and anorexia nervosa. Originally the term "bulimia" meant a voracious, insatiable appetite. Recently the term has been expanded to include terminating of eating binges by purging or other extraordinary efforts to lose weight. Estimates of the incidents of bulimia among teenagers range from 10 to 30 percent. Slightly fewer than one in ten are male.

Anorexia nervosa is a relentless pursuit of thinness by restricting food intake, by exercise, or by chemical agents. About 1 teenager in 250 develops signs of anorexia, though a far larger proportion exhibit restricted eating habits and anxiety about their weight which approaches this disorder. Approximately 95 percent are female.

KANDACE

Well-mannered, organized, and responsible, Kandace was the perfect child. Though she had average ability, Kandace's grades were always high. Teachers at the parochial school she attended in West Hartford, Connecticut, regularly commented on her self-motivation, her determination to do well, neatness and precision, and high energy level. A math teacher in the seventh grade, however, was heard to wonder out loud if perhaps Kandace pushed herself a little too hard.

Kandace and her two younger brothers were close to their parents. They did everything together: ate as a family each night; attended church, movies, and cultural events together; and their parents always took the children with them on vacations.

The summer Kandace was twelve her mother began to worry that she was a little too close to her family and didn't seem to have many friends. Over the loud objections of Kandace, her mother decided she should go to a summer camp in Vermont to develop her social skills. Rather than upset anyone, Kandace went grudgingly. It was a disaster. She didn't like girls whom her letters described as "pretty, spoiled, bitchy, and cliquey." She spent a lot of time reading in her bunk. The previous spring her menstrual cycle had begun and Kandace had started a major growth spurt. As she continued to develop physically over the summer she had a healthy appetite. Though she was by no means obese, she gained considerable weight.

When she found she couldn't fit into last year's clothes, Kandace was concerned. Viewing her small rounded breasts and hips in the mirror, she thought she looked "gross." The last straw was her brother teasing her about having "thunder thighs." She resolved to put herself on a strict diet.

During the next eighteen months she dramatically reduced her food intake, with some days consisting of nothing but sugarless gum and soft drinks. Kandace didn't find it difficult not to eat because she had almost no appetite.

Though she ate little and began to look distinctly undernourished, Kandace was more energetic than ever. In fact she took up distance running and, as a ninth grader, was a member of her school's varsity cross-country team. "She must absorb energy out of the air," her mother worried aloud, "because she isn't getting it from food." Kandace didn't mind being around food and frequently helped her mother prepare meals.

Her mother became increasingly frantic. She bought a doctor's scale and made Kandace weigh in in her presence every morning. She tried everything she could think of to force Kandace to eat normally but she resisted. "Kandace eats three bites and then just pushes the rest of her food around the plate," she said to her husband. As the weight dropped her father threatened her by telling her that if she didn't gain ten pounds he wouldn't allow her to run indoor track. Though she only added six pounds he relented. Right afterward Kandace went on an even stricter eating regimen and lost more weight.

When her periods stopped, her parents' concern changed to alarm. They took her to a specialist in adolescent medicine in Boston. The doctor took one look at her and said that she needed to gain weight. "Gain weight!" Kandace exclaimed, grabbing a hanging fold of skin above her elbow, "See that fat! I have to get rid of it." At the moment Kandace was 5'6" tall and weighed 83 pounds.

HUGH

Hugh's eating problem started just after he successfully auditioned for the spring musical at his suburban Chicago high school. A graceful, outgoing, talented seventeen year old, he was given the lead. In March he saw a videotape of himself at rehearsal and was appalled at how "bloated" he looked. He resolved to lose at least fifteen pounds before opening night by putting himself on a strict diet of carrots, bouillon, appetite-suppressing pills, and vitamins.

Hugh's mother, an accounts manager for an advertising agency, valued being fit and worked hard to stay in shape. By contrast his engineer father was always on the heavy side and seemed impervious to his wife's constant admonitions that he should lose weight. As a child Hugh had always had a healthy appetite. In adolescence he became aware that his mother watched him carefully when he ate, cautioning him not to take in too many calories or he might "develop a pot like Pop's." The smile on her face when she said it did not negate the message.

Hugh did lose almost fifteen pounds on the diet. But as rehearsals intensified in the month before the musical was to open, he became increasingly nervous. Insomnia and stomach problems began to bother him, and he felt increasingly worn out. Hugh had never lost his sweet tooth during his diet. His favorite food was cream-filled chocolate cupcakes. One night he arrived home very tired after rehearsal and sat down to eat something. Before he knew it he had consumed eleven cupcakes and a quart of milk in just under half an hour. His insides felt as though they might explode. Hugh made himself throw up to relieve the pain. Afterward he felt disgusted but more relaxed. Purging himself afterward also eliminated Hugh's worry that his bingeing would make him fat.

During periods of stress over the remainder of his high school years Hugh secretly gorged himself with food and then vomited. Usually he preferred rich food, gobbling packages of cookies and potato chips in addition to cupcakes, barely chewing them.

In the summer prior to his freshman year at college Hugh thought he had the problem licked. But then he started gorging himself and throwing up again. By final exams he was bingeing and purging two to three times a day. Finally his roommate—who knew something was wrong—talked to the resident adviser on their floor. Together they watched him overeat and head for the toilet. While he was throwing up, they walked in and said, "We're really worried about you and think you should talk to someone at the infirmary." Hugh said there was nothing wrong with him except that he had the flu which made him nauseous.

Youngsters in the green zone have a good appetite. At twelve and thirteen they are constantly hungry. The majority of sixteen-year-old youths still eat heartily. Before they are long into adolescence, however, young people understand the relationship of how much they eat to their weight. Even before the present media emphasis on a sleek physique, eleven and twelve year olds watched their waistlines. Today's boys and girls know the time will come when they can no longer eat everything they choose in whatever quantity they desire without putting on unwanted pounds.

TABLE 11.1
Estimating the Severity of Eating Problems

GREEN ZONE—Normal Adaptation

- Good appetite
- Weight conforms to medical standards
- Possible dissatisfaction with weight
- Early self-correction

YELLOW ZONE—Temporary Adjustment Reactions

- Significant variation in eating and weight fluctuations associated with new/greater stress
- Problem recognizable but seen as within control
- Intermittent blocking of reality during eating excesses
- Self-esteem remains positive

ORANGE ZONE—Neurotic Symptoms

- Bulimic or anorexic behavior
- Perfectionistic thinking about weight
- Domination of eating problems, restricting pleasure from other areas
- Family preoccupation with control of eating/weight
- Health a concern

RED ZONE—Severe Maladjustments

- Most characteristics of bulimia or anorexia nervosa exhibited
- Health jeopardized
- Pervasive feelings of inadequacy, depression

Generally the weight of the majority of normal teenagers conforms to medical standards for their sex, age, height, and body frame. Weight expectations for boys and girls ages ten to eighteen is shown in Table 11.2.

TABLE 11.2
Normal Weight by Age, Sex, and Height

	BOYS						GIRLS					
	Height Percentile						Height Percentile					
	10th		50th		90th		10th		50th		90th	
Age	Wt.	Ht.	Wt.	Ht.	Wt.	Ht.	Wt.	Ht.	Wt.	Ht.	Wt.	Ht.
10	56	51″	69	54″	90	57″	57	51″	72	55″	96	58″
11	62	53	78	57	103	60	64	54	82	57	112	61
12	69	55	88	59	116	63	72	56	92	60	124	63
13	79	58	99	62	130	66	80	58	102	62	136	65
14	90	60	112	64	145	69	89	60	111	63	146	67
15	102	62	125	67	159	71	96	60	118	64	153	67
16	113	65	137	68	172	72	101	61	123	64	158	67
17	122	66	146	69	184	73	104	61	125	64	160	67
18	128	67	152	70	195	73	105	62	125	65	159	67

Source: National Center for Health Statistics, Human Resources Administration, Department of Health, Education, and Welfare, Hyattsville, Md. 20782, 1977, pp. 140–41.

Note: Height and weight are rounded to the nearest pound and inch.

Eating habits may exhibit short-term variation causing a youngster's weight to fluctuate. Usually these are seasonal or related to identifiable passing stresses.

It would be a rare group of adolescents who would not tell us they are dissatisifed with their weight. About 75 percent of high school females report "feeling fat" at one time or another and have actively tried to lose weight. Though many more males worry about gaining rather than losing weight, a third of this number have attempted to take off unwanted pounds by the end of their college years.

Self-correction of eating and weight irregularities comes early and without heroic effort. Some of those teens on the heavy side of average try halfheartedly to cut down their caloric intake—one girl may drink a sugar-free soda instead of a regular root beer with her hot fudge sundaes. Others make short runs at losing a few pounds by decreasing how much they eat, eliminating carbohydrates, or going on diets. Before long, their weight and eating patterns return to normal.

Teenagers whose problems fall in the *yellow* zone exhibit significant irregularities in food intake and weight associated with a clear cause. It is part of an adjustment reaction to a new or greater stress. Kandace's weight variation was associated with spending the summer in a camp she disliked. Eating patterns become chaotic for three to six months. They include bingeing, bingeing and purging, crash diets, abuse of chemical agents, or fasting. These chaotic patterns persist three to six months. The weight of these youngsters often varies from 85 to 115 percent of normal expectations. Health is not endangered.

The growth spurt at puberty can be another stressor as it results in weight gain, a change in body size, and in females the development of breasts, a widening of the pelvis, and fatty deposits. A healthy appetite fuels these substantial physical changes. While most teenagers react to these changes positively, others, such as Kandace, are appalled at what nature has done to their bodies.

Youngsters in the yellow zone recognize they have a "problem" but believe it to be within their control. Partly this is because they see the connection between the symptoms and the cause: a boy may binge and purge when he enters his freshman year in college or a girl may exhibit anorexic behavior when she leaves college for a new job in Cincinnati. They are certain that after a period of adjustment they will be back to normal.

Their optimism may be based on an intermittent blocking of reality during bouts of eating irregularities. A boy vowed to keep himself on a twelve-hundred-calorie-a-day diet. One day an extra helping of chicken put him over the maximum. "Then I lost it," he said, "and stuffed myself on cookies. I figured once I broke my pledge I might as well let myself go." When he was gorging himself, he slid into a near trance state where his anxiety diminished for the moment. A girl reported that when she was fasting and exercising vigorously she felt so "high" it was impossible to worry about the damage she might be doing to her body.

Finally a yellow flag is that the adolescent's self-esteem remains essentially positive in spite of eating difficulties. Confidence in themselves is minimally impaired or, if lost, returns quickly. They know they have a problem, are aware that corrective action needs to be taken, and are optimistic about overcoming it.

The most important *orange*-zone indicators are bulimic and anorexic eating behaviors. Teenagers with these problems have some but not all of the diagnostic signs of bulimia and anorexia nervosa shown in Table 11.3.

TABLE 11.3

Characteristics of Bulimia and Anorexia Nervosa

BULIMIA

- Repeated, uncontrolled, secretive binge eating, often terminated by purging
- Excessive sensitivity to weight
- Post-binge relief followed by anguish
- Eating problems experienced as alien and out of control

ANOREXIA NERVOSA

- Substantial self-inflicted weight loss
- Intense fear of fatness
- Distorted self-perceptions
- Preoccupation with food
- Amenorrhea in females, diminished sexual interest

The most noticeable features are overeating, bingeing and purging, and self-inflicted eating restrictions along with considerable weight loss. These are no longer temporary adjustments to stress but persist beyond three to six months in the absence of an obvious cause.

There may be short periods of remission. For instance, Hugh's binge-ing and purging was in reaction to the building tension prior to the high school musical—a yellow flag. Afterward the problem disappeared. In the summer before college Hugh thought he had the eating difficulty licked. Shortly after the freshman year started, however, he began the gorge-purge cycle again, but this time with greater frequency. Before long Hugh lost track of why he was doing it; the bulimic activity seemed to have a life of its own.

As a group people with eating disorders tend to be perfectionistic as well as rigid, ambitious, and demanding of themselves. When these ten-dencies focus on their weight for an extended period, this is an orange flag. They often associate thinness with happiness and become obsessed with losing weight. Yet being slender never brings happiness. They worry constantly that their tight control over their eating habits will break. These individuals have been described as "thin-fat" people. Unless they are eternally vigilant and overcontrol their food intake, they will be help-less to resist gorging themselves and will become fat and miserable.

Perfectionistic thinking about weight often is reinforced at home. Hugh's excessive sensitivity about weight grew out of his mother's con-cern that he avoid becoming obese like his father. Her close monitoring of his eating habits set the stage for his first severe diet when he decided to slim down for opening night.

In the orange zone eating problems dominate the person's life, se-verely restricting pleasure from other areas. Except for her commitment to her schoolwork, other interests fell away as Kandace's anorexic behav-ior persisted. The eating problems impair relationships with friends and loved ones. In spite of his gregarious nature Hugh opted for a single room where he could binge and purge unobserved. Perhaps as a conse-quence of reduced satisfaction from other areas of life, self-esteem di-minishes. A sure orange flag is when youngsters in this zone say that they don't feel as good about themselves as they did before developing this disorder. As teens continue to exhibit anorexic behavior, much of their contact with parents centers on their weight and what they are—and are not—eating. Kandace put it succinctly when she said, "I get so *tired* of talking about my weight all the time. There's more to me than what I eat."

Many who develop eating problems—especially anorexia—come from close families in which overcontrol and overprotection of the children is notable. Kandace's mother and father were constantly worried about her safety and health while regulating her activities carefully. In childhood Kandace was unusually sensitive to parental anxiety. She complied with their wishes before they voiced them. Her willingness to accommodate herself to their needs to control her life kept the peace at home. This intimate, rigid family organization inhibits peer-relationships which are a major vehicle for young adolescents to take greater control of their lives.

Controlling what they eat is one of the few avenues for teenagers to express their growing need for independence. This control results in huge intergenerational conflicts: parents want to dictate how much a child will eat and weigh and the youngster will resist. Elaborate negotiations occur. Bargains are struck: if Kandace put on ten pounds she could go out for the indoor track season was the deal she made with her father. The outcome is often similar to this one: the teenager adds a few pounds —though short of the agreed-upon mark; the adult relents; and this situation is followed by even greater weight loss.

Health becomes a concern. A clear orange-zone indicator is that someone who knows the adolescent well is worried about that youngster's physical welfare. As in Hugh's case, it may be a roommate concerned about his bingeing and throwing up. Or it could be a parent, teacher, or doctor who sees up to 15 percent weight loss or menstrual irregularities in females. All recognize that there is something wrong with these teenagers' eating patterns and something needs to be done to protect their well-being.

Young people in the *red* zone exhibit most of the characteristics of bulimia and anorexia nervosa listed in Table 11.3. The primary red flag signaling bulimia is chronic overeating, often terminated by throwing up, laxatives, suppositories, or enemas. This cycle can occur many times a day. Bulimics plan for their binges: they hoard rolls and butter, muffins or desserts from the cafeteria; or they fill their supermarket carts with food for the next episode. It can be a costly habit. Unlike Hugh, whose disorder was discovered quickly, many adolescents keep their eating problems secret for long periods.

As with Hugh, the eating disorder arises from an excessive sensitivity to the adolescents' weight and in feelings of their bodies being fat. Though a minority of those with this type of eating disorder become overweight for short periods, most are not more than 15 percent over normal weight expectations.

Bulimic youths experience their bingeing and purging as both alien and out of control. Instead of perceiving it as a passing aberration in reaction tension he will rid himself of when he is ready, Hugh finally recognized his gorging and vomiting as a monstrous urge within himself that he could no longer govern.

These adolescents typically feel a little bit better when the cycle is finished. "Stuffing myself and getting rid of it always calms me down," said Hugh. "I guess it's both having your cake and not having it simultaneously that does it," he said with a smile. But the post-binge relief is brief and followed by anguish reminiscent of the alcoholic's. Though they may say "never again" they nearly always do. And, as with the alcoholic, the remorse becomes a source of stress in itself, shortening the time to the next binge-purge cycle.

Substantial self-inflicted weight loss through severe means is the major identifying characteristic of anorexia nervosa. Kandace's actions restricting her food intake and engaging in a heavy exercise program illustrate this feature. Other anorexics lose weight by lengthy fasts, diet pills, and other chemical agents. Some binge and purge.

Some disagreement exists among experts as to what a "substantial" weight loss is. A few maintain it should be 25 percent. Also there is debate as to whether the weight loss should be in reference to the weight prior to the decrease or should be in reference to expectations for age and weight. Since most teenagers are not overweight when they begin an anorexic episode, the more conservative 15 to 20 percent figure or weight loss seems appropriate.

The anorexics' heroic efforts to reduce come from an intense fear of fatness. They are literally terrified of being overweight, are hyperaware of their caloric content in whatever they ingest, don't mind an empty stomach, and love to look thin. Indeed the lives of these teens are organized around the increasing pursuit of thinness: in the grasp of an anorexic episode losing weight was about all Kandace could think about.

Disturbed self-perceptions are notable in anorexics. One manifestation is becoming less in touch with bodily sensations. Though these teenagers eat virtually nothing, they don't feel hungry. Because she had no appetite, Kandace could easily fend off her parents' increasingly anxious efforts to force her to take in something other than no-calorie gum and soda. Another disturbed perception is to feel "fat" in the face of compelling evidence to the contrary. If a group of anorexics are asked to guess the size of their waistlines, they are likely to overestimate their girth. As these same teenagers overcome their eating disorders they will be more accurate in their perceptions of their measurements.

Sometimes these youngsters have strange ideas about what happens to food they consume. Some believe that whatever they eat is automatically converted to fat in their thighs. Others think they have "something inside" themselves and must starve themselves to eliminate it. Others develop delusions: one young woman gorged herself all the time fantasizing she was pregnant and would soon have a baby.

In spite of how little they eat, anorexics exhibit a high energy level. They are found in demanding sports requiring vigorous training—swimming, gymnastics, crew, and track. Indeed a study of "obligatory runners"—those with a single-minded devotion to physical conditioning preempting other satisfactions in life—discovered a similarity between the personalities of these athletes and people with anorexia.

Though they consume little of it, anorexic adolescents are preoccupied with food. Like Kandace they inhabit the kitchen, helping parents prepare meals for the rest of the family. On occasion they engage in rituals about food—copying and recopying recipes, insisting on cooking in copper pans, or eating only natural foods.

The last characteristic of anorexia nervosa is amenorrhea in young women and diminished sexual interests and activity in both sexes. The absence of menses in some young female adolescents is primary, that is, their periods do not begin because of self-starvation. Most of these girls develop secondary amenorrhea which is the absence of menses after their menstrual cycle has begun. Even though teenagers who develop anorexia tend to be socially isolated and have fewer opportunities for heterosexual experience, a lessening of sexual drive occurs as they restrict their food intake.

With both bulimia and anorexia nervosa health is no longer a mere concern. The well-being of red-zone teenagers is in jeopardy. A few of the physical side effects of recurring bulimia include damage to the colon, stomach, or other elements of the GI tract, fluid and electrolyte imbalance leading to dehydration and heart irregularities, and insulin reactions due to low blood sugar. Continuing self-starvation can result in GI problems, skin abnormalities, slowed heart rate, and low blood pressure. Every year young people with anorexia nervosa die because they become so emaciated their bodies can no longer resist disease.

The last red flag is that pervasive feelings of inadequacy abound. Moreover these teenage bulimics and anorexics believe they have no mind of their own and only do things because of others. These inner convictions are in sharp contrast to the way these youngsters are seen by others: during her anorexic episode Kandace was convinced she was a "lazy" student, didn't work hard enough in track, and was helpless to resist doing what others wanted. Associated with this inner experience of ineffectiveness are depressive emotions. They may be constant or intermittent, and they may result from a nutritional deficit as well as despair over how much unhappiness their symptoms cause.

Follow-up

KANDACE

The doctor advised Kandace's parents to admit her into the hospital so her weight could be managed medically. Though Kandace was loudly opposed, they reluctantly agreed. The hospital staff applied a multiple therapeutic approach. A physician directed the overall program and regularly monitored her weight and her vitamin and mineral levels and watched for physical problems associated with anorexia; a nutritionist met with her to plan a tolerable high-calorie menu while assuring her that she would not allow Kandace to become heavy; a psychiatrist saw her two times a week individually to discuss her reactions to the treatment and help her understand how this had happened; and finally she and her parents met with a family therapist regularly.

The doctor—whom she nicknamed "Dirty Harry"—weighed Kandace every Friday. She hated these sessions: "If they've fattened me up he's so happy I could puke," Kandace complained. "But if I haven't gained any weight he yells and threatens to stick a tube in my stomach!"

She was no fan of the psychiatrist either: "All she wants is for me to gain weight too, but she's sneakier about it. It's a waste of time and money." In her therapy sessions Kandace was able to acknowledge that she wanted to be thinner because she would be happier then. But the more weight she lost, the fatter she thought she looked, and the more miserable she became. Yet Kandace worried that if she added enough pounds to be in the normal range for her height and weight she would be desperately unhappy. Kandace felt she was in a box—no matter what she did the result would be unpleasant.

The family therapy was tough going as well. Kandace and her parents were asked to meet with a social worker once a week to help them discover how their relationships may have contributed to her eating problem and might be modified to assist in her recovery. Kandace went grudgingly and her father came willingly. Her mother attended one session and refused to meet again because she was "too busy" and had "no confidence" in the therapist. Nevertheless Kandace and her father continued for several sessions and learned that their family's closeness, high expectations, rigidity, and inability to solve disagreements set the stage for her anorexia.

It was in these meetings that Kandace became aware that the self-starvation began as a way of taking control of her own life. Quickly, however, she found that not eating began to be something she could no longer manage. And it had its pleasant side. "It gave me a rush to eat almost nothing and feel the weight dropping off," she said.

Slowly Kandace filled out. After six weeks the scale read ninety-five pounds when she stepped on it. She was allowed to return home with the understanding that if she did not control her eating she would return to the hospital and the medical staff would take over for her. Though she didn't like it, Kandace agreed. At first she also agreed to continue individual treatment. As soon as she got home however, Kandace stopped seeing the psychiatrist—a move strongly supported by her mother.

All the time Kandace was in the hospital, her teachers sent assignments from the high school so she could keep up with her schoolwork. Summer was uneventful, but when cross-country season began in the fall Kandace started to lose weight again. Her mother became extremely upset and tried to make Kandace weigh herself every day in front of her. When she refused they consulted the doctor again. He told Kandace that she had to regain the lost pounds or she couldn't run cross-country. Moreover, if she lost any more weight she would be put in the hospital again. He then recommended they consult another family therapist. This time her mother agreed to participate.

Perhaps for that reason the family treatment worked a little better. Another contributing factor was that everyone was aware that the eating problem was far from over. The focus of these meetings was on helping the family find ways to accept Kandace's struggle for independence in some other manner than anorexia. Kandace also came to see that if she controlled her eating this could lead to greater freedom, not less. She would be able to continue in sports, do well in school, extend the range of her friendships, and perhaps even find romance.

As much as anything this last realization helped Kandace stabilize her weight—still a little on the thin side for her doctor and a bit too heavy for her. But the anorexia was finally behind her.

HUGH

In spite of Hugh's denial that he was bingeing and purging, his roommate and resident adviser convinced him to see a physician at the college's health service. When the doctor asked him if he had been overeating and throwing up, Hugh said this happened "occasionally," but he had the problem under control now. Unconvinced, the doctor told him to return if he had more of the symptoms. Hugh said he would.

During the remainder of his college career the bulimia gradually worsened. By his senior year the eating problem was a constant companion, occurring eight to ten times a week. During his sophomore and junior years Hugh had a single room so he had no trouble evading detection. To obtain food for the binges, Hugh went to the dining room when it was uncrowded and the serving staff not especially attentive. This enabled him to fill his tray with extra rolls and butter which he hoarded prior to gorging himself. He also found an isolated alcove in the dining room where he could gobble food down undetected if he needed to do so.

Hugh knew he was going to have to do something about his problem when he fell in love with Marilyn in the fall of his senior year. Before long they were spending every weekend together and many nights in between. At Christmas, Marilyn suggested they share an apartment during the spring term. This precipitated an acute conflict. "I want to live with her," Hugh thought to himself, "but I can't because of my eating problem!"

Not knowing what to do, Hugh approached the physician he had seen in his freshman year for help. After diagnosing the problem as bulimia, the doctor referred Hugh to an eating disorder group for treatment. Hugh met with nine others in a treatment program involving sixteen weekly meetings. Led by a psychiatrist and psychologist, these sessions began with a general discussion of bulimia. Gently the participants were encouraged to talk about their own eating difficulties. Like the others, Hugh was surprised at how many characteristics they all shared—including sharing the same isolated alcove to overeat. They were all encouraged to keep a log of the conditions associated with bingeing and purging. They also were asked to be sensitive to barely conscious thoughts and feelings that triggered or accompanied the episode.

Along with several others Hugh identified some of the obvious stressors preceeding his binges. Painfully he recognized other emotional images associated with overeating and throwing up: his desire to please his mother by staying thin and fear of becoming as obese as his father; an association of thinness with success; and an impulse for self-punishment by purging.

Hugh shared with the group another image: that he had a poor body image. "Who doesn't?" responded a young woman. "My roommate, a campus beauty queen, always complains about how deformed she is." The group members agreed that they felt addicted to bingeing and purging. One young man estimated that his "habit" cost him about a hundred dollars a month.

These perceptions fascinated Hugh and he felt better after a session in which he expressed the powerful emotions connected with these understandings. Recognizing the reasons associated with his bulimia and discussing it with others in the group didn't reduce much the frequency of his overeating and vomiting. However, it was becoming more and more something Hugh wanted to rid himself of.

By the sixth meeting the leaders taught Hugh and the others behavioral techniques for controlling the impulse to binge and purge. These included relaxation, self-hypnosis, and guided imagery. After a month Hugh reduced the number of bulimic episodes by half—still too many for him. For those like Hugh who wanted to try for a more complete restoration of normal eating behavior a trial of antidepressant medication was offered.

At the end of the program Hugh, along with about a third of the other members, found to their surprise that their episodes of gorging and purging dropped to zero. Like recovering alcoholics they accepted their remission warily. Four of them decided to join a local chapter of Overeaters Anonymous for continuing support.

What Parents Can Do: Suggestions for Helping

Of all the difficulties afflicting teenagers, eating problems number among the most upsetting and frustrating to the older generation. What might parents do to lower the probability of their children developing an eating disorder? Here are several suggestions that can be helpful.

RECOGNIZE PREDISPOSING VULNERABILITY

Recognize that particular kinds of young people, raised in certain types of families, have a greater chance of developing difficulties with food intake. As children they are unusually ambitious and conscientious, orderly and perfectionistic, and nonassertive and oriented toward pleasing others. Also many may be shy and have few friends.

The families of these boys and girls tend to be close, overprotective, rigid, and lack problem-solving ability. This structure results in the youngsters' accommodating themselves to parental wishes instead of developing a growing sense of autonomy. It is thought that a major reason these compliant young people develop eating disorders in early adolescence is that they're finally shouting "No" to their overcontrolling families.

While most teenagers with these traits raised in families like this don't develop eating or other problems, some do. If you suspect that the mix of your youngster's personality characteristics and the family structure sets that child up to develop an eating problem in adolescence, act to improve the odds against this occurring. A useful approach is to reduce the degree by which you reinforce already overdriven needs for perfection and success. At the same time encourage interest in playful activities that demand neither exactitude nor a high level of achievement. If, for example, your daughter converts tennis—which she began as fun—into a quest for excellence, see if you can find another leisure activity that attracts her attention.

Encourage contact with age-mates. Being part of a peer group supports youngsters in separating from an overweening family influence and developing a sense of independence. A peer group reduces the need for a more dramatic statement of autonomy via an early eating disorder. And since adolescents are strongly influenced by their contemporaries, friends who eat normally will have a positive influence on their food consumption.

WATCH OUT FOR OVERREACTIONS

Parents can help to prevent a brief eating irregularity from becoming a serious problem by monitoring carefully their own overreactions, and trying hard to avoid extended intemperate responses. Fluctuations in their youngster's food consumption or weight worry some parents enormously. It's important to be aware that we are greatly bothered by a son who seems to live on premixed breakfasts, lunches of soft drinks and potato chips, and fast-food hamburgers in the afternoon, or that we become increasingly anxious that a daughter will become obese when she puts on a few pounds during exams.

The awareness that an emotional reflex to these eating variations is out of the ordinary can help us understand its origins: with one boy's mother the source of the overreaction may be the subconscious need to control the youngster's life; with another it may emanate from the need to rescue the child from the potential harm of junk food. Not uncommonly, immoderate responses are rooted in long-standing fears about our own waistlines.

If you can recognize the source of a knee-jerk antipathy to eating irregularities, you are in a far better position to avoid the long, irrational outbursts and efforts to overcontrol which convert a minor variation into a theater for intergenerational conflict. This cognizance also enables you to respond more supportively to teenagers in the yellow zone which will help them regain their eating equilibrium.

INTERVENE AT ONCE

When a young person begins to exhibit a serious eating disorder intervene actively and quickly. The intervention may take the form of sharing your concerns directly: "Kandace, mother and I believe that you haven't been eating properly and we are worried." Ideally the statement of parental anxiety should not compromise the teenager's autonomy by demanding compliance—though that's much easier said than done. Often this confrontation itself is sufficient to jar a teen back to normal. If this return does not happen after a short period, the parents might help the youngster put together a plan for bringing the problem to an end. It is crucial to follow up with the adolescent at short—for example, weekly—intervals to evaluate progress toward regular eating patterns. Changes can be made, with the agreement of the young person, if the program is not effective.

If within a month or so progress is not noticeable, a medical consultation should be sought. Though parents and their children vary greatly in their willingness to consult a doctor, just making the appointment occasionally brings the episode to a halt because it conveys to the youngster that the mother and father take this behavior seriously and worry about the potential menace to health. The visit with a physician also provides a professional opinion about how worried to be and support for the restoration of normal eating habits.

OBTAIN PROFESSIONAL HELP

If the disorder is unresponsive to parental confrontation and a medical consultation, then insist the teenager obtain professional help because of the threat to health. Therapeutic approaches take many forms. Today most include a mix of techniques. At the University of Minnesota, for example, a comprehensive program for bulimics includes twenty-four meetings spread over an eight-week period. During these sessions—some lasting more than five hours—the participants are exposed to lectures on nutrition; they are shown the connection between eating disorders and particular types of thinking, stress, relationships, and depression; they are taught relaxation and assertiveness exercises; they are given information about patterns of recovery; they participate in group therapy to discuss this material with others; and toward the end they are asked to become volunteers to help other bulimics overcome their problem.

At a hospital in suburban Boston a six-to-twelve-month program is organized around treatment with antidepressant medication, but it also includes individual, family, and group treatment along with behavior therapy. Not all approaches are multimodal. Some clinicians report success with medication, group therapy, or hypnosis alone.

Treatment of anorexia is no less comprehensive and may include hospitalization if the youth's health is endangered. In the hospital the goals are to stop the weight loss and assist the patient in redeveloping normal eating habits. Inpatient programs differ greatly as to how much freedom they allow individuals to choose what they eat. For the most part they allow the anorexics to decide *how*—but not *if*—they will maintain an adequate weight. If their physical condition continues to deteriorate because they refuse to eat properly, the matter is taken out of their hands.

Follow-up studies of individuals treated for severe eating disorders in the past century report mixed success. Using restoration of normal weight as the criterion, about half of those with anorexia are cured and another 30 percent are improved several years later. Though far fewer outcome studies have been reported with bulimia, the initial findings suggest the percentages of symptom remission and reduction approximate the anorexia research. Generally speaking, the shorter the period an individual has the eating problem before it is treated, the more favorable the outlook for a complete recovery.

Count on resistance. Teenagers with eating problems are among the most reluctant to accept the idea that they could benefit from professional help. Moreover, even if they enter treatment and clearly benefit from it, their intransigence hardly ever slackens. They abandon therapy at the first opportunity. Usually they leave when they achieve visible improvement. They then pressure their parents to let them "do it on their own," to stop "wasting money" on treatment they no longer need. They insist that the sessions conflict with other worthwhile activities they want to pursue. It is the rare and gifted therapist who does not feel that treatment of the teenager remains incomplete at the time of termination.

12

"Everyone's Doing It"
Drug Use

The use of drugs to induce a sense of well-being, lubricate social relationships, and improve mood is well accepted in most cultures. The beer bust, cocktail party, and "happy hour" are events that bring young people together. Drug promotion is intense and continuous. It is a rare teenager who can go through the day without being invited to get more out of life by switching to a different coffee, being enticed by an attractive and liberated woman to smoke her brand, or being tempted by a man's man to try his beer.

In this context we should not be surprised by Figure 12.1 showing the frequency with which high school seniors tried one of the drugs listed.

Since the percentages concerning drinking behavior haven't changed much in the past five years, we can assume that more than nine tenths of this year's senior class have used alcohol—70 percent in the past month. Consumption of illicit drugs has increased: roughly 60 percent of the twelfth graders in America have tried marijuana; a substantial minority have sampled hallucinogens, "uppers," "downers," cocaine, and heroin. In 1975 the percentage was about half that.

The abuse of drugs—and especially alcohol—has never been greater. Two out of five senior boys who drink admit to problems associated with being under the influence a year before. A quarter of their older male college friends say they have had more than six drinks at least once a week. The proportion of heavy-drinking college females, presently about 12 percent, has just about tripled in the past decade.

Alcohol and other drug-related accidents are the leading cause of death among American youths. Uncontrolled substance abuse exacts

FIGURE 12

Prevalence and Recency of Use of Ten Types of Drugs, Class of 1982 (18,661 Students)

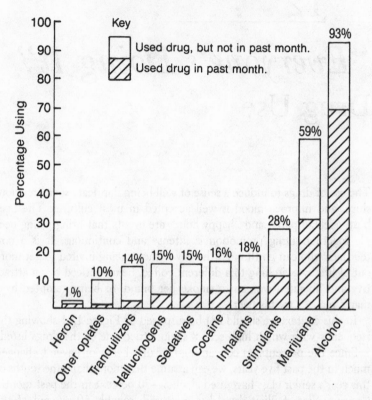

other costs from teenagers—overdoses, medical problems, poor grades in school, uncontrolled violent behavior, vandalism, alienation of loved ones, trouble with the law, job loss and expulsion. Among young drinkers, only a fraction go on to become alcoholics. But 15 to 25 percent of adults who began consuming alcohol as teenagers acknowledge problems connected with its use. The financial cost to the economy of alcohol abuse is well over a hundred billion dollars.

RANDY

Randy was a good linebacker in high school in Charlotte. Because of his size—5'9" and 185 pounds—he decided to accept a scholarship to a small college in North Carolina rather than an ACC university.

The first three months were terrific. He made the varsity, giving him a feeling of belonging. He liked his courses in business administration. He was flattered to be rushed by several fraternities. Finally he settled on the "jock" fraternity known for its good athletes, heavy drinking, wild parties, and poor grades.

The frat's activities were all new and exciting to Randy. At home, raised by a divorced single-parent working mother, Randy never drank or used drugs. Several factors contributed to his abstinence: his father had been an alcoholic, which was the reason for his parents' divorce; he attended a Baptist church which frowned on any form of drug use; he played three sports, worked two jobs, and managed respectable grades; and none of his friends used alcohol.

Things changed quickly for Randy in college. He stopped going to church because none of his new friends bothered to attend. Because of his scholarship Randy didn't have to work during the school year so he had more time to socialize. It wasn't long before Randy was caught up in the after-the-game partying. Along with his teammates he believed he needed to relax after a tough football game by drinking. After all, they were keyed up and had to let off steam.

Alcohol loosened his inhibitions. With a few beers under his belt he felt more relaxed, liked being with his friends more, discovered that he had a sense of humor while he was high at fraternity parties, and was much more confident around young women.

Gradually Randy's alcohol consumption rose. To feel relaxed at a party after the season he needed three or four beers instead of the one or two that provided the desired effect earlier. He also began drinking a little more often; he and some of his friends regularly "started the weekend early" by partying Thursday night—as well as Friday, Saturday, and Sunday afternoons. Randy hardly ever had a hangover and always made it to his Friday and Monday morning classes. His grades were solid.

The only change that anyone noticed in Randy was that he often was aggressive while drinking. Randy and his friends crashed other fraternity parties regularly. Drunk and disorderly, they made themselves obnoxious

—eating their food, drinking their beer, hustling other boys' girlfriends, and threatening to "pound the wimps into the floor" if they objected.

One weekend in late February another student did object to Randy's rowdy behavior and a fight erupted. The campus police took Randy into custody for assault. The next day he appeared before the dean. Randy was contrite, apologetic. He said that he didn't mean to hurt the other student, but he was drunk at the time and things had gotten out of hand. The dean told Randy that violence, committed while drunk or sober, had no place at that college. Moreover, as an athlete trained to control his aggressive feelings, he had less excuse than did other students. Randy was to be suspended for the rest of the year but could apply to return in the fall. The dean strongly suggested to Randy that he involve himself in an alcohol counseling program. "Why do I need to do that?" Randy said. "I'm not an alcoholic!"

HOLLY

Holly grew up in a large old house in Los Angeles near the UCLA campus. A sixteen-year-old tenth grader, she was the youngest of three. Her father was a partner in a large public accounting firm. He compensated for being a workaholic by giving his family anything they wanted or needed. Her mother worked full time as a coordinator of volunteers at an LA hospital. Things were tense between her parents.

A good student and a talented artist, Holly thought that someday she might be a fashion designer, or maybe even an architect. Holly felt she was leading a "double life" with two distinctly different groups of friends. Some of the time she spent with the class "straight arrows" who did well in school, sports, and other activities, and who didn't use drugs. She also hung around with several older members of the school who were artistic, alienated, and poly-drug users. Holly tried alcohol and smoking a little marijuana with her older brother and sister in sixth grade. By middle school she and some of her friends were drinking and getting high at weekend parties. By ninth grade she had tripped with LSD on a half dozen occasions. In the tenth grade she experimented with barbiturates and snorted cocaine.

Holly believed that drugs stimulated her creativity and thus improved the quality of her painting. The art teacher recognized Holly as being both talented and productive and gave her As. The rest of her grades were a mix *of Cs and Bs—down from her As and Bs in middle school. Holly "explained" her mediocre showing in high school by saying that she was planning to become an artist and didn't need to make honor grades in her other subjects.*

In fact, the reason Holly wasn't doing better in school was because she was intoxicated a good deal of the time. She and her friends would often start the day with a beer or two in the parking lot and share a joint at lunch. She got high by herself at night. Weekends were party time and whatever was around she took. Gradually she stopped seeing her straight friends.

In the spring of her sophomore year Holly had trouble affording her drug habit. She partially supported her needs by working as a mother's helper and by dealing. It was the latter source of income that got her into trouble. Because of the death of a student by overdose, the high school cracked down. Several faculty members inspected the students' lockers while they were in class. They found an ounce of marijuana and a bottle of sedatives among Holly's possessions. When her parents were summoned to the school to be told of the discovery, they had different reactions: her father was shattered and wept; her mother said, "You had no right to break into my daughter's locker and I'm going to sue you!" Holly just felt numb.

Adolescents in the *green* zone can comfortably do without drugs and alcohol. The reasons may be their religious or moral convictions, because they don't care for the taste of alcohol or their reactions to drugs, or because they worry about health or fattening effects. Their abstinence may come from the desire to feel as fully and naturally themselves as possible, so they don't choose to ingest any substance that will alter this state of being. Nonuse may be temporary as with young people in training or while driving. Electing not to use drugs does not isolate normal adolescents. They may have friends who regularly get high and will attend parties at which both licit and illicit substances abound. For these teens being a teetotaler is not a heroic self-deprivation, but rather a belief that a full life doesn't require chemical assistance.

Many adolescents experiment with alcohol and other drugs the same way they try out other new experiences. They don't accept the statement that vodka is dangerous because their parents say so; they want to find out for themselves. These teenagers have to try marijuana—even though they've heard that it possibly is the gateway to heroin addiction—be-

TABLE 12.1
Estimating the Severity of Teenage Drug Use

GREEN ZONE—Normal Adaptation

- Comfortable doing without
- Experimentation
- Responsible use
- Infrequent abuse

YELLOW ZONE—Temporary Adjustment Reactions

- Volitional, frequent intoxication
- Use for closeness, release, relief, stimulation
- Negative personality/social effects
- Remorse
- No major trouble

ORANGE ZONE—Neurotic Symptoms

- Substance abuse
- Chronic pain and unhappiness
- Withdrawal from previous sources of pleasure
- Substance use necessary to function
- Temporary restriction of intake

RED ZONE—Severe Maladjustments

- Substance dependence
- Life organized around drugs
- Narrowed behavioral repertoire
- Danger to self, others

cause their friends seem to smoke it with no ill effects. For these young-sters substance consumption is transient and within the context of an otherwise normally functioning personality. Peer pressure can cause them to experiment but not to use alcohol or drugs regularly.

Many experts are highly skeptical of the idea that young people can use intoxicants responsibly. They point to the possible negative effects on attention and memory, psychological and social development, and the assumption of appropriate adult responsibilities. Others see alcohol or marijuana as transitional substances that lead to addiction to harder drugs.

Yet it is also true that the preponderance of teenagers consume these compounds without long-term adverse effects. Much has been said about the irresponsible alcohol and drug use among the young, but little has been written about the moderate consumption which characterizes the majority of adolescents. Though highly controversial, some characteris-tics of responsible use of alcohol and marijuana* include the following:

1. *Time, place, and mental set selective*
   Responsible alcohol and drug users plan when and where. They may drink or smoke at weekend parties with friends, but not usually while studying for exams or working. When drugs are consumed, the individual is in a positive frame of mind, not angry, frustrated, depressed, or anxious because of stressful life circumstances.

2. *With others*
   Virtually no normal adolescent regularly uses alcohol or marijuana alone. It is done with friends and family.

3. *Drug an adjunct*
   Normal young people take drugs to enhance the already positive feelings of being together—to be more comfort-able, relaxed, and open. They do not meet for the purpose of becoming intoxicated. Rather they may get high to in-crease their enjoyment of a walk in the woods, a rock con-cert, a home video movie, a meal, or making love—activi-ties they would engage in without chemicals.

4. *Intoxicant effect controlled and monitored*
   Moderate drug users try to regulate their intake to control the positive effects and minimize the negative ones. They

* Though moderate use of other drugs occurs, no reliable evidence exists describing it.

know their limits. Alcohol is sipped, not gulped, along with
food at the rate sufficient to produce a pleasant high but
not drunkenness. Marijuana is shared with others so that
the time between inhalations allows the individual to monitor his or her degree of intoxication.

Whether it be coffee or cigarettes, alcohol or marijuana, virtually no
one uses drugs without abusing them at one time or another. Teenagers
are no exception. The most temperate of them will have instances when
they become roaring drunk, get totally stoned, wind up feeling panicky
and paranoid instead of pleasantly high. Among normal youths these are
infrequent occasions—once or twice a year—and usually associated with
an exciting or stressful event such as a family wedding or breaking up
with a lover.

Volitional frequent intoxication—defined as becoming inebriated or
excessively high six or more times a year—is a hallmark of the *yellow*
zone. Among young people this condition occurs at weekend parties:
some of Randy's fraternity brothers got regularly plastered on Saturday
nights. Intoxication comes as a result of consciously exceeding their limits: a girl knew when she was overdoing a combination of liquor and
marijuana but continued because she sought the out-of-control sensation.

Everyone has a slightly different combination of symptoms associated
with intoxication. For alcohol these symptoms include one or more of
these physical signs: slurred speech, poor coordination, unsteady gait,
flushing, and rapid involuntary eyeball movement. In addition we may
note mood changes as in a person's greater loquacity, humor, or irritability. Other people become bitter, lacrymose, or affectionate. They may
have an extremely short attention span or be unable to shift their attention: they will listen to the same piece of music a dozen times or want to
tell the same story over and over—thoroughly boring their sober friends.
Teens who abuse marijuana report panic attacks and disturbing suspi-
ciousness. If they smoke at home they worry that their parents will
discover them. Occasional mild hallucinations accompany the suspicion.
When one young woman went to a rock concert, she could not shake the
belief that she had a fleck of marijuana on her lips which would reveal
her to the authorities.

A yellow flag is regular use of drugs to create the illusion of social
intimacy, to release suppressed emotions, to gain relief from stress, or to
attain a desirable mental state not characteristic of sobriety. For some,

beer drinking stimulates the feeling of friendliness. Some like Holly believe their perceptions are intensified which allows them to be more creative. Other youths will say that it's hard for them to feel relaxed without a joint, that a weekend backpacking trip without psychedelics isn't that much fun, getting wasted on Saturday nights is the best way to purge themselves of their accumulated week's tension, or that no natural state produces the euphoria they experience when they inhale cocaine.

Negative personality changes and/or social effects are yellow-zone indicators. Some teens exhibit a dramatic behavioral change when intoxicated, becoming belligerent, sexually aggressive, or boorish. These traits stand in sharp contrast to their sober demeanor—mild-mannered, shy, and sensitive. Friends give them a wide berth when they're inebriated. Eventually many of these teenagers wind up entangled with the law for driving under the influence, fighting, malicious destruction of property, or public drunkenness. People who experience these personality changes typically have a clouded memory of their actions afterward.

Remorse fills their souls the next day. Especially with alcohol abusers regret for having said this or done that is massive. They mount efforts to atone—for example, a young man might send flowers to a girl he insulted at a party and apologize to her boyfriend he nearly beat up when he intervened. The reparation can be subtle: after attending a history class while she was high which was taught by a woman she liked very much, Holly felt badly and was especially nice to the teacher for a week or so afterward. The teacher had no idea why Holly was being so pleasant.

Teenagers in the yellow zone generally escape major trouble. As a rule they limit their drug-using sprees to weekends, vacations, or recreational settings so their intoxication doesn't impair their performance academically, athletically, or occupationally. It is a matter of pride to them that they never miss a class or a day's work even if they overdo the night before. Like Randy, many experience no hangover symptoms. They maintain good health and have had no serious confrontations with the law except perhaps one instance of being arrested for driving under the influence or possession of marijuana. They may acknowledge, however, that they have been very "lucky."

Substance abuse is the primary feature of the *orange* zone of concern. Young people in this group use drugs regularly and, as a result, develop undesirable behavioral changes. No hard-and-fast signs unfailingly point to the teenage alcoholics or pot heads. They don't always have red noses, whiskey on the breath, or the morning shakes; neither are they reliably

runny-nosed, red-eyed, hallucinatory, agitated, or zonked out. Every substance abuser does it in his or her own way. It is the pattern of their drug
intake, and the pain it causes them as well as loved ones, that discriminate them from teens in the yellow zone.

Depending on the substance, the abuse can be seen in getting a buzz
on in the parking lot before school or during lunch, or in the need to
smoke dope at home to relax. Some of the adolescents in the orange zone
limit their abuse to frequent binges. Randy's abstinence during the week
and indulgences Thursday through Sunday exemplify this pattern. Other
teens go on sprees, in addition to regular use, unselectively consuming
whatever compound is available. When one of Holly's friends had hash-
ish she smoked that; when another scored a supply of cocaine she
snorted it; when someone got her hands on pills Holly took those. Whatever drugs they get a hold of they consume.

Substance abuse causes pain and unhappiness to the individual. Frequent episodes of intoxication result in underachievement in school and
on the job; the loss of good friends who tire of the teen's erratic, impulsive, and aggressive actions; physical harm from overdosing, falling down,
being beaten up, and irresponsible driving; legal problems because of
several episodes of driving while under the influence or being apprehended while being in possession of drugs or alcohol. The morning after
is rarely pleasant. There can be severe physical or psychological symptoms. Even though Randy never had a hangover, the blackouts during
several hours the evening before filled him with apprehension. He always
wondered what he might have done. Because adolescents are ashamed of
their actions, they will avoid discussion of how they behaved when they
were high to the point of becoming furious if someone tries to talk to
them about it.

Chronic substance abuse upsets others around the user, but they may
collude with the youngster to pretend that a problem doesn't exist. Holly's parents worried constantly about her when they discovered that she
was taking drugs. Yet they covered up for her, making excuses for her for
missing classes at school or telling relatives that her strange behavior on a
family reunion over the Fourth of July was because of the asthma medication she was taking.

Withdrawal from previous sources of pleasure is a neurotic symptom.
Examples of this withdrawal are quitting a job a teen likes because he's
too hung over to make it to work in the morning; avoiding good friends
because of the embarrassment associated with behavior while intoxi-

cated; giving up a sport or other activity in which the youngster previously excelled—Holly's interest in art dwindled as more and more of her time was devoted to getting high.

In spite of the downside effects of drug abuse, adolescents in the orange zone need it to function. Some require stimulants to study or to get "up" before a game, marijuana to settle down afterward, or psychedelics to free themselves. Unlike other teenagers in the green and yellow zones most of their drug intake is solitary. How much they take is often hidden from others. These youngsters will imbibe alone before a party so that others won't know they've had four beers before the drinking starts.

Young people in the orange zone need to know their favorite drugs are available to them. Alcohol, marijuana, or other substances become a budget item. Being without their means of euphoria for a short period because the sources are unavailable makes them distinctly uneasy. While they don't suffer withdrawal symptoms, the "quality" of their life definitely lacks something.

Temporary restriction of intake is an orange marker. By now these youngsters know that drugs are no longer their friend but their adversary. Following an overdose, accident, alienation from someone especially close, expulsion, or firing, many decide to go on the wagon. These abstinent periods last from a few days to several months before a relapse occurs. Other young people try to cut down: Holly limited her consumption to specific times of the week while Randy tried switching to light beer. It wasn't long before both realized that their total drug intake was unchanged.

Substance dependence marks entry into the *red* zone, which encompasses in more severe form the features of substance abuse along with increased tolerance and withdrawal symptoms. No longer is it possible for the teenagers in the red zone to pretend they function normally. Their drug use results in massive problems in nearly every sphere of life: Holly stopped going to school, could not hold down a job, became estranged from family and friends. She regularly endangered her health with multiple-substance abuse and by not eating properly. She engaged in criminal activities, buying drugs with money stolen from her parents. She began to sell marijuana and pills to finance her growing habit.

Tolerance and withdrawal symptoms characterize drug dependency. Increased amounts of the substance is required to achieve the desired high: by winter Randy found that he required a six-pack to get the same

feeling that two beers had produced in the fall. Withdrawal symptoms
vary with the person and the drug. People dependent on alcohol experience anxiety, irritability, sleeplessness, and clouded awareness as well as
nausea, shakiness, and occasionally hallucinations when they stop drinking. Other agents cause malaise, agitation, bizarre thoughts and feelings,
as well as numerous unpleasant physical sensations upon cessation. Re-
sumption of taking the drug causes these symptoms to vanish.

Teens in the red zone organize their time around obtaining and using
drugs. In contrast to those who take drugs in order to lead some semblance of a normal life, these adolescents live to take drugs. They know
they are hooked but feel both unwilling and unable to stop or reduce
their intake in spite of enormous problems resulting from it. As each day
dawns their first thought is to gain access to enough alcohol, marijuana,
pills, opiates, or whatever to give them peace. Large numbers of them
fall into a life of crime, prostitution, or drug dealing to support their
habits.

Substance dependence diminishes preexisting personality differences
and narrows the behavioral repertoire, making all compulsive drug users
seem much the same. For instance their ways of coping with anxiety are
predictable: they deny how often they are out of control, the adverse
effects of intoxication on their health and the rest of their life, and their
dependency; they "forget" aberrant behavior and bad experiences with
chemicals; they rationalize their continuing misuse, saying they are under too much stress or their friends made them get high; and they have
suspicions that others are always watching them critically which border
on the paranoid. They smell of depression.

Research findings on alcoholics tell a similar story. It was once held
that some youngsters were vulnerable to being dependent because of
predisposing "alcoholic" personality traits. They were thought to possess
an oral fixation, to be dependent, and lack both confidence and willpower. According to this theory, alcoholics' underlying psychopathology
set them up to be unable to deal with the normal frustrations of living
without turning to the bottle. In fact, studies of people before they
become alcoholics suggest the opposite hypothesis, namely, that these
behaviors occur as a *result*, not as the cause, of this continuing substance
abuse. The greater the dependence the more similarly maladjusted these
individuals appear.

Substance-abusing and dependent teenagers menace themselves and
others. Continuous overuse has serious long-term physical consequences.

Depending on the substance, the re... can be damage to the liver, pancreas, and kidneys, increased susceptibi... to infection, cardiac problems, malnutrition, and brain impairment. ... there are unsavory short-term consequences: overdosing, being pois... the ingredients used to cut street drugs, damaging nasal passages by ... the larynx and paralyzing the respiratory system with sp... freezing or contracting hepatitis from dirty needles. Far more leth... inhalants, cents, however, are drug-related accidents, suicides, and ho... adolesMore than half of teenage auto accidents involve alcohol. Many young people who attempt suicide do so while under the influence. Individuals who depend upon drugs are dangerous to be around. They think nothing of stealing the possessions of others to support their habits. While they are high they can be unpredictably violent and can physically abuse loved ones. On occasion their violence results in unintended death.

Follow-up

RANDY

When he returned home, Randy was relieved to find his mother was more worried about him than angry at his being suspended. He told his mother that he had learned his lesson and would never drink to excess again. He didn't see the need for an alcohol-counseling program.

Randy started working construction. It was hard, sweaty labor. Some of the other men drank quite a lot. One fellow's usual lunch was a six-pack. Another nipped rum steadily. After work they gathered for the happy hour at a local hard-hat bar before going home. It wasn't long before Randy joined his co-workers for a draft or two. Gradually this became six or eight beers most nights.

One Thursday evening Randy came home a little under the weather. His mother took a look at him and sobbed. "Oh God, it's starting all over again!" When Randy asked her what she meant, his mother said that she was too upset about it to talk then and he was probably too drunk to understand. They would discuss it the next day.

The next day they both took the day off from work and talked. What had upset Randy's mother the most was that she thought she saw the family alcoholism being passed to the next generation. Not only had

Randy's father been a dr~~ ~~out her own father and sister had drinking
problems. This revelat~~ ~~shook Randy to his toes because he never imagined he could be~~ ~~an alcoholic. He realized how painful this thought
was to both h~~ ~~elf and his mother. It also shook Randy that he was
abusing al~~ ~~again when he had vowed to give it up. Then he knew he
had t~~ ~~p.

~~ ~~dy thought about calling a teenage alcohol-counseling program in
Charlotte. Once he even punched out the number but hung up as soon as
someone answered. The fact was he was ashamed to go. He couldn't
believe that he had fallen into the same drinking pattern that he so
loathed in his father. Still troubled, he went to the library and read everything he could find on alcohol. One statement particularly struck him—if
a parent or close relative was an alcoholic, the child had a five-to-six-times
greater risk of abusing that substance. "If I had only known that," Randy
thought to himself, "I'd have never touched the stuff."

The other related events came together to help Randy abstain. The first
was returning to weekly church attendance. Even though the news of his
problems in college had followed him home, Randy felt acceptance, forgiveness, and support from members of the congregation. It was in church
that he met some other football players from a local college who invited
him to join the Fellowship of Christian Athletes. He liked the young men
and women in this group. They had a great time being together, playing
sports, doing service work in the community, and talking to others about
their beliefs. At one of their regulation weekly meetings, another athlete
talked about his drinking problem. Though Randy said nothing, that
young man's testimonial strengthened his own resolve.

When he returned to college Randy returned to football but dropped
out of the fraternity. "That's just not my scene," he told a friend. He
didn't believe he needed weekend parties to have a good time in college.
But also, down deep, he was terrified that he might start drinking again.
He was sure he was one beer away from being an alcoholic.

HOLLY

Even though he knew that Holly had a drug problem from the evidence
in hand as well as the school grapevine, the principal didn't take his
findings to the police. He didn't want the hassle of a lawsuit and Holly's
mother looked like the sort who would press it. He did warn Holly against

further use of illegal substances and recommended that Holly "see some-one" about her problem.

When they arrived home, her mother lectured Holly about the evils of drugs and said she would tolerate no more of it. They took her to see a psychiatrist specializing in work with adolescents. The doctor was con-cerned about Holly's mental state—the obvious nervousness and depres-sive feelings as well as a sinking academic record. Therapy was recom-mended again but the parents rejected it for the moment because things were better for a while. Holly had no trouble that spring. Her grades picked up a little and she won an award for a painting she created. Privately her father and mother were holding their breaths.

They didn't have long to wait. At a graduation party for several older friends Holly became intoxicated from a mixture of alcohol and mari-juana. As she was driving home, Holly was stopped by the police. By talking to her and giving her several brief behavioral tests—walking a straight line, touching her nose with her finger with her eyes closed, and standing on one leg while counting to thirty—the officer believed that Holly was high. Knowing what the results would show, Holly refused to take a breath, blood, or urine test, though refusal meant automatic suspen-sion of her driver's license for six months. The police took her into protec-tive custody and called her house.

Holly's parents were furious. They grounded her for the rest of the summer and required her to work as a hospital volunteer, and to see the psychiatrist. Unfortunately the job required the use of a car so someone had to drive her each way. Since both parents were busy, it wasn't long before Holly was driving herself, sans license. She stopped seeing the therapist. They knew she was driving and using drugs but felt powerless to stop her.

In the fall of Holly's junior year a rash of burglaries occurred in their affluent suburb. Just before Thanksgiving, Holly was apprehended while serving as a lookout for a group of teenagers who were breaking into a neighbor's house. When her parents confronted Holly in jail, she admit-ted that she and her friends had been breaking and entering for the last three months to steal things in order to have the money to support their drug habits.

Holly was convicted and put on parole for two years. This event finally focused her parents' attention on the seriousness of the problem. At the suggestion of the psychiatrist they sent Holly to a program in Florida for youngsters with drug-related problems. When she arrived Holly told the *director that she didn't want to be there. The director replied, "On the contrary, you've been abusing drugs for the last several years. You must want rehabilitation unless you want to die." The treatment program lasted for eight months. The 120-odd young people began each day with a song and ended it with two hours of vigorous exercise and discussion of their progress. In between they talked about their shared experiences with drug abuse and their motivation for getting high. Their counselors were ex-drug abusers who had graduated from the program. There was little opportunity for deceit. Confrontations were painful but the group support was very warming.*

During this period Holly lived with a foster family who had a child further along in the program. After she "graduated" Holly was asked to stay on as a counselor for another six months. As she helped others she helped herself. During this period she completed sufficient course work to obtain a high school diploma through the local school system.

When Holly left the program she entered UCLA and planned to major in architecture. She elected to live on her own rather than at the college or with her parents. When her friends offered her drugs she would say, "No thanks, they don't work for me."

What Parents Can Do: Guidelines for Helping

The consequences of drug misuse are the greatest hazard facing today's teenagers. Unhappily parents can't count on much help from the schools or the community. On the whole educational efforts to encourage acceptable attitudes to alcohol or to teach responsible drinking habits have not achieved their goals. The success of programs designed to discourage consumption of illicit substances by exaggerating their negative effects has been dubious.

The problem of drug abuse lies squarely in the parents' laps. It is not an easy problem to deal with. Both prevention and intervention in cases of suspected drug-related trouble require a great deal of hard work. Nevertheless, there are several guidelines that can help you help your teenagers to maintain a comfortable abstinence or develop a responsible pattern of substance use.

BE AWARE OF PREDISPOSING FACTORS

Recognize that genetic, family, personality, and peer factors play a significant role in who uses and abuses drugs. There is absolutely no question that a strong hereditary predisposition to alcoholism exists. Moreover, this genetic tendency is stronger than environmental influences. Youths with an alcoholic parent but living in an otherwise stable family may be as much as five times more likely to become problem drinkers as boys and girls from multiproblem families without an alcoholic mother or father.

Family and peers play a role—albeit a smaller one—in adolescent drug use. When parents drink, smoke marijuana, and/or ingest barbiturates or stimulants, a strong likelihood exists that their progeny will follow suit. Older brothers and sisters have almost the same effect. Heavy parental drug consumption predicts higher-level use in their children. We know that peers influence drug experimentation. If your daughter's friends are trying alcohol or marijuana, or sniffing glue, she is probably not far behind.

If you know that your youngster is vulnerable to drug abuse, you can take preventive measures to lower the probability of serious trouble. Communicate information about genetic predisposition to the next generation. If he had known his chances of becoming an alcoholic were 500 percent greater than those of most of his fraternity brothers, would Randy have started drinking? Talk openly about the ambivalence most adults have about the licit and illicit substances they put in their bodies, so that your offspring know the harm caused as well as the benefits. Don't be afraid to say what you think. If you believe that your son shouldn't drink until he graduates from high school, say so—even if he labels you as a refugee from the WCTU. If you think alcohol is okay, say it. But be intolerant of intoxication. Impress upon the teens that drunkenness is neither amusing nor evidence of maturity.

Expect responsible behavior from your teenager. Traditional households—where children have regular chores to do, where doing reasonably well in school is expected, where money is earned and not given, and where teens usually abide by agreed-upon rules for honesty about where they are going on a Saturday night, car use, and curfews—produce adolescents with lower levels of alcohol and drug abuse. Say no to their spending time with friends you don't approve of, or have those friends come to your house. Refuse to give permission for them to attend a rock concert if you know there will be a lot of marijuana around. Be open to discussion about why and consider alternatives. Regulations without affection, however, don't work. For a traditional family to be effective there has to be a good deal of parent-child contact and warmth between the generations.

Try to channel personality traits associated with higher substance use levels into more constructive experiences. The girl who is drawn to getting high to be deviant can be encouraged to try other outlets, for example, the arts or stimulating and challenging activities. The boy who needs beer to be friendly can find an alternative in religious youth groups, outdoor survival programs, or social skills training. Those adolescents who seek to magnify sensory experiences through drugs may try instead yoga, rafting the Snake River, or perhaps a youth tour of New Guinea.

BEGIN DRUG EDUCATION AT HOME

In an ideal world we could prevent our teens from using drugs. Since that is not possible, we must face the reality that drug education begins at home. As in other matters, children are greatly influenced by the deeds and words of their family members. If parents drink they have an opportunity to model appropriate alcohol consumption. For example, children raised in families with a Mediterranean heritage—Italian, Portuguese, Spanish, or Greek—are taught to consume low-proof wine with their meals, and with the family. Drunkenness is condemned. By contrast boys and girls raised in families that vigorously oppose their drinking but tolerate, and perhaps even covertly praise, adults who get roaring drunk are much more likely to have problems with alcohol later on. Parents can show their youngsters how to drink carefully at home under supervision—the way they teach other crucial life cycle tasks. This is a far better introduction to alcohol than gulping gin at an eighth grade party or a chug-a-lugging party freshman year.

It's harder for adults to talk to teenagers about the consumption of illicit drugs such as marijuana or cocaine. Though some youths appear to use them in a controlled manner, much less is known about this subject. In addition to the general principles of responsible substance use, teenagers benefit from information about the harmful consequences of using drugs of unknown ingredients, about lethal combinations such as alcohol and barbiturates, about the unexpected effects of various dosage levels in different settings, about the hazards of drugs with a strong potential for dependence, and about the legal consequences of being caught using them.

Most mothers and fathers don't have this information at their finger-tips. Discovery of what is known, unknown, and subject to speculation can be an interesting and informative shared experience. Facts are avail-able in libraries, at nearby drug-counseling programs, and government-supported institutions such as the National Clearinghouse for Drug Abuse Information (Box 1701, Washington, D.C. 20013).

WATCH OUT FOR YOUR OWN REACTIONS

One of the largest obstacles blocking the ability of parents to talk honestly to their children about responsible drug use are the emotions the subject arouses. Many of the older set have had no formal education on the subject other than media scare tactics. As a result some mothers and fathers overreact, considering experiments with alcohol or marijuana as a road to certain heroin addiction, thereby cutting off communication with their progeny. Others underreact to clear teenage drug misuse be-cause the image they have of someone in trouble is the dope addict or skid row alcoholic. And some parents, such as Holly's mother, deny that a problem exists, pretending it is a minor indiscretion rather than real trouble. Beware of overreacting and labeling these youngsters as drug addicts who are just experimenting. Not only does doing this overstate the role of alcohol, marijuana, or other substances in their lives, but it also undermines your credibility as an understanding parent. Occasion-ally an overreaction sparks a rebellious explosion of drug use in a young-ster who was about to give it up.

Underreaction or denial can lead to serious consequences too. It re-sults in ignoring the message contained in your adolescent's discussion of a friend's drinking. Anytime your youngsters tell you of a friend who's doing drugs, pay attention. Nine times out of ten they are getting ready to try themselves. This is the time to start the discussion. Be slow to rescue a teen from the penalties associated with alcohol or drug misuse. An evening in the drunk tank or having to pay the lawyer's fees for possession of marijuana can be a far more effective object lesson than a lecture or being grounded for a month.

SEEK HELP FOR CONTINUING SUBSTANCE MISUSE

The vast majority of teenagers learn from experimentation and experience how to abstain or use these substances responsibly. If your youngster doesn't learn from experience, or is exhibiting orange- or red-zone characteristics, seek professional help. Physical health takes first priority. With substance-abusing teens who seem all right it is helpful to have a medical checkup to be certain that no physical or mental impairment has been a dividend of the chemicals they've put in their bodies. In cases of overdose, take them to the general hospital emergency room—remembering to collect drug samples or pill bottles that may give a clue what substances they've ingested. Most larger hospitals have detoxification units for heavy alcohol and drug misusers. Typically the youths will remain as inpatients for a week to a month in order to clear their systems of intoxicants.

When the doctors give an adolescent a clean bill of health, the next question facing the parents is whether to hope that the young person has learned his or her lesson or should participate in a drug treatment program. Spontaneous recovery does occur in human beings of all ages for a variety of reasons: having "hit bottom," the recognition of having a lot to lose, the concern of keeping a relationship, or finding a nonchemical alternative. If the teen avers that he or she has seen the light and forswears the drug use, it may be reasonable to give him or her a short trial period—perhaps assisted by changing schools and suggesting activities that may offer both alternatives to getting high with the old peer group.

Should the youngster get intoxicated again anytime in the next calendar year, place that adolescent in a drug treatment program. Plan on resistance. Few teens believe they need help and will not seek it on their own. For alcohol-abusing adolescents, teenage versions of Alcoholics Anonymous is the most successful of the outpatient approaches. Nearly every community has a chapter with regular meetings. More comprehensive programs, many of them based on Alcoholics Anonymous, exist for drug-abusing young people. Examples are the LIFE and STRAIGHT programs in Florida, POSSIBILITIES UNLIMITED in Lexington, Kentucky, and KIDS HELPING KIDS in Cincinnati. Though these approaches differ slightly among themselves, they have common elements: (1) a philosophy condensed to the seven steps shown in Table 12.2 following Alcoholics Anonymous; (2) six to nine months of a daily program; (3) placement with a foster family with a youngster further along in the treatment program; (4) group sessions emphasizing cognitive and behavioral control of the desire to use drugs which include problem solving—ways to say no—and rules to live by; (5) parent groups to help children recognize their feelings about drug use and to support their children in abstinence; (6) exercise and time for emotional release; and (7) positive thinking about progress being made.

TABLE 12.2
The Seven Steps

1. Admit that I'm powerless over drugs and have come to believe in a power greater than myself that can restore me to sanity.

2. Make a decision to turn my will and my life over to the care of God as I understand him.

3. Make a searching and fearless moral inventory of myself daily.

4. Admit to God, myself, and another human being the exact nature of my wrongs immediately.

5. Make direct amends to such persons whenever possible except when to do so would injure myself or others.

6. Seek through prayer and meditation to improve my conscious contact with God as I understand him, praying only for knowledge of his will for me and the power to carry it out.

7. Having received the gift of awareness, I will practice these principles in all of my daily affairs and carry the message to all I can help.

Long-term follow-up studies of individuals involved in the treatment programs such as these have been fragmentary. What has been done suggests these approaches are much superior to other means so far created to treat drug-abusing and dependent youth.

Prevention is still the best way to combat drug misuse. After the 1964 Surgeon General's report made clear the hazards of tobacco, over thirty million smokers have stopped. In the last decade the percentage of high school seniors using tobacco daily has fallen dramatically. The number of college students who now smoke is now estimated to be half of what it was at the time of the Surgeon General's report. This reduction is a direct result of a comprehensive media campaign and educational effort to discourage smoking, the decision of many newspapers and magazines not to accept cigarette advertising, and the efforts of citizen groups to restrict smoking in public places.

Alcohol and drug use can be reduced among our young in the same way if the will and resources are available. We can see evidence of a growing momentum to combat substance use. Here and there church and community groups are organizing to develop nonalcohol and non-drug recreational alternatives for teens. Parents are getting together to influence scattered school systems to build in alcohol- and drug-education programs as well as encouraging a firmer stand against their use. Young people are establishing chapters of Students Against Driving Drunk (SADD) in their high schools. On a broader scale we have the power to lobby with legislators for expanded government-sponsored commercials opposing alcohol and drug use—which now are very nearly drowned out in the Niagara of beer ads.

Unlike swallowing goldfish, drug use is not a passing fad. Our challenge is to educate our teenagers to live knowledgeably and responsibly with this reality.

13

"Who Am I? I Used to Know."
Identity Questions

Adolescence is a period of possibilities and choices. In their teens young people glimpse for the first time the spectrum of values, opportunities, and pathways available to them. They also must select from this array those that seem most compatible with their growing sense of identity. Our identity is a feeling of knowing who we are, what we can do, and where we are headed. The sense of self is not something we "discover" as teenagers. It is an evolutionary process, growing out of the early modeling of parental attitudes and habits, and continuing by means of childhood identifications with significant adults. Our identity continues to develop until close to the end of our lives.

It was once believed that the road to finding ourselves in adolescence is pitted with conflict, regression, and turmoil. More recent research evidence, however, suggests that most teenagers do not go through periods of instability. Rather, the vast majority of high school and college youths enjoy good relationships with family and friends, cope effectively with stress and think well of themselves, and do not experience intense conflict or anxiety. Moreover, identity crises are not a special province of adolescence. They can recur unpredictably throughout the life cycle.

At any given moment, however, a minority of young people do exhibit the confusion, agitation, and distress characteristic of an identity crisis. These tumultuous periods may come on suddenly or emerge gradually.

They range from brief flurries of instability to prolonged periods of doubt, unhappiness, escalating hostilities toward loved ones, relentless self-preoccupation, and a feeling of fragmentation.

JD

Until his junior year things had gone well for JD. An only child, and the only grandson on either side of the family, he received abundant love and attention. His father was a commodities broker in a firm founded by his maternal grandfather. Though he traveled a lot, he and JD were close. JD also loved to fish and hunt with his grandfather for whom he was named.

JD and his parents lived in a nice area just outside of New Orleans. He had attended the same Episcopal day school since kindergarten. In elementary school his grades were high. In fact one of the teachers at a parents' conference was heard to say, "That child is Princeton material." The thought that JD was Ivy League quality caused his father—a college dropout—to feel proud of his son. In the tenth grade JD's report card showed As and Bs. This record was achieved through his hard work and persistence as well as his accommodating nature which occasionally caused faculty to give him the benefit of the doubt academically. Not much of an athlete, JD held a leadership position in a student service club. He was an Eagle Scout.

Disaster struck when the results from the PSATs arrived in the December of JD's junior year. Expecting a total score of between 1200–1300, everyone was surprised by the outcome: Verbal 430, Math 540, Total 970.* JD was devastated. He knew his parents had always planned on his going to a top college, but these numbers were way too low.

His father's reaction was to believe that JD wasn't working hard enough and, uncharacteristically, began nagging him to study more. His mother enrolled him in a tutorial program for the SATs in April. Though JD felt he was doing his best, the winter term grades were slightly lower than those in the tenth grade.

In the spring everything unraveled. JD and his father were barely speaking to each other after a nasty confrontation: his father pointed to JD's sinking effort grades on his report card and said he was getting lazy; furious and frustrated, JD talked back to his father for the first time when

---

* Unlike SATs, PSAT scores omit the final zero, so the results would have read 43 and 54.

*he yelled, "I'm tired of always trying to please you." Then his SATs scores
arrived, and to everyone's dismay they had declined twenty points. The
crowning blow was a meeting with the college adviser. The recommended
list of schools was modest and included no Ivy League schools.*

*While his mother and JD sat numbly, his father ripped into the college
adviser, questioning her qualifications and saying he would speak to the
headmaster. JD's father did talk to him and he confirmed the college
adviser's recommendations. Then JD's father said that he was getting a
pretty poor return on his investment if after twelve years all JD could get
into were a state university and a bunch of colleges no one had ever heard
of. The headmaster replied that if the father felt that way maybe he should
take JD out of the school.*

RACHEL

*Rachel made the decision to leave college the day she returned to
Syracuse for her junior year. But it took her until the end of September to
call her parents with the news. As Rachel anticipated, they were opposed
to the idea. "If you drop out you'll lose all your motivation and will never
go back to college," her mother said after she recovered from her shock.
Her father argued that she would never be able to get a decent job without
a bachelor's degree: "You know, Rachel, the world is not waiting for
another high school graduate."*

*Rachel had been a strong student in high school in Great Neck, Long
Island. She excelled in English, edited the school literary magazine, and
was the high school stringer for the local weekly. Rachel dreamed of being
a newspaper book reviewer someday, or maybe even a writer if she were
talented enough. In addition to being good at English, Rachel played
varsity soccer. Summers were spent at a camp in Maine, first as a camper
and then later as a counselor.*

*Rachel's family was close. Her father ran a printing business in a
nearby town, while her mother worked occasionally for the company and
did volunteer work. A brother three years older was at the Wharton
School. Everyone at home agreed that Rachel was terrific, had a lot of
talent, and would be successful at anything she chose.*

*At Syracuse, Rachel chose to be an English major. She decided not to
try out for soccer or any other activities so she would have more time for
her academic work. Also the competition was tough, "You either have to*

be incredibly talented or a fanatic to do anything around here" is how she explained to her parents why she wasn't going to be involved her freshman year.

Quickly she learned that studying English in college was considerably less enjoyable than before. In high school her teachers encouraged her to think out loud and use her sense of humor; her college professors preferred the sound of their own voices and found nothing amusing in the study of English literature. Rachel also rapidly realized being the best writer in her twelfth grade class didn't guarantee she would be among the one hundredth of 1 percent who can make a living by writing.

Sophomore year she switched to sociology. In addition she was resolved to meet more people. Unfortunately she lived in a high rise which made that task difficult. "It is like living in a New York City apartment building," Rachel explained to her mother. "No one ever talks to anyone." Her roommates were not terrific either: one was a nice, shy premed; another spent all of her time partying; and the third lived mostly with her boyfriend at his dormitory.

Rachel began to be confused about her values and beliefs, about what she was going to do after college, and about herself. At one point she said to one of her friends, "I can't seem to take a stand on anything anymore. I can see all sides of the argument so I wind up believing everything and nothing." There were weeks when she studied vigorously alongside her premed roommate. These alternated with periods when she accompanied the partying roommate on nonstop binges. A brief affair with a fellow in the high rise came to nothing.

When she paged through the course catalogue the first week of her junior year, Rachel couldn't decide what to take. There were so many fascinating possibilities and she could take only four. Not being able to choose, Rachel audited a half dozen courses, hoping to find some that interested her. When the date came to submit her study card and she couldn't pick any, Rachel decided it was time to leave.

In the *green* zone teenagers exhibit growing autonomy from their mothers and fathers. Increasingly they feel they have both the right of and the power for self-governance and they act accordingly. They believe it is legitimate for them to hold opinions that diverge from their parents' and don't mind enlightening the senior set. Their clothes, musical tastes, and reading preferences underline their separateness.

Among normal youths, autonomy is not a high ground to be seized to

TABLE 13.1
Estimating the Severity of Identity Questions

GREEN ZONE—Normal Adaptation

- Growing autonomy
- Unconflicted identity seeking
- Awareness of the not-me

YELLOW ZONE—Temporary Adjustment Reactions

- Normative identity crisis
- De-illusionment
- Sensation of being cut off from the past
- Abundant energy
- Urgency to decide

ORANGE ZONE—Neurotic Symptoms

- Continuing, severe, paralyzing identity confusion
- Oppositional attachment
- Despair over lost promise
- Alienation

RED ZONE—Severe Maladjustments

- Borderline personality organization
- Splitting and projective identification
- Intolerance of being alone
- Feelings of emptiness

win a battle. It develops gradually out of the parent-child relationship, out of the sensitivity to the feelings and needs each generation has for the other. Parents assist the process of autonomy in three ways: (1) by recognizing the teen as a separate person whose independent thoughts and behavior are pleasing rather than threatening; (2) by giving advice but not overcontrolling unless a youngster is in danger; and (3) by relating to the teenager in a more adult manner which recognizes the teen's emerging self-definition.

It is this burgeoning sense of psychological autonomy that sets the stage for another feature of normal teenagers—seeking a workable, cohesive identity. Specifically this process entails teenagers becoming comfortable with the many aspects of their self-image: the experience of their bodies, gender, and sexual roles; race, ethnic, geographical, and social class origins; religious, ethical, and moral values; relationships with others and how these significant individuals perceive them; and occupational plans.

The consolidation of identity among normal youths is not an untroubled pursuit of values and goals that seem worthwhile, nor is it a seamless integration of new self-perceptions and the renouncing of old ones. One or more aspects of a youngster's emerging experience of the self may cause periods of doubt. The upwardly mobile girl with her sights on law school has moments when she questions whether the goal is worth moving away from a comfortable community and friends she can count on. The boy who gives up his Catholicism in college because it's incompatible with his growing intellectual convictions periodically feels a void that his reason does not satisfy.

A green-zone indicator is expanding awareness of the not-me. Knowing who we are is to a large extent based on knowing who we are not. In order to be a conservative an adolescent must be willing to reject being a liberal. A teen majoring in science has to realize this means saying no to the potential satisfactions of the humanities. Another decides she can't worry about everything and comes to the conclusion she has to forget about the plight of the whales to work for a nuclear freeze. As a sculpture is created by chipping away pieces of marble that are not a part of the design, so, too, is an identity largely revealed by giving up some ideals and satisfactions in order to focus energies on other issues more central to the emerging sense of self.

The most dramatic feature of the *yellow* zone is a normative identity crisis. Such a crisis appears in reaction to an environmental stress or without obvious cause. Lasting three to twelve months, it interrupts plateaus of adolescent tranquility with confusion and turmoil. Certainties fade about who they are or what they believe in. One young woman described the sensation as "losing my labels." Teens find it impossible to choose among mutually exclusive values and loyalties. They can argue for or refute any position: like Rachel, they don't know what they stand for anymore. Relationships that a few weeks ago were mutually satisfying become strained because the adolescents are withdrawn, irritable, inconsistent, and preoccupied. We can't understand what has come over them and they can't explain it. Anyone can see that they are nervous, moody, and don't sleep well.

De-illusionment is a yellow-zone flag. Illusions in childhood and adolescence enable us to imagine that we may be able to do something worthwhile or significant with our life, for example, be a professional baseball player, actress, or millionaire. As we grow older, reality scales down these fantasies: we aspire to attend college, have a successful marriage, or choose an occupation that pays a living wage.

De-illusionment occurs when these dreams are radically reduced or laid to waste. A boy might find that college brings none of the joy he anticipated but merely is a continuation of the same academic drudgery in another setting. Or a young woman with a Phi Beta Kappa key in her pocket may find that this honor which she had worked for much of her life doesn't help her get a job unless she can type. The process of de-illusionment triggers intense and diverse emotions from disappointment, bitterness, and grief to relief, wonder, and freedom to form new dreams.

The feeling of being cut off from the past is strong. As one college student put it in the November of his freshman year, "Last spring seems like the Dark Ages." In part this feeling emerges because the dreams guiding adolescents earlier, external beacons marking a pathway to follow, have shut down one after the other, so these young people lose track of where they have been as well as where they are headed. When JD's scores were too low for him to be accepted at colleges he always thought he was going to attend, his whole life plan fell apart. New realities make it difficult to gain pleasure in the same way as before. In college Rachel found that her primary sources of satisfaction—her writing, friends, and sports—were not available to her.

Abundant energy fuels the struggle of youths to discover what is solid within them, what values still work, and re-form a more realistic dream in the light of the changes brought by the identity crisis. Though they may be in considerable emotional pain, they are likely to engage in robust nonstop anguishing about their plight, wearing out family and friends. Some need to be constantly on the move. So long as they are in motion, or planning it, emotional distress is reduced. But it returns as soon as they stop.

The origin of the word "crisis" is the Greek term meaning "to decide." Many people in the yellow zone feel an urgent need to make a decision to end their turmoil. Unfortunately these decisions are unstable because they tend to be made quickly and without careful reasoning. As a result a plan can't resist for very long a competing idea. In her sophomore year Rachel hatched a new program every month to straighten herself out, only to abandon it within two weeks.

Teenagers in the yellow zone communicate to others their urgency to do something to others close to them. They cause friends, family, teachers, and advisers to believe something has to be done *right now* and stimulate them to give advice—much of it unrealistic and conflicting.

Continuing, severe, paralyzing identity confusion characterizes the *orange* zone. Uncertainties and conflicts about the self in adolescence can cause intense emotional distress for the better part of a year. Periods of numbness alternate with depression, anxiety, and anger. "I feel nothing at all and have lost my ability to care what happens to me," a nineteen year old says the afternoon before he is torn awake at night by terrifying fears that he'll never amount to anything.

The identity confusion erodes the most cherished aspects of self-definition: not only was Rachel's vision of herself as a writer blurred in college, but also she began to worry about her capacity to care for others as well as her basic morality. Doubt infiltrates previously secure facets of identity unrelated to the central conflicts. An example is the talented boy with a heterosexual orientation grappling with the question of whether he should become a dancer which would mean giving up the pleasures of college life. As his uncertainty grows he starts to wonder whether his mixed feelings about this vocation are caused by an underlying attraction to men—a totally irrelevant issue for him.

Continuing identity confusion blocks significant satisfaction from the working and loving domains. Students find it impossible to get out of bed, make it to a class on time, or be on time for appointments. Reading an assignment takes forever. JD found himself procrastinating endlessly and his mind wandering all over the place when he tried to study assigned homework—though ironically he had no trouble reading the unassigned chapters or concentrating for hours on an outdoor magazine. These youngsters lose their competitive instinct. Increasingly JD didn't care whether he got a D+ or a C+ rather than a C— or B—, or what his rank in class was.

Relationships with significant others bring largely pain or no satisfaction: Rachel's contacts with her parents were increasingly acrimonious as none of them could understand what was happening to her. She threw herself into a series of affairs but then halted abruptly because they just didn't seem worth it.

Oppositional attachment to parents is a neurotic symptom. Instead of the growing autonomy characteristic of normal maturation, teenagers in this state have enormous difficulty separating themselves from their mothers and fathers. Simultaneously they seem to be holding on and pushing away with all their might. The result is an intrapsychic stalemate in which they damn their parents for overcontrolling their lives but can't disengage from their families to find their own way. Instead they remain locked in a regressive, alien dependency.

In an effort to establish their independence these youngsters act out in opposition to parental values. Their polarization usually includes a divergent choice of dress, friends, language, and values. But it goes much further, expressing itself in self-defeating school failure, delinquency, promiscuity, substance abuse, and car accidents. Periodically these adolescents leave home in an effort to establish themselves, but they return —usually at parental expense—when their money runs out or they can't get along with their traveling companions. They arrive at the doorstep exhausted and meanspirited, angry at themselves and their family for their failure to break away.

Despair over lost promise is widespread. Orange-zone youths believe they have lost their single chance for the greatness and joy they once felt destined to achieve. They dwell on having let opportunities dribble through their fingers, about the teacher who gave them the C+ in a science course which they know will keep them out of medical school, or about random acts of God shattering their dreams. What these melancholy ruminations have in common is the belief that these events are irreversible and will lead to a bleak and cheerless future. Any effort to wring happiness from it is futile.

In this frame of mind these teens will say, "What's the use?" or "Why go on?" or "There's nothing for me anymore." Efforts on our part to reassure them that everyone's life span contains lots of chances, that future accomplishments can compensate for past poor showings, or that their despair may have a large element of rationalization in it will be received with a wry smile that tells us we don't understand how totally hopeless their situation is. These young people contemplate and talk of ending their lives. More than one adolescent has reported that only the thought that they could bring life to an end allowed them to tolerate the psychic pain their inner turmoil produces.

A "solution" to having lost the promise of youth is alienation. Instead of believing that their unhappiness, inner chaos, and inability to get what they want out of life is their personal problem, these adolescents see their state as typical of the human condition. They insist that anyone who looks at the world with a clear eye knows that pain and misery outweigh pleasure and delight; that everyone is propelled by base urges which disrupt any cohesive sense of self; and that any honest individual knows that unpredictable events will surely prevent us from realizing our cherished dreams, and even if we are successful it's all illusion. Diffuse anger spills out at the world, causing them profound misery, as does contempt for those who believe the values of the society in which they live are good, worthwhile, and should be preserved. In contrast to youthful revolutionaries who rebel in the name of a higher value—sexual equality, civil rights, salvaging the environment—these alienated young people do not. They know what they are against but have no alternative program in mind.

Teenagers in the *red* zone show many qualities of less severe states: chronic and free-floating anxiety; uncertainty about identity; sudden, unpredictable, overpowering depression or anger, lasting a few hours to a few days; and episodic alcohol and drug abuse as well as antisocial behavior.

This continuing identity confusion can deteriorate into a borderline personality organization. In this mental condition adolescents frequently exhibit micropsychotic episodes. These are transient periods of sudden personality deterioration and loss of reality testing followed by an equally rapid return to normal. The variations can occur in the same afternoon. For example, after her boyfriend says he wants to break up with her at noontime, a sixteen-year-old girl has a screaming fit. She runs out of school saying she has nothing to live for. At 2 P.M. her mother has to restrain her from taking a kitchen knife to her wrists. An hour later her father makes an appointment for her to see a psychiatrist for an emergency visit. At 5 P.M. she appears in her waitress uniform ready for work as though nothing had happened. Not infrequently teens in the red zone make high marks in school or hold down responsible jobs through all of this emotional instability.

Low-level self-protective responses are much in evidence too. For example, the girl on the way to work in the example just given is likely to deny to her parents that she feels depressed—though she grudgingly acknowledges that she was on the verge of suicide two hours before. Because of their denial these individuals can't feel their depression anymore.

Young people with a borderline personality organization also may exhibit what has been called splitting and projective identification. Splitting is black-and-white thinking. Specific people, values, ideas, or goals are all good or all bad. One of the adolescents who thinks this way might idealize a teacher, imagining that person to possess *the* answer to his identity questions and to be able to straighten him out. Another will believe relief will come by converting to Buddhism, following the precepts of the Divine Light Mission, or traveling to Albuquerque. But the slightest frustration—a teacher who is faintly critical—will cause these youths to shift their perceptions from all good to all bad along with a complete reversal of associated feelings or thoughts.

Projective identification is a special way of provoking others, usually those in authority, to treat these adolescents badly, thus "justifying" their belief that these others have it in for these young people. For instance, a girl in a creative writing class believes a professor hates her because he criticizes one of her stories. Feeling herself to be an assault victim, the student becomes aggressive toward the faculty member. The angry behavior may stimulate retaliation, reinforcing the young woman's belief that her behavior is legitimate. Even if the professor reacts with unusual understanding, tact, and kindness, the girl's antagonism remains because she is convinced she "knows" that the teacher really hates her, no matter what is said.

Adolescents in the red zone cannot bear being alone. They need to be close, to be the center of attention, to be loved. They quickly become dependent upon adults in helping roles, arousing their rescue fantasies, making them believe they are the single person who can help them. These youngsters call at all hours demanding the impossible and become furious or suicidal when their unreasonable demands are not met immediately. In romantic relationships they idealize what the other person can do for them. They close the physical distance quickly. Their exploitation, manipulation, and angry childlike demandingness of those with whom they are involved preclude any other intimacy. When these relationships flounder, they launch themselves into another one as soon as possible because of their inability to tolerate being by themselves.

An empty feeling of self is one of the reasons red-zone teenagers can't stand being alone. They experience their emptiness as a loss of contact with other people. They feel devoid of belief. In contrast to alienated youths who believe in nothing, these youngsters have nothing to believe in. They are drained of enthusiasm for hobbies, pets, or interests they used to enjoy. They may fantasize that the core of themselves has dissolved. Some of these young people go through periods of their life mechanically, doing perfectly well in school or at work, relating congenially to others, but feeling no emotion, interest, or enthusiasm.

A number of young teens try to compensate for their emptiness by filling themselves up with a frantic social life, by staying on the move, by compulsive eating or sexual encounters, or through drugs and alcohol. For a few moments these activities restore a deceptive sense of self. The possibility of substance habituation is very strong among these adolescents.

Follow-up

JD

JD went back to the private school for the twelfth grade and it was the most miserable year of his life. Nothing interested him. He resigned as president of the school service club because he saw no point in what it was doing. Scouting lost its attraction so he dropped out. Feeling cut off from his classmates, he spent most of his spare time in his room listening to music and staring at the wall.

One October weekend he went fishing with his grandfather. When his grandfather asked him what he was going to do the next year, JD replied, "I don't know, I just can't connect with anything, so maybe I'll get a job and forget about college."

Still, JD and his parents visited colleges that fall. "I feel like a robot in the admissions interviews," he told a classmate. He couldn't tell whether or not he liked any of the schools he saw. It seemed to JD that every trip to a college was another opportunity for his father to remind him that they might be looking at the Ivy League if he were a better student.

In December he went into his father's gun cabinet in the study and put a single bullet in a .357 magnum. Spinning the cylinder, JD held the pistol to his head and pulled the trigger. He heard a click. He stared at the gun debating whether to play another round of Russian roulette when his mother came home from shopping.

At first JD's mother didn't understand what he was doing with the gun, but she knew from the look on his face that something was very wrong. Gently she suggested to JD that he return the pistol to the gun cabinet, called his father, and stayed with him. When his father arrived they asked him what he had intended to do with the handgun. JD replied blandly that he didn't know.

The next day JD's mother took him to see a psychiatrist. When the doctor inquired as to what he had had in mind with the pistol, JD said he didn't think it would be much of a loss had he killed himself. The last year had been a disaster, JD reported without emotion, and the future seemed desolate. Everyone would be better off with him gone. "How so?" inquired the psychiatrist.

Over the next twenty-one months JD and the therapist tried to understand what had happened, what his emotions were, and why he felt that way. Bit by bit JD recognized how much invested his father was in his getting into a prestige college. He saw that his unhappiness was much more related to his father's disappointment than his own. Moreover, JD realized how angry he was at his father for turning on him because of his low college boards: "I was the same kid the day after the test scores came in as I was the day before." Gradually JD became aware that his father was using him to fulfill his own frustrated college ambitions and that his mother went along with him. With the therapist's assistance it became clear to JD that his downhill slide at school was a way of disconnecting himself from parental dreams.

JD didn't go right to college. Instead he got a job loading trucks in the warehouse of a brewery. When he saved enough money, JD moved into an apartment with some friends. In the winter following graduation he took two extension courses at a local community college while working full-time. When he discovered he could tolerate studying again and could do reasonably well, JD decided to apply to Tulane for the fall. When his father wondered if he shouldn't apply to a couple of Ivy League schools too, JD replied, "I love you, Dad, but I don't owe you an Ivy League education. Tulane is a fine university, New Orleans is my home, my friends are here, my future is here, and this is where I want to be."

RACHEL

When she arrived home, Rachel was uncommunicative and depressed. She spent long hours playing with her dog. When her mother suggested she take part-time courses at a nearby state university, Rachel declined. When her father advised her to get a job, Rachel agreed, but after circling possible opportunities in the Sunday paper she never got around to pursuing them. Rachel said it was because her resumé wasn't up-to-date.

After a month of doing nothing her parents told Rachel they thought she should consult a therapist. She replied that she wasn't "sick" and didn't need to see a shrink. What she did do was talk to a favorite English teacher at the high school. Finding Rachel apathetic about various low-level job possibilities on Long Island and in the city, he told Rachel that he had heard of another teenager who had found a job abroad through a student exchange program.

Rachel called the student and obtained the phone number and address in New York City. When she visited this organization she found that it could help her obtain a six-month work permit and give her access to jobs in Europe. This seemed right. Rachel decided she would go to London and for the first time in more than a year she was excited about something. She located a friend who was spending a junior year in London so she would have a place to stay until she found an apartment of her own.

In spite of the high unemployment rate in London, Rachel quickly found a job—in fact, two part-time jobs. Most nights she worked as a waitress at a working-class club which featured pop music. During the day she sold fruit in an open market in Covent Garden. Though she often worked over sixty hours a week, Rachel felt better and better. "Having a regular job has settled me down," she wrote. "And it's not too difficult. All I have to do is show up on time, do what I'm supposed to, and be pleasant and my bosses are happy." The holidays were hard, as was being away for her father's fiftieth birthday as well as her own twenty-first. Work was a refuge as was doing things with her three flat-mates. With them she discovered that the theater and musical performances were inexpensive and that she liked to cook.

Rachel had a lot of time to think during these months. Though she reached no profound conclusions, Rachel said in a letter to a friend that she realized she was the kind of person who needed certain things to be satisfied: "When I think about why I'm so content here working incredible hours, separated from my folks by 3,500 miles, and living in the slums, I recognize that pressures and problems bring out the best parts of me. I become stronger, feel more emotion in me, and am certainly responsible and independent. The reason this experience has been good for me is because it's let me see that 'me' is good."

When she arrived home, her mother and father found Rachel quieter and eager to return to college. "I want to go back to college not just to study but to learn"; "I want a political science major and to take courses in art history and music appreciation." She also knew what she didn't want: "I'm through with English," said Rachel. She also decided to be more active at Syracuse: she would try to play soccer, get involved in a congressman's political campaign, and work part-time.

At the end of the fall term Rachel was working fifteen hours a week at a law firm, had made the JV soccer team, and campaigned for an unsuccessful congressman—and her grades were fine. "I think I'm about back to where I was when I started here," she told her parents.

What Parents Can Do: Suggestions for Helping

Moments of instability, uncertainty, anxiety, and conflict about identity occur unpredictably during adolescence. For the most part these are brief and don't affect the overall quality of teens' lives. Parents can assist their teenagers with the process of achieving greater autonomy and developing a congenial sense of self in several ways.

FIND THE RIGHT WORKING DISTANCE

If a teen's questions about the self become a normative identity crisis, parents can do a great deal to minimize the negative effects of this experience and maximize the positive ones. For a parent, the single most important factor in limiting the downside impact is finding the right emotional working distance from the child in turmoil. Our youngsters need to know that we are there to talk to them if they want it or that we remain in the background supplying food and other nutrients on request while they struggle to find their way. The optimal emotional and physical distance between the generations to allow adolescents to benefit from adult support, and not be smothered by it, varies greatly from household to household.

Our own subconscious needs represent the biggest obstacle to maintaining the most helpful distance. No one is immune to the powerful emotions teenagers in the midst of an identity crisis evoke. It's not easy to watch children suffer, and their distress may cause us to want to save them from the pain so necessary to their growth. In this state of mind, young people will be extraordinarily sensitive to parental efforts to govern their thoughts or actions and resist this well-intentioned help. The more we try to make them feel better, the harder they hold us off.

Be careful of overreacting. Identity issues become intensified by parental wishes for the adolescent. JD's problems were considerably worsened by his father's fantasy that he had to receive the prestige education his father never achieved. Similar responses are aroused in parents alarmed by their offspring who play with the idea of giving up medicine for art history, the straight for the gay world, Christianity for Islam, virginity for sexual activity, or ivy-covered walls for the open road. Excessive parental responses can force a premature, antagonistic, reflexive decision by these youths rather than a more painful, but thoughtful, commitment.

But don't be afraid to take a stand. Our offspring count on us to tell them what we believe in and want for them. Sometimes they need us to push up against to overcome their inertia. With teenagers, however, we do well to recognize that they accept and reject our values and desires selectively, as they accept and reject other influences upon their emerging sense of self. They need to have us say what we think is right for them, but not in such a way that we compromise their autonomy— unless their lives are endangered.

PROVIDE INFORMATION

Young people who are in conflict about choices often benefit from information that parents can provide. For instance, Rachel's mother and father could have relieved some of her conflict about dropping out of college by telling her that students usually benefit from taking time off. About half of the freshmen entering higher education do not graduate four years later, but 70 percent of those who leave school eventually return to finish their degrees. Moreover, those who work full-time for a year or more have a higher probability of being successful upon return. Parents also can provide specific information about job possibilities, about how to write a resumé, or they can send them to an expert who can.

Adults can encourage youths with identity problems to follow JD and Rachel's lead and take time off. This is a period of time, perhaps a year or two, in which young people can be free of educational and social obligations so they can delay making decisions about what they are going to do and what sort of adults they plan to be. They are free to head west, to Europe, or down under, to live in an unfamiliar culture, to meet new people, and to support themselves by odd jobs. This time off provides plenty of boredom and time for uninterrupted reflection, listening to music, and reading books unassigned by teachers. It also allows these youths to reestablish a comfortable emotional distance from their parents at this stage of the life cycle. Some youngsters have to be halfway around the world to be able to tell their mothers and fathers they love them.

Not all time off requires a long trip. As JD's case suggests, it can be a guided inward adventure. Countless teenagers benefit from the informal counseling of friends, teachers, clergy, family doctors, and relatives without ever leaving their home or school. Formal psychotherapy with a mental health worker provides a setting in which youths can explore their inner discord and discover which aspects of their identity they wish to retain and which should be left behind.

STAY IN CONTACT

The overwhelming majority of these teens recover spontaneously from identity questions, but a small fraction experience worsening turmoil and confusion. Individuals in a crisis benefit greatly from having parents around them, parents to argue with, parents to care about them. Since in their mental condition they will alienate all but the most tenacious friends, their adult relatives remain a central source of interpersonal support. Ideally, we would like to maintain a light touch in our dialogue with our children, but in fact any sort of dialogue is helpful—irritating or joyous, frustrating or satisfying—so long as human contact remains unbroken.

Being around youths in this much distress is exhausting. It is often necessary to mobilize a network of friends, relatives, and others to assist the troubled boy or girl, providing an ongoing people presence to share the burden.

Staying in touch with teenagers in turmoil allows us to monitor how they are coping with their problems, discouraging self-destructive behavior, providing information that might be helpful, and securing expert help if needed. For instance, our monitoring may tell us that the urgency to decide to do something that promises to relieve their pain for the moment, and the need to detach themselves from the adults whom they believe stand in the way of their finding themselves, is growing rather than diminishing. If it continues to intensify, it may drive the adolescents into making very bad choices. JD's Russian roulette is an extreme example. More common illustrations are failing all classes, drug abuse, antisocial behavior, or joining a cult. By remaining in contact we have a better chance of restraining our youngsters from potentially harmful actions.

Recognize the limits of your control. Being a successful parent entails giving up management of our children's lives as they develop their own individuality, autonomy, and identity. Inevitably in this process our progeny will feel emotional pain from which we could shield or comfort them if they would let us, will make choices we know are unsound, and will want to cut their own trails through their adolescent years when we can point them to a far more efficient and less stressful pathway. Unless their lives are in danger the best we can do is advise them, respect their independence, and maintain our loving contact.

The Japanese symbol for the term "crisis" is composed of two characters. They translate as "danger" and "opportunity." We parents can do little to prevent the hardship associated with identity questions from affecting our youngsters. But we can recognize that this turmoil brings with it the opportunity for positive emotional growth. Through this often painful self-scrutiny, our youths can discover what is solid in themselves, and what is not, can reappraise which values continue to be reliable guideposts and which are illusory, and can learn which aspirations belong to them and which belong to others. Painful though these identity conflicts may be, their scrutiny and resolution frees our young to strike out on a fresh and productive track.

14

Parenting Maturing Teenagers

Our twenty-seven year old can't hold down a job or stay in a relationship with anyone. Now he wants to come home. We've just gotten used to having no kids around the house. What should we do?

My daughter wants to use the money her grandmother left her for graduate school to travel around the world with her boyfriend for the next twelve months. I have no legal way to say no. I feel so powerless.

My son, a college senior, is having knee surgery on Saturday in Montreal. He says he doesn't want me to make the long trip there but sounds so depressed. Should I go?

Our youngster asked for a ten-thousand-dollar loan for a down payment on a condominium in Dallas. We've got plenty of money. What are the pluses and minuses of doing it?

My twenty-five year old is a bank executive in Omaha. She calls me in Kansas City two or three times a week on her office phone just to talk. Can that be normal?

Bookstores allocate large sections for books about how to nurture infants, care for children, and rear adolescents. But virtually nothing has been written about the issues and problems of parenting youngsters in their third decade of life. What are the challenges unique to this stage—for them as well as for us? How do we encourage their growing independence while they remain dependent upon us in so many ways? When does financial and emotional support help the normal maturing process and when does it hinder? Are there better ways than others to influence their choices—or to straighten them out—when they are no longer living under our roof? What do we say when they want to live at home after they've been on their own?

The Maturing Teenager

We know that young adult status can be recognized by specific activities such as a stable sense of self, commitment to an occupation, settling down geographically, getting married—or finding a satisfactory substitute—and for most, making plans for a family.

The process of entering full adulthood is a gradual one, considerably lengthier and more complicated than was imagined as little as a decade ago. Middle-class youngsters with college and extended educational plans today average a dozen years making the transition from adolescent to grown-up status.

Signs that the teenage years are coming to an end can be quite subtle. One indication is pleasure in reminiscing about one's "younger days." At a Thanksgiving family get-together a twenty-four-year-old daughter will delight in going over stories about the stormy confrontations she and her mother had a decade before, while her slightly younger brother and father laugh together about various unsuccessful efforts to pressure him into "living up" to his scholastic ability. Another clue is serious forward-looking speculation about their projected lifestyle. If Jane marries Dick, where will they settle, what type of lifestyle will they lead, what sort of children will they produce?

External events, telling us that our youngsters are growing out of their teens, are far less subtle. Academic milestones mark their progress with the completion of high school, college, graduate or professional school. On the way to young adulthood they move away from the parental orbit of influence and become increasingly autonomous. They travel maximal distance from us geographically and socially, acquainting themselves with diverse ideas, experience, friends, and lovers. In the normal order of things they take responsibility for their health, for their financial support, for picking other adults who will influence them, and for provisional choices about what to do and whom to be with.

More and more these youths make up their own minds about values that influence their behavior. They may differ in small ways from the older generation: a daughter from a family who pays cash for everything might live just slightly beyond her means in anticipation of her next raise. The standards of maturing youths may directly challenge their parents' ideas and values as in the cases of the twenty-four year old raised in the Jewish faith who becomes a born-again Christian, or the scion of an automobile executive who organizes labor in Alabama.

Under the best of circumstances the path from teenage to adult status is hardly tranquil. As an underwater view of synchronized swimmers who seem so relaxed and graceful on the surface reveals the considerable strain and tension necessary to their equilibrium, so, too, does a close look at maturing adolescents reveal the anxiety and conflict behind what appears to be a trouble-free growth process. Though middle-class youngsters have numerous choices available to them, tension comes from the realization that many of the options are mutually exclusive. A decision to be a banker means giving up the idea of being a teacher. Choosing to be with Tom means turning away from Peter. Taking a first job in the Midwest entails forsaking the dream of living on the West Coast. The distress these young people may feel comes from realizing that they will never know the joys along the roads not taken.

A Bittersweet Era

Growing autonomy for children also means greater independence for the parents. They are freed from day-to-day caring and worrying, from the financial burden of tuitions, and from the necessity of organizing their lives around the schedules of the younger generation. No wonder so many middle-aged men and women are exhilarated rather than despairing when the last child leaves home. For the first time since their own youth they have the time and resources for self-indulgence. Without guilt or preoccupation, they can browse and shop, eat out and attend parties, learn a new language and travel, study for a broker's exam, raise roses or puppies, or open up a used bookshop.

But just as teenagers win greater independence at the cost of less intimacy with their parents, mothers and fathers have greater freedom of action in their lives by giving up satisfying day-to-day contact with their offspring. Not infrequently their feelings of loss associated with more autonomy parallels those of their adolescent children.

One loss is the loss of role. As one working woman put it after her fourth and last child left home for college, "What am I going to do now? Being a mother is the only thing I've ever enjoyed doing." Another net loss is the vicarious enjoyment of teenage activities that organize so much of parental lives. A father expressed his sentiments this way: "When our kids were in high school there was always a gang around. Some kind of game—indoors or out—was going on, the TV and the stereos were blaring, and the phone was ringing. I could never keep the refrigerator full. Now they are gone. It leaves such a void."

The departure of teenagers from the family's inner circle can occur around the same period as the first serious illness or the death of a grandparent. The result is a double-barreled loss for these mothers and fathers. Not only is there less closeness with their maturing teenagers but no longer can parents turn to their own parents in some way for comfort. This combination intensifies the reluctance to encourage their young-sters' independence.

The Myth of Leaving the Nest

Perhaps the least accurate metaphor in child rearing is the phrase "leaving the nest." Rarely do we launch our offspring into the world at a certain age so that they infrequently return home. Instead the psychological and physical connection gradually stretches, but the attachment remains firm through the third decade of life.

Consider the item "home address." For example, though a twenty-eight-year-old young woman hasn't regularly lived with her parents in a decade, she still fills in her mother and father's address for her permanent residence. Many of her high school classmates who have married, started families, and have their own homes follow suit.

The parents' house is also where maturing youths come home for rest and relaxation—home for the holidays, home to have a cavity filled or eyes checked, home to have Mom cook their favorite food, home for movies with Dad, home to shop where people know you, home to play with the cat, home to read trashy novels in a familiar bed, home to pretend you are sixteen again.

Just how strong the psychological connection remains to home for young people in the third decade can be seen when parents alter their living arrangements. Not a few youths have been thrown into a decline when their mothers repaper their old bedrooms, give them to younger siblings, and pack their belongings into cardboard boxes in the basement. Others become similarly despondent when their fathers get tired of shoveling snow around the family homesteads, take early retirement, and move to a warmer climate. Parents pulling up roots and living in other circumstances is always difficult for the younger generation because it means saying goodbye to a part of their lives. It is often made more painful when these youths have not yet established their own base of operations.

Young people in North America remain close to their family of origin, strongly resembling their counterparts in Western Europe. In most families the generations are not geographically separated from one another. Three quarters of all parents live within thirty minutes of one child. Though upwardly mobile working-class youths tend to live farther away from their mothers and fathers, telephones shrink the distance. Among many families failure to communicate regularly by phone is considered a serious breach of family obligation.

Guidelines for Parenting Maturing Teenagers

Here are several guidelines for parenting maturing teenagers.

ENCOURAGE DISCRETIONARY DEPENDENCY

One characteristic of a maturing relationship between the generations is mutual discretionary dependency, that is, freely given support which doesn't compromise the youngster's autonomy. Acts of discretionary dependency typically are initiated by the child—a daughter may call her mother three hundred miles away to ask for recipe ideas for a party she and her boyfriend plan for the weekend. This soliciting of support doesn't undermine her competence but enhances it. The young woman knows she can do it all on her own if she has to, but she feels that her capabilities as a cook will be given a boost by conferring with her mother.

Discretionary dependency involves selective acceptance. The girl may conclude that her mother's ideas for the main course are too exotic for her guests' tastes, but her inexpensive mock-crabmeat canapés and macaroon pie are great ideas.

Remember that this is a two-sided relationship. If youths can be dependent at their discretion, so too can their parents be supportive as they choose. We don't always have to be on tap. Sometimes we have neither the time nor the inclination to obsess with a son about whether he should go back to his camp counselor job or work as a paralegal between his junior and senior years in college. Sometimes the best we can say is "You figure it out and let me know what you decide."

CONSULT AND ADVISE STRONGLY, BUT DON'T INSIST

The role for parents of maturing teenagers gradually shifts from day-to-day management to adviser and consultant. As our youngsters move through the second decade we normally encourage greater independence of thought and action, sampling of the world beyond their experience, and even challenging the validity of our ideas and ways of doing things.

This process results in our having less and less control over their destiny. The choice of which college to attend often is the first encounter in which the younger generation has a strong decision-making voice. It's always nice when we agree with our youngsters as to where they should go, but this is not always the case.

Imagine that you and your daughter have different ideas about which college she should attend. You want her to go to a small college near home and she wants to go to a university half a nation away. If you have an opinion about where she should go, don't be nondirective. But also, don't feel you must work your will. Tell her what you think and why. Allow for plenty of time for both sides to digest the other's reasoning. Remind yourself that unless there is a threat to health or welfare the decision should be the young person's to make, even if you disagree. Studies of high school seniors who were allowed to make their own decisions about higher education—even when they ran contrary to parental advice—found that they adjusted better to college than those who were made to follow the advice of the older generation.

Advising youths about money left to them by relatives is always tricky, especially when they don't want to use the wealth the way the giver intended. Say your twenty-three-year-old son inherits twenty thousand dollars from a great-aunt who imagined, but did not stipulate, that the funds would be used for business school. "Invest it," you advise, so it will accrue interest while he decides on where and when to apply for professional training. "I'm going to use half of it to travel to sub-Saharan Africa," your son replies. In cases like this tell him directly what you think, but let him make the final decision even if you are sure it's wrong. Incidentally, this boy's travels stimulated him to give up the idea of business and go into the foreign service. His first assignment was Zaire.

Resist saying, "I told you so!" If a daughter's or son's choice doesn't work out, this is no time to gloat. They know better than anyone that they took the wrong turn. They don't need to be reminded of it or forced to unreasonably defend their judgment. Instead, remember that no one bats 1.000 over a lifetime of decision making. Moreover, failures are inevitably more instructive than successes. Commiserate with them about what went wrong. Help them to learn from experience—What was it that happened that they hadn't anticipated? Were there positive features about the choices they decided against that were overlooked for some reason? Finally, advise them how best to get back on a solid footing.

Don't insist. Eventually many youths discover the truth of Mark Twain's maxim that the older generation seem smarter to them in their twenties than when they were fourteen. Partly this comes from their having tried their own way, without taking into account parental advice, and finding the outcome unsatisfactory. Partly it results from learning that when two opinions exist about a course of action, it's not a question of one person dominating the argument. Advice can be accepted or rejected without undermining the autonomy of either generation.

BE THERE IN ILLNESS AND CRISIS, EXCEPT . . .

Your graduate student son, living all by himself is having knee surgery on a Monday and says there's no reason for you to come. He'll be just fine. Your twenty-seven-year-old daughter's marriage has just failed and she wants to come home with her two year old to pull herself together. Life tends to be "one damned thing after another" and our children are not immune—from illness or injury, the breakup of a primary relationship, flunking out of graduate school or getting fired, sinking heavily into debt, or running into trouble with the law.

We were there for them in illness and crisis when they were growing up. We should continue to play this nurturing role as they move on through their twenties, because they will have not, as a rule, developed patterns of mutual interdependence with others as yet. The twenty-seven year old is not likely to have anyone she can count on as much as her parents when things go really bad.

The problem develops when our thoughts about our children's need to be independent clouds our parental instincts. Somewhere we all learned that at some age we should be able to separate ourselves from being dependent upon parents and to stand on our own two feet. Adults raised in this tradition have a tendency to overthink, to second-guess themselves when their children in their twenties need nurturing. Do we stay at home to reinforce our son's autonomy when he goes under the knife when every impulse urges us to be there? Or do we say no to our daughter who wants to come home because it will be good for her to sort things out on her own.

A useful rule to follow is to be there—be physically present—for your maturing teenagers during times of serious illness or crisis, except when your support perpetuates a chronic inability to cope with normal growth tasks of the young adult era. Giving a son tender loving care after knee surgery is probably not going to make a hypochondriac out of him; neither is giving a daughter and the grandchild a place of refuge while she decides what to do next. On the other hand, being expected to be available for comfort when a twenty-five year old has the flu or is feeling blue does not encourage adult status. Similarly having an open door for a daughter with problems in her marriage can make it excessively easy for her to come home to avoid her problems rather than standing and facing them.

GIVE MATERIAL WEALTH THOUGHTFULLY

The same principles apply to giving material wealth. Be consistent; give it when it is necessary; don't give money when having financial support retards normal adult growth; and be wary of giving gifts to growing children just because they want them.

Every family has a different pattern of giving material wealth to the younger generation. These arrangements don't unfailingly conform to income. A surprisingly high number of offspring from households with a yearly income in seven digits bus tables and sweep floors for spending money as well as paying for a proportion of their education. By the same token many older youths raised in modest circumstances have never worked a day in their lives and have never been denied anything. As a man who supported his family by working as a custodian said of his only daughter, "I've never said no to her. She's always had anything that's been within my power to buy her." Whereas experience indicates that working for money while an adolescent is associated with greater success in adulthood, there is no evidence to indicate that being given a lot as a teen results in becoming a spoiled, dependent grown-up.

Be consistent in your financial dealings with your maturing teenagers. Don't change the way you deal with them just because they turn eighteen, twenty-one, twenty-five, or thirty. If your habit has been to indulge them, don't terminate this behavior abruptly. It can be reasonably traumatic and cause substantial misunderstanding if they are suddenly cut adrift with no material support the day after graduating from college, starting work, or getting married.

There are times in the lives of our maturing teenagers when they require our material help. The daughter trying to make ends meet after a separation or a son living in a dangerous hovel in the big city are examples. In these situations, give them the financial support they need regularly for a finite period of time—for example, three hundred a month for twelve months, to be renegotiated yearly. This gives them the lift they need for a short period along with the expectation that eventually they will be able to manage on their own.

Avoid loans. On the whole our offspring are more conscientious about repaying a bank than they are their parents. They also are less reluctant to square accounts with an anonymous third party. At some level many youths believe their parents should give them money because they need it—just as they did when they were children—and not require reimbursement. When they borrow from the older generation, they may be tempted to ask their parents to take interest-only repayments or skip a month because of other bills.

If your son needs money for a new car for a sales job, co-sign a loan—even if you have the cash to buy it for him. This gives him what he needs, within his budget. It establishes his credit. And it means he has to pay only the bank's interest. In some families the unending emotional interest exacted from the younger generation on parental loans makes the worst loan sharks seem like social workers.

Giving material wealth always has the potential to undermine progress into adulthood. Take the daughter of a wealthy real estate magnate. He has always made a large monthly deposit into her checking account through college and afterward so she can live in the style that pleases him. Then she marries a high school guidance counselor in San Diego. Her father wants to continue to give her money so they can have the things she's always had. The dangers in this uninterrupted subsidy are several. Her father may want to dictate how they will live because he's underwriting a large portion of it. Also the wealth may become a disincentive for the couple to create their own independent financial base. Finally, a sound basis for marriage is shared resources. If the husband's salary is "theirs" but father-in-law's financial support is "hers," trouble is on the horizon.

When you subsidize your maturing teenagers, give them the money the same way you give advice. Tell them what you think they should do with it and let them make the final decision. Be sure the monthly income doesn't discourage their looking for rewarding work. And, when giving to a couple, be sure they know it is for both of them.

There also are moments when our third decade progeny want, but don't need, things. Perhaps a son wants a new home entertainment center with the latest TV, stereo speakers, and a VHS recorder. A daughter would like a trip to Barbados with her boyfriend in February. In these cases remember that much of the joy of the gift is in the giving. It can be extremely enjoyable for parents to think about what their growing-up children would like or need and purchase it for them. For them giving is an act of loving. If it makes you happy to purchase an electronic marvel for your son or send your daughter off to the Caribbean, do it. But if it's hard to say yes, remember that it's also true—to paraphrase a line from a famous play—that "sometimes your prayers are answered and sometimes the answer is no."

GIVE APPROVAL GENEROUSLY

We never outgrow our pleasure in receiving approval from our parents. How many times during the year do those of us who have lost our parents say, "I wish Mother were alive because she would be so happy that. . . ." whether it's completing an arduous surgical residency, buying a first house, getting a promotion, writing a book, or having a child.

If anything the need for parental approval grows as we age. Once we are out of school there are no more grades, awards, varsity letters, write-ups in the campus newspaper, or other community recognition of our achievements. In peoples' twenties many jobs aren't that challenging, progress is slow, raises are small, merit reviews seem lukewarm, and mentors are hard to find. Contemporaries are busy and preoccupied. Even when they possess the desire, they don't have the time and energy to applaud our accomplishments.

This leaves mothers and fathers as the primary cheerleaders. Maturing adolescents need to hear from us that we think they are doing a good job at whatever it is they are doing, that we are glad they have met someone they can stand going out with more than once, that their new drapes look great, that their last party was a smasheroo, that their tennis overhead is improving, that they've lost seven pounds on their new diet. Receiving applause from parents is even more important when the working young person is married to or living with someone who is also career-minded. With dual-career couples, both are often too tired to cheer.

Cheerleaders also give encouragement in bad times. While our nearly adult children may not seem to need to hear from us that we have a high opinion of them when they aren't meeting anyone, when a job isn't working out, when their doctoral thesis seems never ending, or when a winter cold hangs on and on. It's amazing what a tangible expression of approval does to pep them up. This can be in the form of a phone call, a "care" package, a dinner out on us, or a letter telling them we think they are terrific.

Criticize gently. Twenty-five year olds still hear any hint of disapproval with thirteen-year-old ears. Any faultfinding needs to be layered with positive comments.

RESOW THE SEEDS OF LOVE

As we grow older, the loss of loved ones through moving away, death, or alienation is a hardship all of us have in common. This depopulation of our social network makes the departure of our maturing teenagers all the more poignant. To ease these losses we all do well to heed the maxim that we must resow the seeds of love for as long as we live.

In relationships with children, as well as with friends, forgiveness is crucial. No family can live together for long without things being said that wound deeply, without generous acts of caring being repaid with indifference, without being ignored in moments of greatest need, without sacred pledges being broken, and without occasional acts of emotional savagery. It is a rare parent or child who doesn't have legitimate grounds for concluding that the other is "no damn good" and withdrawing. This narrow, legalistic, adversarial thinking does not do justice to the complexities of human relationships. For example, it may ignore the fact of how much pain we have caused people we care most about through our own need to be in control or to be right, through overweening ambition for ourselves and our progeny, through insensitivity and meanness. To continue to love and be loved in return, the assaults upon caring must be forgiven and forgotten.

Age brings with it growing tolerance for diversity so that we are more open to people with different values, attitudes, and backgrounds. A twenty-fifth reunion class will find they've had a lot of common life experiences, and a lot to talk about, no matter what their present station in life. Also our facility to love grows as we age. On the whole older men and women are more competent and practiced at being sensitive, open, honest, and caring than they were at a younger age.

Watch for opportunities to make friends among the younger generation. Something in us resists doing this, but it is vitally important. Natural sources for repopulating the shrinking circle of loved ones are nieces and nephews, youthful friends of our children, children of our friends, and younger colleagues. As the file of names of people in our generation on the Christmas card list shrivels, we can offset these gaps by adding these maturing young people. Establishing and maintaining affectionate bonds with the younger generation is good insurance against an old age of loneliness.

No matter how troubled their teenage years, the vast majority of young people turn out to be well-balanced, effective adults. Some take a longer, more taxing route than others do. Our efforts to understand the seriousness of adolescent problems and provide appropriate assistance when necessary both shorten the period of travail and give comfort during these hard times.

Even though our relationship with our grown-up children is increasingly adult to adult, the one role from which we can never fully retire is that of being mothers and fathers. As our adult children in their turn become concerned about their own teenagers, we might help both generations by recollecting with them our own struggles, recognizing that we both survived, and that the bonds of affection remain intact.

REFERENCE NOTES

Chapter 1

2   **one teenager in ten** The figures for the percentage of emotional disorders among adolescents vary considerably from about 5 percent to as high as 20 percent depending on the population studied and the criteria used to define mental disturbance. See Michael Rutter, *Changing Youth in a Changing Society: Patterns of Adolescent Development and Disorder* (Cambridge, Mass.: Harvard University Press, 1980), ch. 1.

2   **normal variants** An exception is Karl Menninger (with Martin Mayman and Paul Pruyser), *The Vital Balance: The Life Process in Mental Health and Illness* (New York: Viking, 1967).

3   **teenager** Though considerable overlap exists among the stages, clinicians and researchers in human development discriminate among "early adolescence"—ages about eleven to fourteen, "adolescence proper"—fifteen to eighteen, "late adolescence"—eighteen to twenty-one, and "youth"—twenty-two to twenty-five. See Peter Blos, *On Adolescence: A Psychoanalytic Interpretation* (Chicago: University of Chicago Press, 1962), pp. 75–158; Harry S. Sullivan, *Interpersonal Theory of Psychiatry* (New York: Norton, 1953), pp. 245–310; James S. Coleman, ed., *Youth: Transition to Adulthood* (Chicago: University of Chicago Press, 1974), pp. 1–7; and Kenneth Keniston, *Youth and Dissent: The Rise of the New Opposition* (New York: Harcourt Brace Jovanovitch, 1971).

4   **growing maturity** Described in J. M. Tanner, "Sequence, Tempo, and Individual Variations in the Growth and Development of Boys and Girls Aged Twelve to Sixteen," *Daedalus* 100 (1971): 907–30.

5   **junior high school** Noted by Jerome Kagan, "A Conception of Early Adolescence," *Daedalus* 100 (1971): 997–1012. Middle schools usually encompass grades six to eight while junior high school grades typically are made up of seven through nine.

6   **best friend**   One of the first to describe the importance of the best
         friend in normal development was Sullivan, *Interpersonal Theory*,
         ch. 16.

6   **clique**   The importance of social acceptance in early adolescence
         and how this success can be blocked by achievement has been
         described by James S. Coleman, *The Adolescent Society* (New
         York: Free Press, 1961).

7   **work laws**   Described in Grace Abbott, "State Child Legislation,"
         in *The Child and the State*, ed. Grace Abbott, vol. I of *Legal Status
         in the Family, Apprenticeship and Child Labor: Selected Docu-
         ments. With Introductory Notes* (New York: Greenwood, 1968).

7   **regulate the labor**   See Joseph Kett, "History of Age Grouping in
         America"; and Robert Brenner, "Rights of Children and Youth,"
         both in Coleman, *Youth*.

         Chapter 2

13   **little difference**   See William James, "The Will To Believe," in
         Pragmatism and Other Essays (1896; reprint, New York: Pocket
         Books, 1975). p. 257.

13   **these youngsters**   The classical statement of the characteristics of
         adolescents was presented by G. Stanley Hall, *Adolescence: Its Psy-
         chology and Its Relation to Physiology, Anthropology, Sociology,
         Sex, Crime, Religion and Education* (New York: Appleton, 1904),
         vols. I and II. Many modern clinicians continue to adhere to these
         views of the teenage years.

14   **abnormal**   From Anna Freud, "Adolescence as a Developmental
         Disturbance," in *The Writings of Anna Freud* (New York: Interna-
         tional Universities Press, 1971), vol. 7.

14   **rather than dramatic revolution**   Studies of normal high school
         and college youth are reported in Daniel Offer, Eric Ostrov, and
         Kenneth I. Howard, *The Adolescent: A Psychological Self-Portrait*
         (New York: Basic Books, 1981); Douglas H. Heath, *Maturity and
         Competence: A Transcultural View* (New York: Gardner Press,
         1977); Stanley H. King, *Five Lives at Harvard* (Cambridge, Mass.:
         Harvard University Press, 1973); Daniel Offer, *The Psychological
         World of the Teenager: A Study of Normal Adolescent Boys* (New
         York: Basic Books, 1969); and Joseph Katz et al., *No Time for
         Youth: Growth and Restraint in College Students* (San Francisco:
         Jossey-Bass, 1968).

14   **most challenging tasks**   Anna Freud has said that differentiating
         temporary turmoil from true pathology is a very difficult task. See

A. Freud, "Adolescence," in *The Writings of Anna Freud* (New York: International Universities Press, 1969), vol. 5.

18   **primary features** The dimensions for assessing adjustment have been described in one form or another by philosophers, clinicians, and researchers through the centuries. A summary of their thinking is contained in Douglas H. Powell, *Understanding Human Adjustment: Normal Adaptation Through the Life Cycle* (Boston: Little, Brown, 1983), chs. 1 and 9.

19   **no different** See Sigmund Freud, "Five Lectures on Psychoanalysis," in *The Standard Edition of the Complete Psychological Works of Sigmund Freud,* trans. and ed. James Strachey, in collaboration with Anna Freud (London: Hogarth Press, 1953–64), vol. 11, p. 50.

21   **mood of youth** See Offer, Ostrov, and Howard, *Adolescent,* p. 105.

21   **humor** See George E. Vaillant, *Adaptation to Life* (Boston: Little, Brown, 1977), p. 386.

22   **resources** Research on the importance of resources is summarized in Powell, *Human Adjustment,* pp. 21–23, 87–88.

22   **more ways of being normal** Clinicians working with mentally disturbed individuals note a limited repertoire of behavior and sameness about these individuals. On the other hand, research with normal adolescents shows them to differ substantially among themselves. See, for example, Paul R. Singer, "Psychological Testing: Thematic Apperception Test, Rorschach Test, and WAIS Vocabulary Scale," in Daniel Offer, *The Psychological World of the Teenager* (New York: Basic Books, 1969). This also is true for grown-ups. Studies of adult drinkers found that early-stage problem drinkers are far more heterogeneous psychologically than are severe alcoholics. See Leslie C. Morey, Harvey A. Skinner, and Roger K. Blashfield, "A Typology of Alcohol Abusers: Correlates and Implications," *Journal of Abnormal Psychology* 93 (1984): 408–17.

23   **suddenly reversed** Excellent clinical descriptions of this period of instability are contained in Anna Freud, "Adolescence." Also see Erik H. Erikson's *Identity: Youth and Crisis* (New York: Norton, 1968).

23   **this instability** Adjustment disorders are summarized in the *DSM-III: Diagnostic and Statistical Manual of Mental Disorders,* 3d ed. (Washington, D.C.: American Psychiatric Association, 1980), pp. 299–302.

23   **acting out** See Peter Blos, "The Concept of Acting Out in Relation to Adolescent Process," in *The Psychology of Adolescence:*

Essential Readings, ed. Aaron H. Esman (New York: International Universities Press, 1975).

24   **"hyper-"**   These defenses associated with the first level of dysfunction are described in Karl Menninger (with Martin Mayman and Paul Pruyser), *The Vital Balance: The Life Process in Mental Health and Illness* (New York: Viking, 1967), ch. 8.

25   **Familiar stress symptoms**   Ibid.

25   **three to six months**   *DSM-III*, pp. 65–67, describes the criteria for two major neurotic disorders of youth—identity and oppositional disorders—as lasting three to six months, respectively. This seems consistent with the experience of most parents and clinicians.

27   **Compulsive disobedience**   See A. Freud, "Adolescence," p. 158.

28   **Overdriven behaviors**   Characterized in Robert W. White and Norman F. Watt, *The Abnormal Personality*, 5th ed. (New York: Wiley, 1981), ch. 3.

28   **Mental functioning**   Drawn from Mardi G. Horowitz et al., "Signs and Symptoms of Post-traumatic Stress Disorders," *Archives of General Psychiatry* 37 (1980): 85–92.

30–31 **reactive and process psychoses**   A concise summary of the differences between reactive and process psychoses is contained in White and Watt, *Abnormal Personality*, ch. 13.

Chapter 3

34   **Socrates**   Attributed to Socrates by E. James Anthony, "The Reactions of Adults to Adolescents and Their Behavior," in *The Psychology of Adolescence: Essential Readings*, ed. Aaron H. Esman (New York: International Universities Press, 1975).

34   **normal event**   The most eloquent spokesperson for this thesis has been Anna Freud, "Adolescence as a Developmental Disturbance," in *The Writings of Anna Freud* vol. 5 (New York: International Universities Press, 1971). Also, Peter Blos, "The Initial Stage of Male Adolescence," in *The Adolescent Passage: Developmental Issues* (New York: International Universities Press, 1979).

35   **Rustam and Sohrab**   Leon Sheleff describes the Rustam Complex and summarizes the evidence for and sources of potential hostility toward their offspring in his *Generations Apart: Adult Hostility to Youth* (New York: McGraw-Hill, 1981).

35   **children determine**   See Richard Q. Bell and Lawrence V. Harper, *Child Effects on Adults* (Hillsdale, N.J.: Erlbaum, 1977).

35   **emotional tenor**   Data presented in a study by Laurence D. Steinberg, "Transformations in Family Relations at Puberty," *Developmental Psychology* 17 (1981): 833–40.

36   **temperament**   For a description of the ways in which personality styles have been described throughout history, see Douglas H. Powell, *Understanding Human Adjustment: Normal Adaptation Through the Life Cycle* (Boston, Little, Brown, 1983), ch. 4.

36   **three types of temperament**   These characterizations are drawn from two sources: Arnold A. Gesell, Frances L. Ilg, and Louise B. Ames, *Infant and Child in the Culture Today: The Guidance of Development in Home and Nursery School*, rev. ed. (New York: Harper & Row, 1974); and Alexander A. Thomas and Stella Chess, *Temperament and Development* (New York: Bruner/Mazel, 1977).

37   **remain consistent**   This research reported by Jerome Kagan, *The Nature of the Child* (New York: Basic Books, 1984).

38   **work, love, and play**   For a summary of the developmental tasks of teenagers and adults, see Powell, *Human Adjustment*, chs. 6, 7, and 8.

40   **Generativity**   The term "generativity" was coined by Erik H. Erikson. See his "Reflections on Dr. Borg's Life Cycle," *Daedalus* 105 (1976): 1–28.

43   **preexisting illusions.**   Several of the specific adult illusions about adolescents are drawn from the following sources: E. James Anthony, "Reactions," in *Psychology of Adolescence:* ed. Esman; and Peter Blos, "The Generation Gap. Preoedipal Factors in the Etiology of Female Delinquency," in Blos, *Adolescent Passage.*

46   **"good enough" parents**   For a further elaboration, see Anthony, "Reactions."

48   **clinicians have long noted**   See David G. Cooper, *The Death of the Family* (New York: Pantheon, 1970).

Chapter 4

51   **loving contact**   This research is reported in Robert Sears, Eleanor Maccobby, and Harry Levin, *Patterns of Child Rearing* (Evanston, Ill.: Row/Peterson, 1957).

51   **healthy families**   Two recent summaries of the differences between healthy and less well-functioning families are contained in Froma Walsh, "Conceptualizations of Normal Family Functioning," in *Normal Family Process,* ed. Froma Walsh (New York: Guilford, 1982); and Jerry M. Lewis et al., *No Single Thread: Psychological Health in Family Systems* (New York: Bruner/Mazel, 1976).

51   **good relationships**   See the summary of research contained in Michael Rutter, *Changing Youth in a Changing Society: Patterns of Adolescent Development and Disorder* (Cambridge, Mass.: Harvard

University Press, 1980), ch. 3; and Karl Menninger (with Martin Mayman and Paul Pruyser), *The Vital Balance: The Life Process in Mental Health and Illness* (New York: Viking, 1967), pp. 294–95.

51   **opposite of love** See George W. Goethals, "Love, Marriage, and Mutative Relationships," in *On Love and Loving*, ed. Kenneth Pope (San Francisco: Jossey-Bass, 1980).

53   **percentage doubles** Reported in the U.S. Department of Labor, *Handbook of Labor Statistics* (Washington, D.C.: U.S. Government Printing Office, 1980).

53   **Working teens** See Ellen Greenberger, Laurence D. Steinberg, and Alan Vaux, "Adolescents Who Work: Health and Behavioral Consequences from Job Stress," *Developmental Psychology* 17 (1981): 691–703. Research on Depression youth was carried out by Glen H. Elder, Jr., *Children of the Great Depression* (Chicago: University of Chicago Press, 1974).

53   **A group of boys** Longitudinal studies of working blue-collar young people was reported in George E. Vaillant and Caroline O. Vaillant, "Natural History of Male Psychological Health, X: Work as a Predictor of Positive Mental Health," *American Journal of Psychiatry* 138 (1981): 1433–40.

54   **"loving"** Loving as an active process has been described by Erich Fromm, *The Art of Loving* (New York: Holt, Reinhart & Winston, 1956). Types of love are described concisely in C. S. Lewis, *Four Loves* (New York: Harcourt Brace Jovanovitch, 1960).

54   **Eighty percent** Comprehensive summaries of this research are contained in Rutter, *Changing Youth*, ch. 1; and Wenda Dickens and Daniel Perlman, "Friendship Over the Life Cycle," in *Developing Personal Relationships*, ed. Steve Duck and Robin Gilmore, vol. 2 of *Personal Relationships* (London: Academic Press, 1981).

55   **Table 4.1** Inspired by W. Stephen Royce and Hal Aukowitz, "Multi-Model Evaluation of Practice, Interaction as Treatment for Social Isolation," *Journal of Consulting and Clinical Psychology* 46 (1978): 239–45.

56   **play** An extended description of play—including forms characteristic of teenagers—can be found in Douglas H. Powell, *Understanding Human Adjustment: Normal Adaptation Through the Life Cycle* (Boston: Little, Brown, 1983), ch. 8.

56   **inner and outer stresses** See Rutter, *Changing Youth*, ch. 3.

57   **function normally** A graphic portrayal is the case of Eddie in Selma Fraiberg, *The Magic Years* (New York: Scribner Lyccum, 1959), pp. 289–90.

57   **adaptation** Drawn from a much more elaborate description by

Heinz Hartmann, *Ego Psychology and the Problem of Adjustment* (New York: International Universities Press, 1958).

58   **conscious of immediate reactions** This process has been called appraisal and reappraisal. See Richard S. Lazarus, James R. Averill, and Edward M. Opton, "The Psychology of Coping: Issues of Research and Assessment," in *Coping and Adaptation*, ed. George L. Coelho, David R. Hamburg, and John E. Adams (New York: Basic Books, 1974).

61   **studies of youths** See George E. Vaillant, *Adaptation to Life* (Boston: Little, Brown, 1977), ch. 15.

62   **Strong evidence** Contained in Norma Haan, *Coping and Defending: Processes of Self-environment Organization* (New York: Academic Press, 1977), ch. 10.

63   **Babies** These studies are presented in Lois B. Murphy and Alice E. Moriarty, *Vulnerability, Coping and Growth: From Infancy to Adolescence* (New Haven: Yale University Press, 1976).

63   **competence** See Robert W. White, *The Enterprise of Living: Growth and Organization in Personality* (New York: Holt, Rinehart and Winston), 1972.

63   **Eighteen year olds** This research was carried out by Emmy E. Werner and Ruth S. Smith, *Vulnerable but Invincible: A Longitudinal Study of Resilient Children and Youth* (New York: McGraw-Hill, 1982).

64   **research shows** Observed by George E. Vaillant, *The Natural History of Alcoholism: Causes, Patterns, and Paths to Recovery* (Cambridge, Mass.: Harvard University Press, 1983).

64   **students at a California college** Reported by Rudolph H. Moos, "Creating Healthy Human Contexts: Environmental and Individual Strategies" (Paper presented at the annual meeting of the American Psychological Association, Los Angeles, 1981); also, his *Evaluating Educational Environments* (San Francisco: Jossey-Bass, 1979).

64   **belief** Recent converts to four religious groups—Jewish and Catholic, Bahai and Krishna—had experienced traumatically unhappy childhoods and teenage years much more frequently than nonconverts. See Chana Ullman. "Cognitive and Emotional Antecedents of Religious Conversion," *Journal of Personality and Social Psychology* 43 (1982): 183–92.

65   **pets** Boris Levinson has written two excellent books describing the value of pets in enhancing normal development and as an adjunct to dealing with emotionally disturbed children: *Pets and Human Development* (Springfield, Ill.: Charles Thomas, 1972); and

Pet-Oriented Child Psychotherapy (Springfield, Ill.: Charles Thomas, 1969).

66   **studies of men and women**   Contained in Vaillant, *Adaptation.* Also, Marjorie F. Lowenthal et al. *Four Stages of Life: A Comparative Study of Men and Women Facing Transition* (San Francisco: Jossey-Bass, 1976).

66   **we know that**   This research summarized by Carlyle H. Folkins and Wesley E. Sime. "Physical Fitness and Mental Health," *American Psychologist* 36 (1981): 373–89.

67   **treatment of adolescents**   In Anna Freud, "Adolescence," in *The Writings of Anna Freud* (New York: International Universities Press, 1969), vol. 5.

68   **nearly all**   See Rutter, *Changing Youth,* pp. 74–76.

Chapter 5

73   **affects 2–4 percent**   Reported in Philip J. Graham, Epidemiological Studies," in *Psychopathological Disorders of Children,* ed. Herbert C. Quay and John S. Wherry, 2d ed. (New York: Wiley, 1979).

76   **reason is stronger than anxiety**   See Daniel Offer, Eric Ostrov, and Kenneth I. Howard, *The Adolescent. A Psychological Self-Portrait* (New York: Basic Books, 1981).

78   **absences**   Personal communication to the author from Frank P. Krypel, vice-principal, Concord-Carlise Regional High School, Concord, Massachusetts, and Louis Arieti, Director of Guidance, Brockton High School, Brockton, Massachusetts. Absences in less college-oriented communities are higher.

79   **history of successfully managing**   These are called Type I school phobics. They are more often younger, are from well-functioning families, have no history of school refusal, show fear specific to school, and the problems seem to be associated with recent stressful events. See Wallace A. Kennedy, "School Phobia: Rapid Treatment of 50 Cases," *The Journal of Abnormal Psychology* 70 (1965): 285–89.

79   **impairs reason**   Impairment of reason by anxiety is noted by Isaac M. Marks, *Living With Fear: Understanding and Coping with Anxiety* (New York: McGraw-Hill, 1978), p. 147.

79   **school phobia**   For a classical psychoanalytic perspective on school phobia based on a pathological mother-child relationship, refer to John C. Coolidge et al., "Patterns of Aggression in School Phobia," *The Psychoanalytic Study of the Child* 17 (1962): 319–33; John C. Coolidge et al., "School Phobia in Adolescence: A Manifestation of

Severe Character Disturbance," *American Journal of Orthopsychiatry* 30 (1960): 599–607; and Melitta Sperling, "School Phobias: Classification, Dynamics, and Treatment," *Psychoanalytic Study of the Child* 22 (1967): 375–401.

81 **separation anxiety** This condition is described concisely in the *DSM-III, Diagnostic and Statistical Manual of Mental Disorders*, 3d ed. (Washington, D.C.: American Psychiatric Association, 1980), pp. 50–53.

85 **act promptly** Nearly all experts on transitional anxiety agree that acting promptly to return a child to school is appropriate except in chronic or especially difficult cases in which a more comprehensive program is required. See Marks, *Living with Fear*, ch. 7.

85 **Experience suggests** See Gerald Weinberger, Theodore Leventhal, and George Beckman, "The Management of a Chronic School Phobic Through the Use of Consultation with School Personnel," in Howard L. Millman et al., *Therapies for School Behavior Problems: A Handbook of Practical Interventions* (San Francisco: Jossey-Bass, 1980).

87 **a mix of approaches** Research evidence in this country and in Great Britain indicates that this multiple therapeutic approach works successfully in over 80 percent of young people with severe transitional anxiety. See N. R. Blagg and W. Yule, "The Behavioural Treatment of School Refusal—A Comparative Study," *Behaviour Research and Therapy* 22 (1984): 119–27; and H. Thompson Prout and John R. Harvey, "Applications of Desensitizing Procedures for School-Related Problems: A Review," in Millman et al., *Therapies*.

88 **same-sex surrogates** Reported by Arnold LeUnes and Sandra Siemsglaz, "Paraprofessional Treatment of School Phobia in a Young Adolescent Girl," in Millman et al., *Therapies*.

Chapter 6

89 **varies greatly** Differences in early adolescent maturation are summarized in J. M. Tanner, "Sequence, Tempo, and Individual Variations in the Growth and Development of Boys and Girls Aged Twelve to Sixteen," *Daedalus* 100 (1971): 907–30.

89 **sexually active earlier** See Alfred C. Kinsey et al., *Sexual Behavior in the Human Male* (Philadelphia: Saunders, 1948), pp. 297–325; Alfred C. Kinsey et al., *Sexual Behavior in the Human Female* (Philadelphia: Saunders, 1953), pp. 302–4; and more recently, S. Jean Emans, "The Sexually Active Teenager," *Journal of Developmental and Behavioral Pediatrics* 4 (1983): 37–42.

90   **all-time high** The birthrate from unmarried women fifteen through nineteen increased 2 percent in 1981. See National Center for Health Statistics, *Monthly Vital Statistics Report*, vol. 32, no. 6 (Washington, D.C.: U.S. Department of Health and Human Services, Public Health Service, 1983). The rate for primary and secondary syphilis has continued to increase through 1983 among fifteen to nineteen year olds, though the rate for gonorrhea has declined slightly. See Centers for Disease Control, *Sexually Transmitted Disease Statistics 1983*, no. 133 (Washington, D.C.: U.S. Department of Health and Human Services, Public Health Service, 1985).

93   **biggest change** See Ellen Porter Honnet, "The Loss of Virginity: A Major Milestone or a Minor Event (Qualifying paper submitted to the Harvard School of Education, Harvard University, January 1983); and Carol A. Wagner, "Sexuality of American Adolescents," *Adolescence* 15 (1980): 567–80.

93   **love and sex** Summarized in George W. Goethals and Dennis Klos, *Experiencing Youth: First Person Accounts*, 2d ed. (Boston: Little, Brown, 1976), p. 269.

95   **fidelity** See Paul A. Walters, Jr., "Promiscuity in Adolescence," *American Journal of Orthopsychiatry* 35 (1965): 670–75.

95   **celibacy** Presently this trend is growing among older youths and young adults. Refer to Gabrielle Brown, *The New Celibacy: Why More Men and Women are Abstaining From Sex—And Enjoying It* (New York: McGraw-Hill, 1980).

96   **uniformism** Portrayed by Peter Blos, *On Adolescence: A Psychoanalytic Interpretation* (Chicago: University of Chicago Press, 1962), pp. 117–18.

96   **reality of their fantasies** See Peter Blos, "The Concept of Acting Out in Relation to Adolescent Process," in *The Adolescent Passage: Developmental Issue* (New York: International Universities Press, 1979).

96   **rush to physical intimacy** This applies to heavy petting as well as coitus in young teens. See Thomas J. Cottle, "The Connections of Adolescence," *Daedalus* 100 (1971): 1177–1219.

97   **boy crazy** Being "boy crazy" is only one of several reactions to puberty. See Karen Horney, "Personality Changes in Female Adolescents," *The American Journal of Orthopsychiatry* 5 (1935): 19–26.

97   **excessive intellectualization** See Goethals and Klos, *Experiencing Youth*, pp. 274–75.

98   **painful isolation** Summarized in John H. Gagnon, William Si-

mon, and Alan J. Berger, "Some Aspects of Sexual Adjustment in Early and Late Adolescence," in *The Psychopathology of Adolescence*, ed. Joseph Zubin and Alfred Freedman (New York: Grune and Stratton, 1970).

98   **most common**   Many of the features of the oppositional personality are contained in these socially and sexually precocious youngsters. See the *DSM-III, Diagnostic and Statistical Manual of Mental Disorders*, 3d ed. (Washington, D.C.: American Psychiatric Association, 1980), p. 65.

98   **negative picture**   See Jerald G. Bachman and Patrick M. O'Malley, "Self-Esteem in Young Men: A Longitudinal Analysis of the Impact of Educational and Occupational Attainment," *Journal of Personality and Social Psychology* 35 (1977): 365–80.

99   **Delinquency and promiscuity**   Examples are provided by Blos, *Adolescent Passage*.

99   **problems with sexual functionings**   Summarized in the *DSM-III*, pp. 261–83.

Chapter 7

109   **one teenager in three**   A summary of the research in this area is contained in Arlette Lefebvre and William Hawke, "Learning Disorders in Children and Adolescence," in *Psychological Problems of the Child in the Family*, ed. Paul D. Steinhauer and Quentin Rae-Grant 2d ed. (New York: Basic Books, 1983).

114   **selective attention**   See Alan O. Ross, *Psychological Aspects of Learning Disabilities and Reading Disorders* (New York: McGraw-Hill, 1976).

115   **their own control**   This concept was developed by Julian B. Rotter, "Generalized Expectancies of Internal Versus External Locus of Control of Reinforcement," *Psychology Monographs* 80 (1966): 1.

116   **cower and buller**   The differences between these two learning styles are drawn from William G. Perry, Jr., "Examsmanship and the Liberal Arts: A Study in Educational Epistemology," in *Examining Harvard College: A Collection of Essays by Members of the Harvard Faculty*, ed. Lee Bramson (Cambridge, Mass.: Harvard University Faculty of Arts and Sciences, 1963).

118   **thirty-five percentile points**   Personal communication to the author on September 24, 1984, by Professor Richard J. Light, author of (with David B. Pillamer) *Summing Up: The Science of Reviewing Research* (Cambridge, Mass.: Harvard University Press, 1984).

118   **"superficial-passive"**   A fuller description of the superficial-passive

learning style and related research is given by Noel Entwhistle, *Styles of Learning and Teaching: An Integral Outline of Educational Psychology for Students, Teachers, and Lecturers* (New York: Wiley, 1981), pp. 77–78.

118   **overinclusive attention**   Such teenagers are not suffering from an attention deficit disorder because the distractibility, difficulty concentrating, and overactivity is not noticeable in other areas of self-directed activities. See the *DSM-III: Diagnostic and Statistical Manual of Mental Disorders*, 3d ed. (Washington, D.C.: American Psychiatric Association, 1980), pp. 41–45.

119   **helplessness**   Learned helplessness has been described by Lyn Y. Abramson, Martin E. P. Seligman, and John D. Teasdale, "Learned Helplessness in Humans: Critique and Reformulation," *Journal of Abnormal Psychology* 87 (1978): 49–74.

119   **avoid failure**   This tendency has been called the motive to avoid failure. See John W. Atkinson. "The Mainsprings of Achievement-Oriented Activity," in *Motivation and Achievement*, ed. John W. Atkinson and Joel O. Raynor (New York: Wiley, 1974).

121   **depression**   Depression is a notable symptom in a minority of younger teens. See David T. Stevenson and David M. Romney, "Depression in Learning Disabled Children," *Journal of Learning Disabilities* 17 (1984): 579–82.

121   **behave antisocially**   Studies of the relationship between delinquency and underachievement in London is contained in Michael Rutter et al., *Fifteen Thousand Hours: Secondary Schools and Their Effects on Children* (Cambridge, Mass.: Harvard University Press, 1982), ch. 5; and in the United States by C. D. Porumba, "Learning Disabilities, Youth and Delinquency: Programs for Intervention," in *Progress in Learning Disabilities*, ed. Helmer R. Myklebust (New York: Grune and Stratton, 1975), vol. 3.

124   **lag behind**   Refer to Louise B. Ames, Clyde Gillespie, and John W. Streff, *Stop School Failure* (New York: Harper & Row, 1972), ch. 3.

124   **Follow-up studies**   Research in the effects of repeating immature children is overwhelming positive. See Louise B. Ames, *Is Your Child in the Wrong Grade?* (New York: Harper & Row, 1970).

125   **other physical difficulties**   A survey of the physical as well as of other factors contributing to underachievement is contained in Ames, Gillespie, and Streff, *School Failure*, ch. 3; and Lefebvre and Hawke, "Learning Disorders."

125   **attention deficit disorders**   See the *DSM-III*, pp. 41–45; and

Klaus Minde, "Disorders of Attention," in Steinhauer and Rae-Grant, *Psychological Problems.*

125 **Studies of overactive children** Hyperactive children, however, did have greater trouble as adolescents with poor school performance and more delinquent behavior, and as adults with greater impulsivity, accidents, and less well-developed social skills. See Gabrielle Weiss and Lily Hechtman, "The Hyperactive Child Syndrome," *Science* 205 (1979): 1348–53.

128 **Harvard Bureau of Study Counsel** Drawn largely from unpublished materials produced by the staff of the Harvard Bureau of Study Counsel: especially, (1) "A Guide to Study at Harvard," ed. Carla Jones and Kathleen Marshall, 1983; (2) "Some Hints for Studying," ed. Kiyo Morimoto, 1982; and (3) A Guide to Study: A Synopsis of Ideas Originally Proposed by the Efficacy Group for Students at Harvard and Radcliffe, ed. Jeff Howard, Michael Paine, and Anita Howard, 1981, and ed. Peter Hardie, 1977.

133 **low teacher expectations** See Robert Rosenthal and Lenore Jacobson, *Pygmalion in the Classroom: Teacher Expectation and Pupil's Intellectual Development* (New York: Holt, Rinehart and Winston, 1968); and more recently, Monica Harris and Robert Rosenthal, "The Mediation of Interpersonal Expectancy Effects: 31 Meta-Analyses," *Psychological Bulletin* 97 (1985): 363–86.

133 **majority of young people** This research is presented in Gene V. Glass et al., *School Class Size: Research and Policy* (Beverly Hills, Calif.: Sage, 1982).

133 **individual teacher** Research summarized by Jeanne S. Chall, "A Decade of Research on Reading and Learning Disabilities," in *What Research Has to Say About Reading Instruction,* ed. S. Jay Samuels (Newark, Del.: International Reading Associates, 1978).

134 **77 percent** See Jeannette Jansky and Katrina deHirsch, *Preventing Reading Failure* (New York: Harper & Row, 1972).

134 **produce graduates** In Rutter et al., *Fifteen Thousand Hours,* chs. 7 and 10.

135 **a helpful technique** The seminal thinking on this subject is contained in Joseph Wolpe, *The Practice of Behavior Therapy,* 2d ed. (New York: Pergamon, 1973), chs. 6 and 7.

135 **pessimistic thoughts** This approach combines ideas drawn from David H. Meichenbaum, *Cognitive-Behavior Modification: An Integrative Approach* (New York: Plenum, 1977); Aaron T. Beck, *Cognitive Therapy and Emotional Disorders* (New York: International Universities Press, 1976); and Albert Ellis, *The Essence of*

Rational Psychotherapy: A Comprehensive Approach to Treatment (New York: Institute for Rational Therapy, 1970).

135   **reward system**   For a brief review of the positive effects of rewards on student preparation, see Charles E. Schaeffer and Howard I. Millman. *How to Help Children with Common Problems* (New York: Van Nostrand Reinhold, 1981), pp. 402–5.

136   **doing something**   Clinical research in schools aiming to match particular treatment modes to particular problems among "at-risk" children found that a variety of interactions were successful with many types of youngsters. See Israel Kolvin et al., *Help Starts Here: The Maladjusted Child in the Ordinary School* (London: Tavistock, 1981).

136   **neurotic symptoms**   For a comprehensive survey of the persistent psychological forces at work that inhibit learning in low aptitude readers, see Peter H. Johnson's article, "Understanding Reading Disability: A Case Study Approach," *Harvard Educational Review* 55 (1985): 153–77.

Chapter 8

138   **direct opposition**   This description of the passive-aggressive syndrome is drawn from elements of the Passive-Aggressive Disorder in the *DSM-III: Diagnostic and Statistical Manual of Mental Disorders,* 3d ed. (Washington, D.C.: American Psychiatric Association, 1980), pp. 63–65 and 328–29; and from the expanded portrayal in Theodore Millon, *Disorders of Personalities: DSM-III: Axis II* (New York: Wiley, 1981).

141   **comfortable assertiveness**   Characteristics of assertiveness behavior are contained in Arthur J. Lange, "Cognitive-Behavioral Assertion Training," in *Handbook of Rational-Emotive Therapy,* ed. Albert Ellis and Russell Geiger (New York: Springer, 1977).

141   **a right to be heard**   An excellent treatment of normal disagreement in early to middle adolescence is contained in Arnold Gessel, Frances L. Ilg, and Louise B. Ames, *Youth: The Years from Ten to Sixteen* (New York: Harper and Brothers, 1956).

143   **Absolutist thinking**   Described by Peter Blos, "The Split Parental Imago in Adolescent Social Relations: An Inquiry into Group Psychology," in *The Adolescent Passage* (New York: International Universities Press, 1979).

143   **goofing off**   Summarized by Robert B. Everhart, "The Nature of 'Goofing Off' Among Junior High School Adolescents," *Adolescence* 17 (1982): 177–81.

144 **provides diversion** See Jeffrey W. Reimer, "Deviance as Fun," *Adolescence* 16 (1981): 39–43.

144 **active and passive** Descriptions of active and passive forms of oppositional behavior in the yellow and orange zones are drawn from Millon, *Disorders*, ch. 9; and the *DSM-III*, pp. 63–65 and 328–29, unless otherwise noted.

147 **unrealistically high goals** See Irving B. Weiner, "Psychodynamic Aspects of Learning Disability: The Passive-Aggressive Under-achiever," in *Adolescent Behavior and Society: A Book of Readings*, ed. Rolf E. H. Muuss (New York: Random House, 1980).

147 **chronic exhaustion** See George K. Montgomery, "Uncommon Tiredness Among College Undergraduates," *The Journal of Consulting and Clinical Psychology* 51 (1983): 517–25.

147 **discomfort dodging** Described by William J. Knaus, *Do It Now: How to Stop Procrastination* (Englewood Cliffs, N.J.: Prentice-Hall, 1979).

148 **Masochist manipulation** Drawn from the thinking about masochism by Wilhelm Reich, *Character Analysis*, 3d ed. (New York: Orgone Institute Press, 1949); and Karen Horney, *New Ways in Psychoanalysis* (New York: Norton, 1939).

152 **less is known** This is most obvious from the scant literature on the subject. See Richard D. Parsons and Robert J. Wicks, eds., *Passive-Aggressiveness: Theory and Practice* (New York: Bruner/Mazel, 1983).

152 **games** These self-perpetuating maladaptive scenarios were first described by Eric Berne, *Games People Play* (New York: Grove Press, 1964).

153 **not impressive** See Parsons and Wicks, *Passive-Aggressiveness;* and Millon, *Disorders*.

153 **inconsistency** These patterns are concisely summarized by Millon, *Disorders*.

154 **reduce the likelihood** An overview of the research bearing on appropriate handling of disobedience in children is contained in Charles E. Schaeffer and Howard I. Millman, *How to Help Children with Common Problems* (New York: Van Nostrand Reinhold, 1981), pp. 274–94.

155 **assertive behavior** The steps in teaching assertive behavior are contained in Arthur J. Lange and Patricia Jakubowski, *Responsible Assertive Behavior: Cognitive Behavioral Procedures for Trainers* (Champaign, Ill.: Research Press, 1976).

155 **becoming angry** See James R. Averill, "Studies on Anger and

Aggression: Implications for Theories of Emotion," *American Psychologist* 38 (1983): 1145–60.

Chapter 9

158   **moodiness**   The classic clinical description of moodiness in teenagers was written years ago by Hall, vol. 2, 1905, pp. 76–78.

158   **most adolescents**   Data on teenage depression are reviewed in George M. Chartier and Daniel J. Rainieri, "Adolescent Depression: Concepts, Treatments, and Prevention," in *Adolescent Behavior Disorders: Foundations and Comtemporary Concerns. Advances in Child Behavior Analysis and Therapy*, ed. Paul Karoly and John J. Steffen (Lexington, Mass.: Heath, 1984), vol. 3.

158   **may be nearly equal**   An interesting and carefully done study found that about 7 percent of men and women under observation for eight months experienced depression for the first time. See Christopher S. Amenson and Peter M. Lewinsohn, "An Investigation into the Observed Sex Difference in Prevalence of Unipolar Depression," *Journal of Abnormal Psychology* 90 (1981): 1–13.

161   **worrying**   Research about normal worrying among college students was carried out by Thomas D. Borkovec, et al., "Preliminary Exploration of Worry: Some Characteristics and Processes," *Behaviour Research and Therapy* 21 (1983): 17–27.

163   **loneliness**   See Harry S. Sullivan, *Interpersonal Theory of Psychiatry* (New York: Norton, 1953), pp. 260–62.

163   **pessimistic personality style**   A summary of this and other personality styles is contained in Douglas H. Powell, *Understanding Human Adjustment: Normal Adaptation Through the Life Cycle* (Boston: Little, Brown, 1983), ch. 4.

163   **transient depressions**   A comprehensive summary of the thinking of many experts about types of adolescent depression is presented by E. James Anthony, "Depression in Adolescence: A Psycho-dynamic Approach to Nosology," in *The Adolescent and Mood Disturbance*, ed. Harvey Golombek and Barry D. Garfinkel (New York: International Universities Press, 1983).

164   **grief reactions**   This is called "uncomplicated bereavement" in the *DSM-III, Diagnostic and Statistical Manual of Mental Disorders*, 3d ed. (Washington, D.C.: American Psychiatric Association, 1980). It has several features in common with the Major Depressive Episodes and the Post-Traumatic Stress Disorder.

165   **two to six months**   The cognitive and emotional symptoms associated with acute trauma diminished in six to twenty-eight weeks among subjects studied by Mardi G. Horowitz et al., "Signs and

Symptoms of Post-Traumatic Stress Disorders," *Archives of General Psychiatry* 37 (1980): 85–92.

165   **helplessness** A basic work on helplessness is Lyn Y. Abramson, Martin E. P. Seligman, and John D. Teasdale, "Learned Helplessness in Humans: Critique and Reformulation," *Journal of Abnormal Psychology* 87 (1978): 49–74.

165   **masked depressions** Considerable disagreement exists whether depression in children and adolescents is in fact masked by other symptoms or co-exists with, preceeds, or succeeds the depressive state. Current evidence supports both positions. The concept remains useful, however, as it encourages us to look beyond the superficial behavior to determine if these may be indirect expressions of depression. See Gabrielle A. Carlson, "Overview of Masked or Alternative Forms of Depression," in *Affective Disorders in Childhood and Adolescence: An Update*, ed. Dennis P. Cantwell and Gabrielle A. Carlson (New York: Spectrum, 1983).

166   **chronic depressed mood** This syndrome is sometimes called a Dysthymic Disorder or depressive neurosis. The major criteria are presented in the *DSM-III*, pp. 220–22.

167   **ambivalence** The first description of this phenomenon is Sigmund Freud's *Mourning and Melancholia*, vol. 14 of *The Standard Edition of the Complete Psychological Works of Sigmund Freud*, ed. and trans. James Strachey with Anna Freud (London: Hogarth Press, 1953–64), pp. 243–58.

167   **Distorted negative thinking** One of the first to recognize the cognitive elements associated with depression in adults was Aaron T. Beck, *Depression: Clinical, Experimental, and Theoretical Aspects* (New York: Harper & Row, 1967). Since his initial work considerable research has been carried out with adolescents, much of it confirming aspects of his thinking. See the review of the literature by Chartier and Rainieri, "Adolescent Depression"; and a classic article, Lyn Y. Abramson and Harold A. Sackeim, "A Paradox in Depression: Uncontrollability and Self-blame," *Psychological Bulletin* 84 (1977): 838–51.

168   **"go with"** Numerous empirical studies of depressed children generally support this view. An example is Gloria R. Leon, Phillip C. Kendall, and Judy Garber, "Depression in Children: Parent, Teacher, and Child Perspectives," *Journal of Abnormal Child Psychology* 8 (1980): 221–35.

168   **suicidal thoughts and talk** For a concise summary of research on suicidal ideation and behavior among normal and emotionally disturbed youngsters, see Gabrielle A. Carlson, "Depression and Sui-

cidal Behavior in Children and Adolescents, in Cantwell and Carlson, eds., *Affective Disorders.*

169   **physical harm**   Described by E. Mansell Pattison and Joel Kahan, "The Deliberate Self-Harm Syndrome," *American Journal of Psychiatry* 140 (1983): 867–72.

169   **Major depressions**   The description of the primary features of major depression along with anhedonia and physical and mental slowing are taken from the *DSM-III*, pp. 210–15; and Gabrielle A. Carlson and Michael Strober, "Affective Disorders in Adolescence," in Cantwell and Carlson, eds., *Affective Disorders.*

170   **five thousand young people**   In 1982, 5,025 young people ages fifteen through twenty-four took their lives. In 1962, 1,502 youths committed suicide. From National Center for Health Statistics, *Advanced Report of Final Mortality Statistics. 1982,* vol. 33, No. 9 (Washington, D.C.: U.S. Department of Health and Human Services, Public Health Service, 20 December 1984).

170   **suicidal attempt**   References of interest are John E. Mack and Holly Hickler, *Vivienne: The Life and Suicide of an Adolescent Girl* (Boston: Little, Brown, 1981); Paul C. Hollinger and Daniel Offer, "Perspectives on Adolescent Suicide," *Research in Community and Mental Health* 2 (1981): 139–57; Keith Petrie and Kerry Chamberlain, "Hopelessness and Social Desirability as Moderator Variables in Predicting Suicidal Behavior," *Journal of Consulting and Clinical Psychology* 51 (1983): 485–87; and Barry D. Garfinkel and Harvey Golombek, "Suicidal Behavior in Adolescence," in Golombek and Garfinkel, *Adolescent.*

170   **Suicidal acts**   See Edwin S. Shneidman, Norman L. Farbarow, and Robert E. Litman, *The Psychology of Suicide* (New York: Science House, 1970).

173   **slightly greater tendency**   Evidence for the biological component in depression among the young is accumulating. Of interest are William R. Beardslee et al., "Children of Parents with a Major Affective Disorder: A Review," *American Journal of Psychiatry* 140 (1983): 825–32.

173   **overwhelming majority**   Research on the parental factors associated with stress-resistant children is provided by Emmy E. Werner and Ruth S. Smith, *Vulnerable but Invincible: A Longitudinal Study of Resilient Children and Youth* (New York: McGraw-Hill, 1982); and Michael Rutter, *Maternal Deprivation Reassessed,* 2d ed. (London: Penguin, 1981).

175   **moderate exercise**   See Carlyle H. Folkins and Wesley E. Sime, "Physical Fitness and Mental Health," *American Psychologist* 36

(1981): 373–89; and Elizabeth J. Doyne, Diane L. Chambless, and Larry E. Beutler, "Aerobic Exercise as a Treatment for Depression in Women," *Behavior Therapy* 14 (1983): 434–40.

175   **positive thinking**   For a survey of some of the cognitive patterns sustaining a depressed mood and techniques for altering these thoughts, see Lynn Rehm, "Self-Management in Depression," in *The Psychology of Self-Management: From Theory to Practice*, ed. Paul Karoly and Frederick Kanfer (New York: Pergamon, 1982); also Leonard A. Doerfler and Steven C. Richards, "Self-Initiated Attempts to Cope with Depression," *Cognitive Therapy and Research* 5 (1981): 367–71.

177   **caffeine**   Noted by David M. Veleber and Donald I. Templer, "Effects of Caffeine on Anxiety and Depression," *Journal of Abnormal Psychology* 93 (1984): 120–22.

177   **most typical outpatient treatment**   Refer to Joel Hershowitz and N. Paul Rosman, *Pediatrics, Neurology, and Psychiatry—Common Ground: Behavioral, Cognitive, Affective, and Physical Disorders in Children and Adolescents* (New York: Macmillan, 1982), ch. 6.

178   **negative mental set**   See Aaron T. Beck et al., *Cognitive Theory of Depression* (New York: Guilford, 1979).

178   **coping with depression course**   Described by Peter M. Lewinsohn et al., in *The Coping with Depression Course* (Eugene, Oreg.: Castelia, 1984).

178   **versions of this approach**   Several of these programs are detailed by Janice W. Wetzel, *Clinical Handbook of Depression* (New York: Gardner, 1984), ch. 6.

178   **suicide attempts**   See Carl L. Tishler, Patrick C. McKenry, and Karen C. Morgan, "Adolescent Suicide Attempts: Some Significant Factors," *Suicide and Life Threatening Behavior* 11 (1981): 86–92.

180   **rebound from periods of gloom**   One of the first of the modern clinicians to take an interest in this topic was Gregory Rochlin in his book, *Grief and Discontents: The Forces of Change* (Boston: Little, Brown, 1965), chs. 4 and 5. Recently, André Haynal has addressed the same topic in *Depression and Creativity* (New York: International Universities Press, 1985).

Chapter 10

181   **hormonal changes**   The precise biochemical origins of increased aggression around puberty have yet to be clearly established and are intertwined with social and psychological factors. See reviews by Gerald C. Brown, "Aggression, Adolescence, and Psychobiology," in *The Aggressive Adolescent: Clinical Perspectives*, ed. Charles R.

Keith (New York: Free Press, 1984); and Morris A. Sklansky, "The Pubescent Years: Eleven to Fourteen," in *The Course of Life: Psychoanalytic Contributions Toward Understanding Personality Development* (DHHS Publication (ADM) 79–600150), ed. Stanley I. Greenspan and George H. Pollack (Washington, D.C.: U.S. Government Printing Office, 1980).

181   **juvenile misconduct** For a review of this literature in England and the United States, see Michael Rutter, *Changing Youth in a Changing Society: Patterns of Adolescent Development and Disorder* (Cambridge, Mass.: Harvard University Press, 1980), chs. 1 and 3.

181   **not pranks** See the descriptions of Conduct Disorders, Disorders of Impulse Control Not Otherwise Classified, and the Antisocial Personality Disorders in the *DSM-III, Diagnostic and Statistical Manual of Mental Disorders*, 3d ed. (Washington, D.C.: American Psychiatric Association, 1980), pp. 45–50, 291–98, and 317–21.

181   **Within this population** These patterns are summarized in Theodore Millon, *Disorders of Personalities: DSM-III: Axis II* (New York: Wiley, 1981), ch. 7.

184   **Rugged individualism** See ibid., ch. 7.

184   **anger usually doesn't** This pattern has shown clearly in James R. Averill, "Studies on Anger and Aggression: Implications for Theories of Emotion," *American Psychologist* 38 (1983): 1145–60.

186   **Nine out of ten** Inferred from data presented in William J. Kirk, "Juvenile Justice and Delinquency," in *Adolescent Behavior and Society: A Book of Readings*, ed. Rolf E. H. Muuss (New York: Random House, 1980); and Delbert S. Elliott and Harwin L. Voss, *Delinquency and Dropout* (Lexington, Mass.: Heath, 1974).

187   **explosive outbursts** The aggressive aspects of conduct problems in the yellow and orange zones are largely drawn from Millon, *Disorders*, ch. 7, except where otherwise indicated.

187   **one million** Personal communication from William Treanor, director, American Youth Work Center, a Washington, D.C.based lobbying organization for runaways. January 31, 1986.

189   **other forms** See the *DSM-III*, pp. 291–98.

190   **disappear** Inferred from personal communication with Treanor; and, Federal Bureau of Investigation, *Uniform Crime Reports: Crime in the United States, 1984* (Washington, D.C.: United States Printing Office, July 23, 1985).

190   **intense depression and anxiety** For a comparison of normal and delinquent American adolescents, see Daniel Offer, Eric Ostrov,

and Kenneth I. Howard, *The Adolescent: A Psychological Self-Portrait* (New York: Basic Books, 1981), app. E.

190 **four subtypes** Drawn from the description of Conduct Disorders in the *DSM-III*, pp. 45–52.

191 **morality and remorse** See Millon, *Disorders*, ch. 7.

192 **3 to 5 percent** Presented in Elliott and Voss, *Delinquency*.

196 **higher rate of persistence** See Simon Dinitz and John P. Conrad, "Who's in That Dark Alley?" in *Handbook of Longitudinal Research*, vol. 2, *Teenage and Adult Cohorts*, ed. Sarnoff A. Mednick, Michael Harway, and Karen M. Finello (New York: Praeger, 1984); and Rutter, *Changing Youth*, ch. 1.

196 **genetic** For a concise review of the possible biological factors associated with the aggressive personality, see Millon, *Disorders*, ch. 7.

196 **less misconduct** See Elliott and Voss, *Delinquency;* and T. E. Moffitt et al., "Socioeconomic Status, IQ, and Delinquency," *Journal of Abnormal Psychology* 90 (1981): 152–56.

197 **Being unclear** This parent-child pattern seems to be characteristic in all forms of antisocial behavior. This research is summarized by Rutter, *Changing Youth*, ch. 3; and Rolf Loeber and Thomas J. Dishion, "Early Predictors of Male Delinquency: A Review," *Psychological Bulletin* 94 (1983): 68–99.

197 **Home atmospheres** See Rutter, *Changing Youth*, ch. 3.

197 **aggression begets** For example, Jerry Neopolitan, "Parental Influences on Aggressive Behavior: A Social Learning Approach," *Adolescence* 16 (1981): 831–40.

198 **understand why** A summary of the motives for stealing in children and appropriate parental response is contained in Charles E. Schaefer and Howard I. Millman, *How to Help Children with Common Problems* (New York: Van Nostrand Reinhold, 1981), pp. 303–10.

199 **Empathy** The absence of empathy in delinquents is described in Phillip L. Ellis, "Empathy: A Factor in Antisocial Behavior," *Journal of Abnormal Child Psychology* 10 (1982): 123–34.

200 **sports** For a discussion of the values of sport in controlling aggression, refer to Konrad Lorenz, *On Aggression* (New York: Harcourt Brace and World, 1966).

201 **big brother** See Douglas H. Powell and Michael W. Hurst, *Do Big Brothers Matter: An Evaluation Study of the Impact of Big Brothers on Boys* (Boston, Mass.: Big Brother Association of Boston, 1972); and Fredrick W. Seidele, "Big Sisters: An Experimental Evaluation," *Adolescence* 17 (1982): 117–28.

201   **cognitive-behavioral** Some therapists using this mix of treatment modalities call it rational-emotive therapy. See John T. Watkins, "Rational-Emotive Dynamics of Impulsive Disorders," in *RET: Handbook of Rational-Emotive Therapy*, ed. Albert Ellis and Russell Grieger (New York: Springer, 1977).

201   **stress inoculation** Two slightly different approaches are: Raymond W. Novaco, "Anger and Coping with Stress: Cognitive Behavioral Interventions," in *Cognitive Behavior Therapy: Research and Applications*, ed. John P. Foreyt and Diana P. Rathjen (New York: Plenum, 1978); and Eva L. Feindler and William J. Fremouw, "Stress Inoculation Training for Adolescent Anger Problems," in *Stress Reduction and Prevention*, ed. Donald Meichenbaum and Matt E. Jaremko (New York: Plenum, 1983).

202   **Most rejoin** See David B. Adams, "Adolescent Residential Treatment: An Alternative to Institutionalization," *Adolescence* 15 (1980): 521–27. A variation of this program in England, called "Achievement Place," is described by Rutter, *Changing Youth*, ch. 3.

Chapter 11

203   **on a continuum** The concept that eating problems occur on a continuum is stated clearly in Paul E. Garfinkel and David M. Garner, *Anorexia Nervosa: A Multi-Dimensional Perspective*, (New York: Bruner/Mazel, 1982), ch. 2.

203   **Two types** Definitions of, and data about, bulimia and anorexia nervosa are drawn from the *DSM-III, Diagnostic and Statistical Manual of Mental Disorders*, 3d ed. (Washington, D.C.: American Psychiatric Association, 1980), pp. 67–71; Christopher G. Fairburn, "Bulimia: Its Epidemiology and Management," *Psychiatric Annals* 13 (1983): 953–61; Marlene Boskind-White and William C. White, Jr., *Bulimarexia: The Binge-Purge Cycle* (New York: Norton, 1983); and Hilde Bruch, "Anorexia Nervosa: Therapy and Theory," *American Journal of Psychiatry* 139 (1982): 1531–38.

209   **A third** See Garfinkel and Garner, *Anorexia Nervosa*, ch. 5.

209   **significant irregularities** Criteria for distinguishing less from more serious eating problems are contained in Nancy Rollins and Eugene Piazza, "Diagnosis of Anorexia Nervosa: A Critical Reappraisal," *The Journal of the American Academy of Child Psychiatry* 17 (1978): 126–37.

209   **chaotic** Chaotic eating patterns are described in Robert L. Palmer, "The Dietary Chaos Syndrome: A Useful New Term?" *British Journal of Medical Psychology* 52 (1979): 187–90.

limia: Preliminary Experience and Practical Recommendations," *Journal of Clinical Psychopharmacology* 3 (1983): 274–81.

Not all approaches For example, see Harrison G. Pope, Jr. et al. "Bulimia Treated with Imipramine: A Placebo-Controlled Double-Blind Study," *American Journal of Psychiatry* 140 (1983): 554–58; John D. Boyd, "Effects of a Hypnotherapy Treatment for Bulimarexia: A Preliminary Investigation" (Paper presented at annual meeting of the American Psychological Association, Washington, D.C., August 1982); and Boskind-White and White, *Bulimarexia.*

taken out of their hands See W. Stewart Agras and Helena C. Kraemer, "The Treatment of Anorexia Nervosa: Do Different Treatments Have Different Outcomes?" *Psychiatric Annals* 13 (1983): 928–35; and Neuman and Halvorson, *Anorexia Nervosa,* ch. 3.

Follow-up studies Summarized in Schwartz and Thompson, *"Anorectics."*

percentages of symptom remission See Katherine A. Halmi, "Anorexia Nervosa and Bulimia," *Psychosomatics* 24 (1983): 111–29.

Chapter 12

Figure 12.1 Lloyd D. Johnston, Jerald G. Bachman, and Patrick M. O'Malley, *Student Drug Use, Attitudes, and Beliefs: National Trends 1975–1982* (Washington, D.C.: U.S. Government Printing Office, 1982).

percentages Drug use patterns among American youths are drawn from the following sources: ibid.; Richard Jessor, James A. Chase, and John E. Donavan, "Psychosocial Correlates of Marijuana Use and Problem Drinking in a National Sample of Adolescents," *American Journal of Public Health* 70 (1980): 604–13; David J. Hanson and Ruth C. Engs, "College students' Drinking Attitudes: 1970–1982," *Psychological Reports* 54 (1984): 300–302; Joseph D. Matarazzo, "Behavioral Health's Challenge to Academic, Scientific, and Professional Psychology," *American Psychologist* 37 (1982): 1–14; and U.S. Department of Health, Education, and Welfare, Public Health Service, Office of the Assistant Secretary for Health and the Surgeon General, *Healthy People: The Surgeon General's Report on Health Prevention and Disease Prevention* (Washington, D.C.: U.S. Government Printing Office, 1979).

15 to 25 percent See the *DSM-III, Diagnostic and Statistical Manual of Mental Disorders,* 3d ed. (Washington, D.C.: American

210   **Table 11.3**   Table 11.3 is based on the *DSM-III*, pp.
         cia A. Neuman and Patricia A. Halvorson, *Anorexia*
         Bulimia: A Handbook for Counselors and Therapist.   2
         Van Nostrand Reinhold, 1983); Bruch, "Anorexia N
         finkel and Garner, *Anorexia Nervosa;* and Rollins and
         agnosis."

211   **"thin-fat"**   This classic description was by Hilde Bru
         Disorders: Obesity, Anorexia Nervosa and the Person
         York: Basic Books, 1973).

211   **overcontrol and overprotection**   See Salvador Minuc   2
         L. Rosman, and Lester Baker, *Psychosomatic Famili*
         Nervosa in Context (Cambridge, Mass.: Harvard Univ
         1978).

213   **15 to 20 percent**   Refer to Garfinkel and Garne
         Nervosa; and Rollins and Piazza, "Diagnosis."

213   **overestimate their girth**   See P. D. Slade and G. F.
         "Awareness of Body Dimensions in Anorexia Nervosa.
         tional and Longitudinal Studies," *Psychological Medicir*
         188–99.

214   **have a baby**   Though the case for binge eating and
         scious desire for impregnation has been largely disco
         story of Laura shows that the relationship between th
         occur from time to time. See Robert Lindner, *The F*
         Hour: A Collection of True Psychoanalytic Tales (New
         Aronson, 1982).

214   **"obligatory runners"**   See Alayne Yates, Kevin Leehey,
         erine M. Shisslak, "Running—An Analog of Anorexia?"
         England Journal of Medicine 308 (1983): 251–55.

214   **jeopardy**   About 6 percent of patients diagnosed as h
         orexia nervosa die from self-starvation. Data contained i
         W. Schwartz and Michael G. Thompson, "Do Anore
         Well? Current Research and Future Needs," *American*
         Psychiatry 138 (1981): 319–33.

214   **feelings of inadequacy**   See Hilde Bruch, "Psychothera;
         mary Anorexia Nervosa," in *The Psychiatric Treatment o*
         cents, ed. Aaron H. Esman (New York: International Un
         Press, 1983).

219   **shouting "No!"**   Refer to Bruch, "Psychotherapy."

221   **University of Minnesota**   Described in Neuman and H;
         Anorexia Nervosa, pp. 238–39.

221   **a hospital**   This program reported in Harrison G. Pope,
         Hudson, and Jeffrey M. Jonas, "Anti-Depressant Treatmen

Psychiatric Association, 1980), p. 168; and George E. Vaillant, *The Natural History of Alcoholism: Causes, Patterns, and Paths to Recovery* (Cambridge, Mass.: Harvard University Press, 1983), ch. 3.

224 **hundred billion dollars** In 1980 the total cost was estimated at just under 90 billion. Assuming a 5 percent yearly inflation rate, the total in 1986 would be over 120 billion. Refer to Henrick J. Harwood et al. *Economic Costs to Society of Alcohol and Drug Abuse and Mental Illness: 1980* (Research Triangle Park, N.C.: Research Triangle Institute, June, 1984).

227 **do without** Reasons not to use drugs, especially alcohol, are described by Charles E. Schaefer and Howard I. Millman, *How to Help Children with Common Problems* (New York: Van Nostrand Reinhold, 1981), pp. 354–55; and Vaillant, *Alcoholism*, ch. 4.

227 **experiment** It is possible to describe three broad categories of young drug users—experimental, depressive, and characterlogical. Each needs a different helping response. See Stephen Proskauer and Ruick S. Rolland, "Youth Who Use Drugs: Psychodynamic Diagnosis and Treatment Planning," *Journal of the American Academy of Child Psychiatry* 12 (1973): 32–47.

229 **Many experts** For example, Diana Baumrind, *A Developmental Perspective on Adolescent Drug Use*. National Institute on Drug Abuse Research Monograph Service. In Press.

229 **responsible use** The guidelines for responsible use are drawn from the research done with youths and adults in Norman E. Zinberg, *Drug, Set, and Setting: The Basis for Controlled Intoxicant Use* (New Haven: Yale University Press, 1984); Vaillant, *Alcoholism;* and Schaefer and Millman, *Common Problems*, pp. 355–56.

230 **six or more** In addition, problem drinkers have experienced negative consequences of their alcohol intake at least twice in at least three of five areas: trouble with teachers, criticism from dates, difficulties with friends, trouble with police, and driving while under the influence. See Jessor, Chase, and Donavan, "Correlates of Marijuana."

230 **intoxication** Summarized in the *DSM-III*, pp. 129–32.

230 **abuse marijuana** See Zinberg, *Basis*, ch. 4.

231 **euphoria** Research with animals, still in its beginning stages, speculates that "pleasure centers" exist—brain circuits that provide a positive feeling when stimulated. These are triggered by the ingestion of alcohol, barbiturates, stimulants, opiates, and other drugs. According to this theory we consume these substances because of the euphoria they produce, not because of the addiction.

See Michael A. Bozarth and Roy A. Wise, "Anatomically Distinct Opiate Receptor Fields Mediate Reward and Physical Dependence," *Science* 224 (1984): 516–17; and Roy A. Wise, "Action of Drugs of Abuse on Brain Reward Systems," *Pharmacology, Biochemistry, and Behavior* 13 (1980): 213–23.

231 **dramatic behavioral change** Though it occurs with other substances, this is more characteristic of alcohol intoxication. See the *DSM-III*, p. 132.

231 **substance abuse** Characteristics of substance abuse and dependence are summarized in ibid., pp. 164–76; Vaillant, *Alcoholism*, ch. 9; and Zinberg, *Basis*, chs. 2, 3, and 4.

234 **much the same** See Vaillant, *Alcoholism*, ch. 2.

237 **behavioral tests** In suburban Los Angeles, drivers stopped and suspected of being intoxicated are given several behavioral tests. Then they have a choice of breath, blood, or urine tests. Personal communication to the author from the Westwood, California, police department, July 24, 1984.

238 **has been dubious** See Zinberg, *Basis*, ch. 7; and Department of Health, Education, and Welfare, *Healthy People*, ch. 10.

239 **hereditary predisposition** See Donald W. Goodwin, *Is Alcoholism Hereditary?* (New York: Oxford University Press, 1976).

239 **Family and peers** See Judith S. Brook, Martin Whiteman, and Ann S. Gordon, "Stages of Drug Use in Adolescence: Personality, Peer, and Family Correlates, *Developmental Psychology* 19 (1983): 269–77; and Grace M. Barnes, "The Development of Adolescent Drinking Behavior: An Evaluation Review of the Impact of the Socialization Process in the Family," *Adolescence* 12 (1977): 571–91.

240 **Drunkenness is condemned** An excellent survey of the literature as well as of his own research on ethnic differences in alcohol intake as a function of family attitudes is contained in Vaillant, *Alcoholism*, ch. 2.

240 **much less is known** Refer to Zinberg, *Basis*, ch. 7.

242 **Spontaneous recovery** See Vaillant, *Alcoholism*, ch. 4.

242 **comprehensive programs** These programs are far more comprehensive than outlined here. For instance, they emphasize maintaining physical, emotional, and spiritual health; developing an ongoing life plan that includes honesty with the self and personal improvement; rebuilding satisfying family relationships; creating significant drug-free friendships; and continuing educational, vocational, leisure time, and community interests. My thanks to Dr. George Ross, director of *Possibilities Unlimited*, and Ms. Helen

Petermann, program director of *Life*, for describing their excellent programs for drug-abusing young people.

243   **follow-up studies** Refer to Dennis Hoogerman et al. "Effective Early Intervention for Adolescents Harmfully Involved in Alcohol and Drugs," *The Journal of the Florida Medical Association* 71 (1984): 227–32; and Thomas E. Bratter, "Treating Alienated, Unmotivated Drug-Abusing Adolescents," *American Journal of Psychotherapy* 27 (1973): 585–98.

244   **recreational alternatives** Summarized in two publications by Marsha Monatt, *Parents, Peers and Pot* and *Parents, Peers and Pot II: Parents in Action* (Washington, D.C.: U.S. Government Printing Office, 1979 and 1983).

Chapter 13

245   **identity** The person who first defined identity as an important element in human development was Erik H. Erikson. See his *Dimensions of a New Identity: The 1973 Jefferson Lectures in the Humanities* (New York: Norton, 1974), p. 124.

245   **once believed** Freud's daughter, Anna, said, "the upholding of a steady equilibrium during the adolescent process is in itself abnormal." See "Adolescence," in *The Writings of Anna Freud* (New York: International Universities Press, 1969), vol. 5, p. 164.

245   **the vast majority** Most longitudinal researchers agree with the "no turmoil" theory of adolescence. See the studies of normal high school and college youth reported in Daniel Offer, Eric Ostrov, and Kenneth I. Howard, *The Adolescent: A Psychological Self-Portrait* (New York: Basic Books, 1981); Douglas H. Heath, *Maturity and Competence: A Transcultural View* (New York: Gardner Press, 1977); Stanley H. King, *Five Lives at Harvard* (Cambridge, Mass.: Harvard University Press, 1973); Daniel Offer, *The Psychological World of the Teenager: A Study of Normal Adolescent Boys* (New York: Basic Books, 1969); also see Joseph Katz et al., *No Time for Youth: Growth and Restraint in College Students* (San Francisco, Calif.: Jossey-Bass, 1968).

245   **recur unpredictably** See Daniel J. Levinson et al., *Seasons of a Man's Life* (New York: Knopf, 1978).

248   **self-governance** Many of the ideas in this section are based on the works of Peter Blos on the second individuation process, especially "Phases of Adolescence," in Peter Blos, *On Adolescence: A Psychoanalytic Interpretation* (Chicago: University of Chicago Press, 1962); and "The Second Individuation Process of Adoles-

cence," in Peter Blos, *The Adolescent Passage: Developmental Issues* (New York: International Universities Press, 1979).

250   **three ways**   See George W. Goethals and Dennis S. Klos, *Experiencing Youth: First Person Accounts* (Boston: Little, Brown, 1970 and 1976).

250   **this process entails**   The dimensions of identity with rich clinical examples are portrayed in ibid.

250   **not-me**   See Erik H. Erikson and Joan M. Erikson, "On Generativity and Identity: From a Conversation with Erik and Joan Erikson," *Harvard Educational Review* 51 (1981): 249–69.

250   **normative identity crisis**   A classic description of this condition is summarized in Erik H. Erikson, *Identity: Youth and Crisis* (New York: Norton, 1968).

251   **de-illusionment**   See Levinson, *Seasons,* p. 195.

252   **identity confusion**   Described in Erikson, *Identity,* pp. 165–72; also, Salman Akhtar, "The Syndrome of Identity Diffusion," *American Journal of Psychiatry* 14 (1984): 1381–85.

254   **alienation**   The first modern writer to capture the flavor of youthful alienation is Kenneth Keniston in *The Uncommitted: Alienated Youth in American Society* (New York: Harcourt Brace and World, 1965).

254   **borderline personality**   This description of the borderline personality organization is drawn from the *DSM-III, Diagnostic and Statistical Manual of Mental Disorders,* 3d ed. (Washington, D.C.: American Psychiatric Association, 1980), pp. 321–23; and from the work of Otto Kernberg, especially *Borderline Conditions and Pathological Narcissism* (New York: Aronson, 1975).

254   **transient periods**   Portrayed in Paul A. Andrulonis et al., "Borderline Personality Subcategories," *Journal of Nervous and Mental Disease* 170 (1982): 670–79.

255   **splitting and projective identification**   See Kernberg, *Borderline Conditions,* ch. 7; also John Zinner and Roger L. Shapiro. "Projective Identification as a Mode of Perception and Behavior in Families of Adolescents," *International Journal of Psycho-Analysis* 53 (1972): 523–30.

256   **empty feeling of self**   This pattern has been called the "as if" personality. See Helene Deutsch, "Some Forms of Emotional Disturbance and Their Relationship to Schizophrenia," in Helene Deutsch, *Neuroses in Character Types: Clinical Psychoanalytic Studies* (New York: International Universities Press, 1965).

260   **about half**   This research summarized in Douglas H. Powell, *Un-*

derstanding Human Adjustment: Normal Adaptation Through the Life Cycle (Boston: Little, Brown, 1983), ch. 6.

261   **time out** This time out has been called a "psychosocial moratorium" by Erik H. Erikson, *Identity*, pp. 156–58.

261   **dialogue** See James Lynch, *The Broken Heart: The Medical Consequences of Loneliness* (New York: Basic Books, 1979).

Chapter 14

265   **lengthier and more complicated** See Daniel J. Levinson et al., *Seasons of a Man's Life* (New York: Knopf, 1978), ch. 5 and 6; and Roger L. Gould, *Transformations and Change in Adult Life* (New York: Simon and Schuster, 1978), sects. 2 and 3.

265   **increasingly autonomous** The growth of autonomy in maturing young people is concisely described by Douglas H. Heath in his article, "Wanted: A Comprehensive Model for Health Development," *The Personnel and Guidance Journal* 59 (1980): 391–99.

265   **normal order of things** See Gould, *Transformations*, sect. 3.

266   **distress** The classical types of conflict caused by selecting among mutually exclusive alternatives were originally described by Kurt Lewin in *A Dynamic Theory of Personality* (New York: McGraw-Hill, 1935).

268   **remain close** See Ethel Shanas et al., *Older People in Three Industrial Societies* (New York: Atherton, 1968).

268   **thirty minutes** See Jan Stehouwer, "The Household and Family Relations of Old People," in Shanas et al., *Older People*.

268   **regularly by phone** Reported by Azubike F. Uzoka, "The Myth of the Nuclear Family: Historical Background and Clinical Implications," *American Psychologist* 34 (1979): 1095–1106.

269   **high school seniors** This research is described by Earle Silber et al., "Competent Adolescents Coping with College Decisions," *Archives of General Psychiatry* 5 (1961): 517–27.

270   **Mark Twain's maxim** Quoted in Caroline F. Harnsberger, *Mark Twain at Your Fingertips* (New York: Beechurst, 1948).

273   **"no"** this line is paraphrased from the play, *Sister Mary Ignatius Explains It All For You*, by Christopher Durang.

274   **resow** See George E. Vaillant, *Adaptation to Life* (Boston: Little, Brown, 1977).

275   **tolerance for diversity** Men and women in their sixties exhibited a taste for friends exhibiting a wider range of interests than did cohorts in their forties, twenties, and late teens. See Marjorie F. Lowenthal et al., *Four Stages of Life: A Comparative Study of Men and Women Facing Transition* (San Francisco: Jossey-Bass, 1976).

275   **majority of young people**   Numerous studies support the observa-
           tion that most young people grow out of problems that beset them
           when they are teenagers. See Jancis V. Long and George E. Vail-
           lant, "Natural History of Male Psychological Health: XI. Escape
           From the Under Class," *American Journal of Psychiatry* 141
           (1984): 341–46; and Loretta K. Cass and Carolyn B. Thomas,
           *Childhood Pathology and Later Adjustment: The Question of Pre-
           diction* (New York: Wiley, 1979).

Name Index

Subject Index

Absolutist thinking, 144
Academic performance
    aversion to "owning," 119–20
    and control of fate, 119
    correlation with school enjoyment, 53
    disparity between ability and, 118
    predisposition to, 124–26
    report cards, 112, 115, 118
    and risk taking, 119, 131–32
    and teacher expectations, 133
    variations in, 115–21
    See also Underachievement
Accommodation by others, 28–29
Accountability, teen, 197
Acting out, 23–24, 253
Adaptation, 57, 58
Adjustment mechanisms, 60, 61
    See also Self-protective responses
Adolescent, adolescence. *See* Teenager,
    Youth
Afterglow, following play, 29
Aggression. *See* Anger
Alcohol
    cost to economy, 224, 301n.
    percentage of teens abusing, 223, 224
    See also Drugs
Alex, case of normal adjustment, 10, 11
Alienation 254, 256
A-literate, 117
Altruism, 54
Amenorrhea, 214
Anger, 28, 30
    control of, 199, 200
    in delinquent behavior, 188, 189
    identity confusion, 252, 254
    as stress response, 184
    See also Assertiveness
Anhedonia, 169

Anorexia nervosa
    characteristics of, 204, 210, 211, 212,
        213, 214, 215
    and distorted bodily perceptions, 213
    and health, 212, 214, 299n.
    significant weight loss in, 213
Anticipation, 60, 61
    See also Self-protective responses
Anti-depressant medication, 177
Antisocial behavior
    characteristics of, 181, 189
    and identity confusion, 254
    parental confrontation of, 198, 199
    See also Conduct disorders,
        Delinquency
Anxiety, 22, 28, 30, 31
    attacks, 121
    and depression, 166, 168
    and identity crisis, confusion, 252, 254
    and physical symptoms, 79, 80
    and reason, 79
    reduction of, 88, 135
    See also Meditation, Phobias,
        Relaxation
Appetite, 203, 209, 213
    See also Eating disorders, Health
Assertiveness, 141, 155, 199
Assistance seeking: academic, 115
Attention
    overinclusive, 118–19, 288n.
    selective, 114
Attention deficit disorder (ADD), 125–
    26, 288n.
Autonomy
    and eating disorders, 212, 219
    limited by intergenerational conflict,
        48
    promoting, 248, 250, 260, 262, 269–70

JD: case of identity confusion, 246–47, 256–58
Jobs. *See* Work
Jonathan: case of underachievement, 110–11, 121–22
Junior high school, 5, 277n.
See also Education

Kandace: case of anorexia nervosa, 204–5, 215–17
Ken: case of social and sexual precocity, 91–92, 102–3

Learning disabilities
characteristics of, 125
early diagnosis of, 53
tutorial help for, 126
Learning from experience
and academic performance, 132
and adaptation, 58
and adjustment, 21, 25
encouraging, 270
and self-protective responses, 60, 61
Learning strategies, 114, 129–31
Learning styles
characteristics of, 116–17, 118
fit with teacher and school, 132–33
See also "Buller," "Cower," Superficial-passive
Leaving the nest: myth of, 267–68
Life cycle tasks
contrasts as source of conflict, 38–41
in young adulthood, 7, 265–66
in youth, 265–66
Lisa: case of a temporary adjustment reaction, 11–12
Loneliness, 22, 163
Love: loving
and adjustment, 19, 23, 25
altruistic, 54
between generations, 40, 51
family as center of, 54
loss of, 267
resowing seeds of, 274–75
See also Friends
Lower school, 5
See also Education

Marijuana, 224
See also Drugs
Masochistic manipulation, 148

Medical examination: indications for, 87, 125, 134, 177, 220–21, 242
Meditation, 88
See also Anxiety, Relaxation
Menstruation, 4, 89
See also Puberty
Mental health. *See* Green zone
Mental organization functioning
and adjustment, 21, 25, 28, 29, 31
in depression, 166, 177
in identity confusion, 252–53
in underachievement, 117, 118
See also Attention, Concentration, Reason
Michelle: case of procrastination, 140–41, 151–52
Middle school, 5
See also Education
Minimal brain dysfunction. *See* Attention Deficit Disorder
Moodiness, 21, 23, 158, 161, 163
See also Depression
Mother-child relationship
and aggressive behavior, 35
inhibiting autonomy, 81, 87
in separation anxiety, 81–82
See also Family, Parent-child, Parents
Motility
characteristics of, 59, 60–61
in depression, 165–66
in identity crisis, 252, 256
See also Self-protective responses
Motivation
contrast between parent and child, 39, 40, 41
contrast between school and work, 117–18
See also Goals
Multiple therapies, 87–88, 177, 178, 221, 242–43
See also Cognitive-behavioral therapy, Psychotherapy

National Clearing House for Drug Abuse Information, 241
Negative thinking
altering, 175–77
in depression, 167–68
See also Pessimistic personality style
Neurotic symptoms, 26–29
See also Orange zone